The Ultimate Istan

MW01538981

All You Need to Know Before You Go with Recommendations on Must-See Attractions, Things to Do, Hidden Gems, Where to Stay, Places to Eat, and Ways to Save

Sebastian Felix

Disclaimer Notice

The information provided in this book is intended for general informational purposes only and reflects the author's research and personal experiences. While every effort has been made to ensure the accuracy and reliability of the content, the author and publisher make no guarantees or warranties regarding the completeness, timeliness, or applicability of the information contained herein. Readers are encouraged to seek professional advice and conduct their research before making decisions based on the contents of this book. The author and publisher shall not be held liable for any errors, omissions, or actions taken based on the information presented.

Contents

Chapter 1: Introduction

Welcome to Istanbul

Welcome to Istanbul, a city where the East meets the West in a spectacular blend of cultures, traditions, and history. Straddling two continents, Europe and Asia, Istanbul offers a unique experience with its rich heritage, stunning architecture, vibrant markets, and bustling street life. From the grandeur of the Hagia Sophia and the Blue Mosque to the lively atmosphere of the Grand Bazaar and the serene beauty of the Bosphorus, Istanbul captivates every traveler with its timeless charm and dynamic energy.

Cultural Crossroads: Discover the diverse cultural influences that have shaped Istanbul over millennia, from Byzantine and Ottoman legacies to modern-day vibrancy.

Historic Landmarks: Explore the city's iconic historical sites, including palaces, mosques, churches, and ancient ruins that narrate the story of empires past.

Scenic Beauty: Enjoy breathtaking views of the Bosphorus, the Golden Horn, and the city's skyline, adorned with minarets and domes.

Modern Metropolis: Experience the dynamic life of contemporary Istanbul, with its trendy neighborhoods, bustling markets, and vibrant nightlife.

Overview of Istanbul

Geography: Istanbul is uniquely situated on both sides of the Bosphorus Strait, which separates Europe and Asia. The city is divided into the European side, with historic and commercial districts, and the Asian side, known for its residential areas and green spaces.

Districts: Istanbul is composed of several districts, each offering unique attractions and experiences:

- **Sultanahmet (Historic Peninsula):** Home to iconic landmarks like the Hagia Sophia, Blue Mosque, Topkapi Palace, and Basilica Cistern.
- **Beyoğlu:** Known for its lively nightlife, shopping streets like Istiklal Avenue, and cultural sites such as Galata Tower and Taksim Square.
- **Kadıköy:** A vibrant neighborhood on the Asian side with bustling markets, trendy cafes, and the historic Haydarpaşa Train Station.
- **Üsküdar:** Features beautiful mosques, scenic waterfronts, and views of the Maiden's Tower.
- **Besiktas:** A hub for nightlife, shopping, and dining, with attractions like Dolmabahce Palace and the lively Ortaköy district.
- **Fatih:** Encompasses the historic heart of the city, including the Grand Bazaar and Suleymaniye Mosque.
- **Eminönü:** Known for its bustling ferry docks, the Spice Bazaar, and the New Mosque.

Population: Istanbul has a population of approximately 15 million people, making it one of the most populous cities in the world. Its diverse population reflects the city's rich cultural tapestry.

Economy: Istanbul is the economic powerhouse of Turkey, with a robust economy driven by finance, trade, tourism, and manufacturing. The city is a key financial center and a hub for international business.

Transportation: Istanbul boasts an extensive transportation network, including trams, buses, metro lines, ferries, and taxis, making it easy to navigate the city. Istanbul Airport (IST) and Sabiha Gökçen Airport (SAW) serve as major international gateways.

History of Istanbul

Ancient Byzantium: Founded as Byzantium in the 7th century BC, the city became an important Greek colony and later a Roman city.

Constantinople: Renamed Constantinople in 330 AD by Emperor Constantine the Great, it became the capital of the Byzantine Empire and a major center of Christianity.

Ottoman Era: Conquered by the Ottomans in 1453, the city was renamed Istanbul and became the capital of the Ottoman Empire, flourishing as a cultural, political, and economic center.

Republic of Turkey: Following the fall of the Ottoman Empire and the establishment of the Republic of Turkey in 1923, Istanbul retained its significance as the country's cultural and commercial heart.

Modern Istanbul: Today, Istanbul is a dynamic and cosmopolitan city, seamlessly blending its rich history with contemporary life and development.

How to Use This Guide

This guide is designed to help you explore Istanbul, offering practical advice, insider tips, and recommendations to ensure you make the most of your visit.

Planning Your Trip: Essential information on when to visit Istanbul, entry requirements, travel insurance, health tips, currency exchange, and packing essentials for different seasons.

Getting to and Around Istanbul: Detailed guides on arriving in Istanbul by air, train, or road, as well as navigating the city efficiently using public transportation, ferries, and taxis.

Where to Stay: Recommendations for accommodations across Istanbul, from luxury hotels and boutique inns to budget-friendly hostels and guesthouses.

Top Attractions: A comprehensive list of must-see sights and activities, including museums, historic sites, parks, shopping streets, and scenic viewpoints, with tips for exploring each destination.

Cultural Experiences: Insights into Istanbul's vibrant cultural scene, including art galleries, theaters, music venues, and local festivals.

Dining and Nightlife: Recommendations for dining out in Istanbul, from gourmet restaurants and street food markets to traditional Turkish eateries and trendy bars, as well as nightlife spots and entertainment options.

Outdoor Activities: Suggestions for outdoor enthusiasts, including Bosphorus cruises, hiking trails, parks, and seaside promenades.

Family-Friendly Activities: Fun-filled attractions and activities for families, including interactive museums, theme parks, kid-friendly parks, and educational tours.

Practical Information: Useful tips on tourist information centers, emergency contacts, local customs and etiquette, internet connectivity, and postal services in Istanbul.

Maps and Navigation: Detailed maps of Istanbul's districts, public transportation networks, and tourist routes, facilitate easy exploration and navigation during your stay.

Final Tips and Recommendations: Insider advice on hidden gems, lesser-known attractions, seasonal events, and local insights to enhance your visit to Istanbul and create lasting memories.

Appendices: Additional resources, including a glossary of Turkish phrases, conversion charts, emergency phrases, recommended reading, and an index for quick reference.

With this guide, you'll embark on a journey through Istanbul's historical landmarks, cultural treasures, outdoor adventures, and modern attractions, ensuring an enriching and unforgettable experience in this magnificent city where East meets West.

Why Visit? Top Reasons to Visit Istanbul, Turkey

1. Rich Historical Heritage

Istanbul is a city where East meets West, boasting a rich tapestry of history that spans centuries. As the former capital of empires such as the Roman, Byzantine, and Ottoman, it offers an array of historical landmarks. Explore the magnificent Hagia Sophia, originally a cathedral, then a mosque, and now a museum, where stunning mosaics and architectural brilliance tell stories of the past. The Topkapi Palace, once the residence of Ottoman sultans, invites visitors to marvel at its opulent rooms and lush gardens while offering insights into the imperial life of the era.

2. Breathtaking Architecture

The architectural diversity in Istanbul is awe-inspiring. The Blue Mosque (Sultan Ahmed Mosque) stands out with its striking blue tiles and six minarets, creating a harmonious silhouette against the skyline. Meanwhile, the Basilica Cistern, an underground reservoir supported by grand columns, provides a mystical atmosphere that transports visitors to ancient times. Each structure encapsulates the city's historical layers and artistic endeavors.

3. Vibrant Culture and Traditions

Istanbul's culture is a blend of various influences, reflected in its art, music, and cuisine. The city hosts numerous festivals celebrating everything from film to jazz, providing a glimpse into its vibrant cultural life. Engage with local artists in the neighborhoods of Karaköy or Balat, where colorful street art adorns the walls, showcasing contemporary creativity alongside traditional crafts.

4. Culinary Scene

Turkish cuisine is a gastronomic treasure. From mouthwatering kebabs to sweet baklava, the flavors are diverse and rich. Visit the bustling Grand Bazaar to taste street food like simit (sesame bread) and gözleme (stuffed flatbread). Don't miss dining at a traditional meyhane, where you can enjoy a feast of meze (small dishes) paired with raki, the anise-flavored national drink while soaking in the lively atmosphere.

5. Stunning Views and Bosphorus Cruises

The Bosphorus Strait, separating Europe and Asia, offers some of the most picturesque views in Istanbul. A ferry ride provides a unique vantage point to admire the city's skyline, dotted with palaces, mosques, and charming waterfront homes known as yalis. Sunset cruises are particularly enchanting, as the golden light bathes the city in a warm glow.

6. Unique Shopping Experience

Shopping in Istanbul is an adventure in itself. While the Grand Bazaar is famous for its labyrinthine layout and vibrant stalls, selling everything from jewelry to spices, the Spice Bazaar (Egyptian Bazaar) enchants visitors with its aromatic delights. For a modern twist, explore Nişantaşı and Kadıköy, where boutique shops and local designers offer unique finds away from the tourist crowds.

7. Historical Sites and Museums

Beyond the well-known attractions, Istanbul is home to numerous lesser-known gems. The Chora Church (Kariye Museum), with its stunning mosaics, is often overlooked but offers breathtaking artistry. The Istanbul Archaeological Museums house an extensive collection of artifacts, including the famous Alexander Sarcophagus, showcasing the region's rich history.

8. Cafés and Tea Gardens

Istanbul's café culture is a vital part of daily life. Sip on traditional Turkish tea or coffee in a cozy café overlooking the Bosphorus or nestled in a bustling neighborhood. The Çamlıca Hill tea garden offers panoramic views and a tranquil setting, perfect for enjoying a relaxing afternoon amidst nature.

9. Dynamic Nightlife

The nightlife in Istanbul is diverse and exciting. Areas like Taksim and Beyoğlu are filled with lively bars, rooftop lounges, and nightclubs. Experience traditional live music at a meyhane or dance the night away at a trendy club. The city's nightlife scene offers something for everyone, from laid-back venues to vibrant dance floors.

10. Warm Hospitality

The warmth of Turkish hospitality is palpable throughout Istanbul. Locals are known for their friendliness and eagerness to share their culture. Engaging with residents, whether in a market, café, or on the street, often leads to meaningful exchanges and unforgettable memories, making your visit truly special.

By exploring these aspects of Istanbul, visitors can immerse themselves in a city that seamlessly blends ancient history with modern vibrancy, offering an unforgettable travel experience.

Chapter 2: Know Before You Go

Best Time to Visit

Istanbul, with its unique position straddling two continents, boasts a rich blend of history, culture, and vibrant city life. The best time to visit Istanbul largely depends on what you're looking to experience. Here's a detailed guide to help you plan your visit:

Spring (March to May)

Weather:

Spring is one of the most popular times to visit Istanbul. During this season, the weather is mild and pleasant, with average temperatures ranging from 10°C (50°F) in March to around 20°C (68°F) in May. This makes it an ideal time for outdoor activities and sightseeing.

Highlights:

- **Tulip Festival:** April marks the annual Istanbul Tulip Festival, where the city's parks and gardens are adorned with millions of tulips, creating a stunning visual treat.
- **Less Crowded:** Early spring can be less crowded compared to the peak summer months, allowing for a more relaxed experience at popular tourist spots.

Activities:

- **Sightseeing:** Ideal for exploring historical sites like Hagia Sophia, Topkapi Palace, and the Blue Mosque.
- **Bosphorus Cruise:** A cruise on the Bosphorus offers a refreshing view of the city's skyline and historical landmarks.
- **Outdoor Cafes:** Enjoy the burgeoning café culture in neighborhoods like Karaköy and Bebek.

Summer (June to August)

Weather:

Summer in Istanbul can be hot and humid, with temperatures often reaching up to 30°C (86°F) or higher. The heat can be intense, particularly in July and August.

Highlights:

- **Festivals and Events:** Summer hosts numerous festivals, including music and arts festivals, such as the Istanbul Jazz Festival and the Istanbul International Music Festival.
- **Extended Daylight:** Longer days provide more time for exploration and enjoying outdoor activities.

Activities:

- **Beach Trips:** Escape the city heat with a trip to nearby beaches along the Marmara Sea or the Black Sea.
- **Evening Strolls:** Cooler evenings are perfect for walking along Istiklal Street or enjoying the nightlife in the Beyoğlu district.
- **Dining:** Experience rooftop dining with panoramic views of the Bosphorus.

Considerations:

- **Crowds and Costs:** Summer is peak tourist season, meaning attractions can be crowded, and accommodation prices may be higher.
- **Sun Protection:** Ensure you carry sunblock and hats, and stay hydrated.

Autumn (September to November)

Weather:

Autumn is another excellent time to visit Istanbul, with temperatures cooling down to a comfortable range between 15°C (59°F) and 25°C (77°F). The weather remains pleasant through September and October, gradually becoming cooler in November.

Highlights:

- **Fewer Crowds:** With the summer rush over, popular sites are less crowded, making it a more peaceful time to visit.
- **Autumn Colors:** Parks and gardens transform with beautiful autumn foliage, providing picturesque settings for walks and photography.

Activities:

- **Cultural Events:** Autumn is rich in cultural events, such as the Istanbul Biennial, showcasing contemporary art, and the Akbank Jazz Festival.

- **Food and Wine:** Harvest season brings an abundance of fresh produce and local wines. Enjoy the rich flavors of seasonal Turkish cuisine.
- **Sightseeing:** Ideal conditions for exploring both indoor museums and outdoor landmarks.

Winter (December to February)

Weather:

Winter in Istanbul can be chilly and wet, with temperatures ranging from 3°C (37°F) to 10°C (50°F). Snowfall is possible but not frequent.

Highlights:

- **Lower Prices:** Winter is the off-peak season, so you can find better deals on accommodation and flights.
- **Winter Charm:** The city has a unique charm during winter, with fewer tourists and a quieter ambiance.

Activities:

- **Indoor Attractions:** Perfect time to visit museums, palaces, and historic sites without the crowds.
- **Shopping:** Enjoy the Grand Bazaar and local markets at a more leisurely pace.
- **Turkish Baths:** Experience traditional Turkish baths (hamams) to warm up and relax.
- **Festive Season:** December is festive with Christmas markets and New Year celebrations.

Best Time to Visit Istanbul Based on Interests and Preferences

Here's a comprehensive guide to the best times to visit Istanbul based on various interests:

1. Historical and Cultural Exploration

Best Time: Spring (April to June) and Autumn (September to November)

During these periods, the weather is mild and pleasant, perfect for exploring Istanbul's numerous historical sites such as Hagia Sophia, Topkapi Palace, and the Blue Mosque. The city is less crowded compared to the peak summer season, allowing for a more relaxed and immersive experience at museums, mosques, and historical landmarks.

2. Cultural Festivals and Events

Best Time: Throughout the Year

Spring (April - June):

- **Tulip Festival (April):** Istanbul's parks and gardens, especially Emirgan Park, are adorned with millions of tulips.
- **Istanbul Film Festival (April):** A major event for cinema enthusiasts.

Summer (July - August):

- **Istanbul Music Festival (June - July):** Classical music, opera, and ballet performances.
- **Jazz Festival (July):** Renowned jazz musicians from around the world.

Autumn (September - November):

- **Contemporary Istanbul (September):** An international art fair showcasing contemporary art.
- **Istanbul Biennial (every two years, September - November):** A prestigious art exhibition.

Winter (December - March):

- **New Year's Eve:** Festivities and fireworks, especially around Taksim Square and the Bosphorus.

3. Culinary Experiences

Best Time: Year-Round, with Spring and Autumn being Ideal

Istanbul's culinary scene is a year-round delight, but spring and autumn offer the most comfortable weather for exploring street food markets, open-air restaurants, and food festivals. Enjoy seasonal specialties like fresh seafood in the autumn and an array of fruits and vegetables in the spring.

4. Bosphorus Cruises and Outdoor Activities

Best Time: Late Spring (May to June) and Early Autumn (September to October)

These periods provide the best weather for taking scenic Bosphorus cruises, visiting the Princes' Islands, and engaging in outdoor activities. The temperatures are comfortable, and the skies are generally clear, offering stunning views of Istanbul's skyline and waterfront.

5. Shopping

Best Time: Year-Round, with Sales and Discounts in January and July

Istanbul is a shopping paradise with its grand bazaars, local markets, and modern malls. Winter (post-New Year) and summer (July) are the best times for shopping enthusiasts due to major sales and discounts. The Grand Bazaar and Spice Bazaar are open year-round, providing a unique shopping experience at any time.

6. Beaches and Seaside Leisure

Best Time: Summer (June to August)

For those looking to enjoy Istanbul's beaches and seaside, summer is the ideal time. The weather is hot, making it perfect for sunbathing and swimming. Popular beaches include Kilyos on the Black Sea coast and the Marmara Sea's Florya and Menekse beaches.

7. Nightlife and Entertainment

Best Time: Spring to Autumn (April to October)

Istanbul's nightlife is vibrant year-round, but the best time to experience it is during the warmer months when rooftop bars and outdoor venues are open. Areas like Beyoglu and Kadikoy are bustling with nightlife options, from chic bars and nightclubs to live music venues and cultural performances.

Summary

Spring (April to June): Ideal for historical exploration, festivals, and pleasant weather for outdoor activities.

Summer (June to August): Best for beachgoers, open-air events, and the height of the tourist season.

Autumn (September to November): Great for cultural events, culinary experiences, and comfortable weather.

Winter (December to March): Perfect for those who enjoy fewer crowds, winter sales, and New Year celebrations.

Month-by-month Guide to Visiting Istanbul

January:

January in Istanbul is chilly, with average temperatures ranging from 3°C to 8°C (37°F to 46°F). It's the coldest month of the year, and you can expect occasional rain and even snow. Tourist crowds are minimal, making it a peaceful time to explore the city's famous landmarks like the Hagia Sophia and the Blue Mosque without long lines. The New Year celebrations can add a festive charm, with fireworks and events taking place in various parts of the city.

February:

February remains cold, with similar temperatures to January, but the days start getting slightly longer. It's still the off-season, so you can enjoy discounted rates on hotels and fewer tourists at popular attractions. This is a great time to indulge in Istanbul's indoor attractions like the Grand Bazaar, Topkapi Palace, and the numerous museums. Valentine's Day might bring some special events and romantic setups in restaurants and hotels.

March:

March marks the beginning of spring, with temperatures ranging from 6°C to 12°C (43°F to 54°F). The weather can be unpredictable, with a mix of sunny and rainy days. Tourist activity starts picking up, but it's still not peak season, so you can enjoy relatively uncrowded experiences. Tulips begin to bloom, especially in parks like Emirgan Park, heralding the start of the Istanbul Tulip Festival, which peaks in April.

April:

April is one of the best times to visit Istanbul. The city comes alive with the Istanbul Tulip Festival, showcasing millions of tulips in full bloom. Temperatures range from 9°C to 16°C (48°F to 61°F), making it pleasant for outdoor activities and sightseeing. Major attractions might see an increase in visitors, but the vibrant colors and mild weather more than compensate for the larger crowds. This is also a great time to explore the Bosphorus Strait by boat.

May:

May offers warmer weather, with temperatures between 14°C and 22°C (57°F to 72°F). It's an ideal time for exploring Istanbul's outdoor attractions, like the Princes' Islands, parks, and waterfronts. The crowds grow as the city gears up for the peak tourist season, but it's still manageable. Various cultural events and festivals take place, providing a rich experience of Turkish arts and traditions.

June:

June sees the onset of summer, with temperatures ranging from 18°C to 26°C (64°F to 79°F). The weather is warm but not excessively hot, perfect for enjoying Istanbul's beaches and open-air cafes. This is the start of the high tourist season, so expect more crowds and higher accommodation prices. It's a great time for evening strolls along the Bosphorus and attending outdoor concerts and events.

July:

July is hot, with temperatures between 21°C and 29°C (70°F to 84°F). The city is bustling with tourists, and all major attractions can be crowded. However, the vibrant atmosphere, long days, and numerous summer festivals make it an exciting time to visit. Beaches and waterfront areas are popular for cooling off. It's advisable to book accommodations and tickets for major attractions in advance.

August:

August is the hottest month, with temperatures often exceeding 30°C (86°F). While the heat can be intense, Istanbul offers plenty of ways to stay cool, from air-conditioned museums to refreshing Bosphorus cruises. The crowds remain, and prices for hotels and flights are at their peak. Despite the heat, the lively atmosphere continues, with festivals, nightlife, and cultural events in full swing.

September:

September brings relief from the summer heat, with temperatures ranging from 18°C to 26°C (64°F to 79°F). It's a favorite month for many visitors, as the weather is still warm but more comfortable. The tourist crowds start to thin out, making it a perfect time to explore the city's historical sites, markets, and neighborhoods. The Istanbul Biennial, held every two years, often begins in September, attracting art lovers from around the world.

October:

October offers mild weather, with temperatures between 14°C and 20°C (57°F to 68°F). It's an excellent time for sightseeing, as the fall colors add a picturesque backdrop to the city's landscapes. The crowds continue to decrease, and accommodation prices start to drop. October also hosts the Akbank Jazz Festival, featuring performances by international and local artists in various venues across the city.

November:

November sees cooler temperatures, ranging from 9°C to 15°C (48°F to 59°F). The weather can be a bit unpredictable, with occasional rain, but it's still a good time for indoor attractions and cultural experiences. Tourist numbers are lower, allowing for a more relaxed exploration of Istanbul's famous sites. The city's culinary scene becomes even more appealing, with hearty Turkish dishes providing comfort against the cooler weather.

December:

December is cold, with temperatures between 5°C and 11°C (41°F to 52°F). The city takes on a festive vibe, with Christmas markets, lights, and decorations, particularly in areas frequented by tourists. It's a great time to experience Turkish hospitality in cozy cafes and restaurants. While it's off-season for tourism, the New Year's Eve celebrations bring a brief spike in visitors, with fireworks and parties taking place across Istanbul.

Getting to Istanbul

By Air

Major Airports

Istanbul is served by two major airports:

a. Istanbul Airport (IST)

Location: Located on the European side, about 40 km (25 miles) northwest of the city center.

Facilities: One of the largest airports in the world, featuring a wide range of amenities including lounges, duty-free shops, restaurants, and hotels.

Airlines: The main hub for Turkish Airlines, offering numerous international and domestic flights.

Connectivity: Well-connected with direct flights from major cities around the world, including New York, London, Paris, Dubai, Tokyo, and many more.

b. Sabiha Gokcen International Airport (SAW)

Location: Located on the Asian side, about 45 km (28 miles) southeast of the city center.

Facilities: Smaller than Istanbul Airport but still offers various services including lounges, shopping, and dining options.

Airlines: A base for Pegasus Airlines and serves a variety of international and domestic carriers.

Connectivity: Provides flights from European, Middle Eastern, and Asian cities.

Transportation from Airports

a. Istanbul Airport (IST):

Metro: The M11 metro line connects the airport to the city center.

Havaist Buses: Comfortable shuttle buses that operate 24/7 to various parts of the city.

Taxis: Available 24/7 with metered fares.

Private Transfers: Can be pre-booked for convenience.

b. Sabiha Gokcen Airport (SAW):

Havabus Shuttles: Operates to Taksim Square, Kadikoy, and other key locations.

Taxis: Readily available with metered fares.

Private Transfers: Pre-booked options for door-to-door service.

By Train

a. International Train Services

The Bosphorus Express: Connects Istanbul with Bucharest, Romania. A scenic route offering sleeper and couchette services.

Trans-Balkan Express: Links Istanbul with Belgrade, and Serbia, passing through Sofia, Bulgaria. Provides comfortable sleeper cars.

b. Domestic Train Services

Marmaray Line: An underground railway that connects the European and Asian sides of Istanbul, passing under the Bosphorus.

YHT High-Speed Trains: Connects Istanbul with other major Turkish cities such as Ankara, Eskişehir, and Konya. Comfortable and efficient for long-distance travel within Turkey.

By Bus

a. International Bus Services

Eurolines: Offers routes from various European cities to Istanbul.

Metro Turizm and Ulusoy: Turkish bus companies providing services from Balkan countries, Greece, and other neighboring regions.

b. Domestic Bus Services

Bus Terminals: The two main bus terminals are Esenler (European side) and Harem (Asian side). They serve various destinations within Turkey.

Major Companies: Include Kamil Koç, Pamukkale, and Metro Turizm. Buses are modern with amenities like Wi-Fi and refreshments.

By Car

Driving to Istanbul

European Routes: From Europe, drivers can use major highways like the E80 (Trans-European Motorway) that connects to the Turkish border.

Asian Routes: From Asia, drivers typically enter through border crossings from Iran or Georgia.

Car Rentals

Availability: Numerous international and local car rental agencies at airports and within the city.

Driving Conditions: Modern highways, but heavy traffic can be a challenge, especially during peak hours.

Documentation: An international driving permit (IDP) may be required, along with your home country's driver's license.

By Sea

International Ferry Services

From Greece: Ferries operate from Greek islands like Lesbos and Chios to Turkish ports, with connections to Istanbul.

From Ukraine and Russia: Limited ferry services are available, mostly for freight but occasionally for passengers.

Domestic Ferry Services

Sehir Hatlari: Operates traditional ferry services across the Bosphorus, connecting the European and Asian sides of the city.

IDO (Istanbul Deniz Otobüsleri): Provides fast ferries to nearby cities like Bursa and Yalova.

Arrival Tips

Currency Exchange: Available at airports, and major train and bus stations, but often with better rates in the city.

SIM Cards: Available at airports and various locations in the city for mobile connectivity.

Language: Basic English is commonly spoken in tourist areas, but learning a few Turkish phrases can be helpful.

Local Transport: The Istanbul Card (Istanbulkart) is a reusable travel card for public transport, including buses, trams, and ferries.

Visa and Entry Requirements

Visa Exemption:

Citizens of several countries do not require a visa to enter Turkey for tourism or business purposes for stays up to 90 days within 180 days. This includes citizens of the European Union member states, the United States, Canada, Australia, and many others. The exact list can vary, so it's essential to check with the Turkish Ministry of Foreign Affairs or the nearest Turkish consulate/embassy for the latest information specific to your nationality.

E-Visa:

For citizens of countries that require a visa, Turkey offers an electronic visa (e-Visa) application system, which allows travelers to obtain a visa online before traveling to Turkey. The e-Visa is valid for tourism or business purposes and allows stays up to 90 days within 180 days. The process is straightforward and can be completed via the official Republic of Turkey e-Visa website.

To apply for an e-visa, you will need:

- A valid passport (with an expiration date at least six months beyond the duration of your stay in Turkey).
- A credit/debit card for payment.
- A valid email address to receive the e-visa.

The e-visa is usually processed quickly (often within minutes to hours), and once approved, it is sent to the applicant via email. Travelers are advised to apply for their e-Visa well in advance of their travel dates to avoid any last-minute issues.

Visa on Arrival:

Turkey also offers a visa-on-arrival option for citizens of some countries who do not qualify for an e-visa. This option is generally available at Turkish airports and allows for a single-entry stay of up to 30 days. However, it's crucial to check the latest updates and confirm eligibility before traveling, as visa policies can change.

Work and Residence Permits:

For those planning to work, study, or reside in Turkey for longer periods, different visa and permit requirements apply. Work permits, residence permits, and student visas have specific application processes and requirements, often requiring documentation such as proof of employment, student enrollment, or financial means.

Entry Requirements:

Passport Validity: Your passport should be valid for at least six months beyond your intended stay in Turkey.

Return Ticket: It is advisable to have a return or onward ticket when entering Turkey, as immigration officials may ask for proof of departure.

Proof of Funds: Although not always requested, having proof of sufficient funds to cover your stay in Turkey can be helpful.

Important Notes:

Border Crossings: If you plan to enter Turkey via a land border, check the specific entry requirements and visa policies, as they may differ from those at airports.

Travel Advisories: Before traveling, it's wise to check travel advisories issued by your home country and the Turkish government for any updates or advisories regarding safety, health, or entry requirements.

Budgeting and Costs

Planning a budget for a vacation in Istanbul involves considering various aspects such as accommodation, food, transportation, sightseeing, and miscellaneous expenses. Here's a detailed breakdown to help you estimate your travel costs:

Transportation Costs

Transportation in Istanbul is relatively affordable and efficient, with various options available, including public transport, taxis, and ride-sharing services.

Public Transport: The Istanbulkart is a rechargeable smart card that can be used on buses, trams, metro, ferries, and funiculars. A single trip costs around 7.67 TL (approximately USD 0.80) with the Istanbulkart, which can be purchased and topped up at various kiosks and stations. Public transport is the most cost-effective way to get around the city.

Taxis and Ride-Sharing: Taxis are plentiful but can be more expensive, especially during peak hours or heavy traffic.

The starting fare is around 9.8 TL (USD 1), and the fare increases by 6.3 TL (USD 0.65) per kilometer. Ride-sharing apps like Uber and BiTaksi are available and might offer promotions or discounts.

Walking: Many of Istanbul's key attractions are within walking distance of each other, especially in the Sultanahmet area. Walking not only saves money but also allows you to explore the city's hidden gems and enjoy its vibrant street life.

Accommodation Costs

Accommodation in Istanbul ranges from budget hostels to luxury hotels. Prices vary significantly based on the location, type of accommodation, and time of year.

Budget Accommodation: Budget hotels and hostels range from $10 to $30 per night. These are ideal for solo travelers and backpackers.

Mid-Range Accommodation: Mid-range hotels cost between $60 and $150 per night, offering a balance of comfort and affordability.

Luxury Accommodation: Luxury hotels and boutique stays range from $200 to $600 per night, providing high-end amenities and services.

Food and Dining Costs

Istanbul offers a wide variety of dining options, from street food to fine dining, catering to different budgets.

Street Food: Street food is both delicious and affordable. Popular options include simit (a sesame-coated bread ring) for 5 TL (USD 0.50), döner kebabs for around 30 TL (USD 3), and balik ekmek (fish sandwich) for about 40 TL (USD 4).

Local Restaurants: Dining at local restaurants or cafes costs between $5 and $15 per meal. Traditional dishes like kebabs, mezes, and pide (Turkish pizza) are both filling and reasonably priced.

Fine Dining: Fine dining restaurants can cost anywhere from $30 to $100 per person, offering a more upscale experience with gourmet Turkish and international cuisine.

Attraction Costs

Many of Istanbul's attractions are either free or inexpensive, but some major sites have entrance fees.

Free Attractions: Visiting iconic landmarks like the Blue Mosque, Grand Bazaar, and Spice Bazaar is free. Walking tours and exploring neighborhoods like Sultanahmet and Galata are also cost-free.

Paid Attractions: Entry fees for top attractions like Hagia Sophia (300 TL/$30 USD), Topkapi Palace (320 TL/$32 USD including the Harem section), and the Basilica Cistern (190 TL/$19 USD) can add up, so budgeting for these is important.

Museum Pass Istanbul: For 700 TL (USD 70), the Museum Pass provides access to multiple museums and historical sites over five days, potentially saving money if you plan to visit several attractions.

Money-Saving Tips

1. **Use Public Transportation:** The Istanbulkart provides discounted fares across all public transport. It's economical and convenient for getting around.
2. **Stay in Budget or Mid-Range Accommodation:** Look for deals and book in advance to secure better rates. Consider staying in neighborhoods slightly outside the main tourist areas for lower prices.
3. **Eat Local:** Enjoying street food and dining at local restaurants can significantly reduce food expenses. Sampling traditional Turkish cuisine at affordable eateries provides an authentic experience without breaking the bank.
4. **Visit Free Attractions:** Take advantage of the many free attractions in Istanbul, such as mosques, markets, and public parks. Plan your visits to paid attractions and consider purchasing the Museum Pass for cost savings.
5. **Travel Off-Peak:** Traveling during the shoulder seasons (spring and fall) can result in lower accommodation rates and fewer crowds, enhancing your experience and saving money.
6. **Book Online in Advance:** Many attractions, tours, and transportation services offer discounts for online bookings made in advance. This also helps avoid long queues at popular sites.

7. **Negotiate Prices:** In markets like the Grand Bazaar and Spice Bazaar, haggling is expected. Polite negotiation can lead to significant savings on souvenirs and goods.
8. **Use Local Currency:** Paying in Turkish Lira (TL) instead of foreign currency ensures you get the best exchange rate and avoid additional fees.

Daily Budget Estimate for Istanbul

Budget Traveler ($40 - $60 per day)

- **Accommodation:** $10 - $20 (Hostels or budget hotels)
- **Food:** $10 - $15 (Street food and budget eateries)
- **Transportation:** $5 (Public transport with Istanbulkart)
- **Attractions:** $5 - $10 (Free attractions and a couple of paid sites)
- **Miscellaneous:** $5 - $10 (Snacks, souvenirs)

Mid-Range Traveler ($100 - $150 per day)

- **Accommodation:** $50 - $80 (Mid-range hotels)
- **Food:** $20 - $30 (Mix of local restaurants and occasional street food)
- **Transportation:** $10 (Public transport and occasional taxi or ride-sharing)
- **Attractions:** $10 - $20 (A mix of paid and free attractions)
- **Miscellaneous:** $10 (Snacks, small purchases)

Luxury Traveler ($200 - $400+ per day)

- **Accommodation:** $150 - $300 (Luxury hotels and boutique stays)
- **Food:** $50 - $100 (Fine dining and high-end restaurants)
- **Transportation:** $20 - $30 (Taxis, ride-sharing, and possibly private transfers)
- **Attractions:** $20 - $30 (Entrance fees for multiple sites and possibly guided tours)
- **Miscellaneous:** $20 - $50 (Shopping, high-end souvenirs, extra services)

By carefully planning and utilizing these money-saving tips, you can enjoy all that Istanbul has to offer while keeping your expenses in check. Whether it's savoring local cuisine, exploring historic sites, or simply soaking in the vibrant culture, Istanbul offers a wealth of experiences that cater to every budget.

Travel Insurance

Travel insurance is an essential consideration for anyone planning a trip to Istanbul, or anywhere else for that matter.

Here's a comprehensive overview of what travel insurance typically covers and why it's important for visitors to Istanbul:

Importance of Travel Insurance

Medical Emergencies: Travel insurance provides coverage for medical emergencies, including doctor visits, hospital stays, and emergency medical evacuation. In Istanbul, having insurance ensures access to quality medical care in case of unexpected illness or injury.

Trip Cancellation/Interruption: It reimburses non-refundable trip costs if your trip is canceled or interrupted due to covered reasons, such as illness, injury, or natural disasters. Istanbul, like any travel destination, can be affected by unforeseen events that might disrupt your plans.

Lost or Delayed Baggage: Insurance covers costs associated with lost, stolen, or delayed baggage. In a bustling city like Istanbul, this coverage can be crucial for replacing essential items if your luggage is lost or delayed.

Travel Delays: It provides compensation for additional expenses due to travel delays, such as accommodation and meals, if your trip is delayed for a certain amount of time (typically 6-12 hours) due to reasons like weather, airline strikes, or mechanical failures.

Personal Liability: Coverage for legal expenses and damages if you're held liable for injury or property damage to others while in Istanbul.

Emergency Assistance Services: Most travel insurance policies offer 24/7 emergency assistance services, including help with medical emergencies, legal referrals, translation services, and travel arrangements.

What to Consider When Buying Travel Insurance for Istanbul

Coverage Limits: Ensure the policy limits are sufficient to cover potential expenses in Istanbul, where healthcare costs can vary.

Exclusions: Review the policy exclusions carefully to understand what situations are not covered. For instance, certain activities like extreme sports may require additional coverage.

Pre-Existing Conditions: Some policies may exclude coverage for pre-existing medical conditions unless a waiver is purchased or conditions are met.

Length of Coverage: Determine if the policy covers the entire duration of your stay in Istanbul, including any side trips or extensions.

Policy Reviews: Read reviews and check the reputation of the insurance provider to ensure they have a good track record of handling claims, especially internationally.

Where to Purchase Travel Insurance

Online Providers: Numerous online platforms offer comparative quotes and comprehensive coverage options tailored to international travelers.

Travel Agencies: Many travel agencies and tour operators offer travel insurance as part of their packages.

Credit Cards: Some credit cards provide limited travel insurance coverage if you purchase your trip with the card, though coverage may be less comprehensive compared to standalone policies.

Chapter 3: Accommodation

Types of Accommodations in Istanbul

Luxury Hotels

Istanbul boasts a wealth of luxury hotels that offer a blend of modern amenities and rich historical charm. These five-star establishments are often situated in prime areas such as Sultanahmet, Taksim, and along the Bosphorus, providing stunning views and easy access to major attractions. Luxury hotels in Istanbul feature lavish rooms with high-end furnishings, and marble bathrooms, and often include access to on-site spas, gourmet restaurants, and rooftop bars with panoramic city views. The service is impeccable, with personalized attention and a range of concierge services. Popular choices include the Ciragan Palace Kempinski and the Four Seasons Hotel Istanbul at Sultanahmet. The price range for luxury hotels in Istanbul typically starts from around 5,000 TRY ($180) per night and can go upwards depending on the suite and season.

Boutique Hotels

Boutique hotels in Istanbul offer a more intimate and personalized experience, often set in charming, historic buildings that have been meticulously restored. These hotels are scattered throughout the city, with notable concentrations in the Beyoğlu, Karaköy, and Galata districts, where the blend of history and modernity creates a unique atmosphere. Rooms are typically well-appointed with stylish décor that often reflects the local culture and heritage, offering guests an authentic Turkish experience. Amenities can include on-site cafes, cozy lounges, and sometimes small, private courtyards or terraces. Prices for boutique hotels range from 2,000 to 4,500 TRY ($70-$160) per night, making them an excellent option for travelers seeking comfort and style without the grandeur of larger luxury hotels.

Mid-Range Hotels

For those seeking comfort without the hefty price tag, Istanbul's mid-range hotels offer a balance between affordability and quality. These hotels are often located in central districts like Şişli, Beşiktaş, and Kadıköy, providing easy access to public transportation and popular sites. Rooms are generally spacious and well-maintained, with essential amenities such as Wi-Fi, air conditioning, and breakfast services. Many mid-range hotels also feature on-site restaurants and business facilities, making them a good choice for both leisure and business travelers. The price range for these accommodations typically falls between 1,000 to 2,500 TRY ($35-$90) per night, offering good value for money in a city known for its diverse lodging options.

Budget Hotels and Hostels

Budget-conscious travelers will find numerous options in Istanbul, from budget hotels to hostels that cater to a younger crowd or those looking to stretch their travel budget. These accommodations are commonly found in districts like Fatih, Sultanahmet, and Taksim, close to major tourist sites. While rooms are basic, they are clean and functional, often with shared or private bathrooms. Hostels typically offer dormitory-style rooms with shared facilities, communal kitchens, and social areas where travelers can meet. Some budget hotels may also include simple breakfast offerings. Prices for budget hotels range from 500 to 1,000 TRY ($18-$35) per night, while hostel beds can start as low as 150 TRY ($5) per night, making them an ideal choice for backpackers and solo travelers.

Apartments and Vacation Rentals

For those who prefer the comforts of home, Istanbul offers a wide range of apartments and vacation rentals. These accommodations are particularly popular in neighborhoods like Beyoğlu, Nişantaşı, and Kadıköy, where modern, fully-equipped apartments provide a home-like atmosphere. Apartments vary in size, from studios to multi-bedroom units, and include amenities such as kitchens, laundry facilities, and often, living and dining areas. Some even offer balconies or terraces with city views. Vacation rentals are ideal for families, groups, or travelers planning an extended stay, offering the flexibility to cook meals and live like a local. Prices for vacation rentals range from 1,500 to 5,000 TRY ($50-$180) per night, depending on the location and size of the apartment.

Historical Inns (Konaks)

For a truly unique experience, staying in one of Istanbul's historical inns, known as konaks, can offer a deep dive into the city's rich past. These accommodations are typically set in restored Ottoman-era mansions, providing a blend of historical architecture and modern comfort. Konaks are often found in areas like Sultanahmet, with some located near iconic landmarks like the Blue Mosque and Hagia Sophia. Rooms are decorated with traditional Turkish furnishings, and many inns feature beautiful courtyards, lush gardens, and sometimes, panoramic rooftop terraces.

Staying in a konak offers a more personalized experience, often with fewer rooms and more attentive service. Prices generally range from 2,500 to 4,500 TRY ($90-$160) per night, offering a luxurious yet intimate stay steeped in history.

Waterfront Hotels

Waterfront hotels in Istanbul offer stunning views of the Bosphorus Strait or the Sea of Marmara, providing a tranquil escape within the bustling city. These hotels are often located in the Beşiktaş, Ortaköy, and Üsküdar districts, allowing guests to enjoy the scenic beauty of Istanbul's iconic waterways. Rooms in waterfront hotels are typically designed with large windows or balconies to maximize the views, and many offer luxury amenities such as in-room jacuzzis, private terraces, and access to exclusive piers. Guests can enjoy on-site fine dining restaurants that serve fresh seafood and Turkish cuisine, often with outdoor seating areas that overlook the water. These hotels are ideal for romantic getaways or special occasions, with prices ranging from 4,000 to 8,000 TRY ($140-$280) per night, depending on the location and the level of luxury offered.

Eco-Friendly and Sustainable Hotels

Istanbul has seen a rise in eco-friendly and sustainable hotels, catering to environmentally-conscious travelers. These hotels are often located in quieter, more residential areas like Cihangir and Moda, though some can also be found in central locations. Sustainable hotels in Istanbul emphasize the use of natural materials, energy-efficient systems, and locally sourced products. Rooms are designed with eco-friendly features such as organic linens, low-energy lighting, and recycling programs. Many of these hotels also offer plant-based dining options, support local artisans, and provide guests with information on how to explore the city in an eco-friendly manner. Prices for sustainable hotels range from 2,000 to 4,500 TRY ($70-$160) per night, making them an attractive option for those looking to minimize their environmental impact while enjoying a comfortable stay.

Family-Friendly Hotels

Family-friendly hotels in Istanbul cater to the needs of travelers with children, offering spacious accommodations and amenities designed to make family stays enjoyable. These hotels are often located in neighborhoods like Sultanahmet and Kadıköy, close to family-oriented attractions such as parks, museums, and the Istanbul Aquarium.

Rooms in family-friendly hotels are larger, often with the option for adjoining rooms or suites, and are equipped with cribs, extra beds, and childproofing features. On-site facilities may include kid-friendly dining options, play areas, and sometimes even babysitting services. Many family-friendly hotels also offer special packages that include tickets to local attractions or discounts on family activities. Prices typically range from 1,500 to 3,500 TRY ($50-$120) per night, depending on the size of the room and the amenities provided.

Traditional Turkish Guesthouses (Pansiyons)

Traditional Turkish guesthouses, or pansiyons, offer a warm, homely experience that is often more affordable than staying in a hotel. These accommodations are typically run by local families and are found in various neighborhoods across Istanbul, including Sultanahmet, Fatih, and Üsküdar. Rooms are usually simple but comfortable, often decorated with traditional Turkish textiles and furnishings. Staying in a pansiyon provides an opportunity to experience Turkish hospitality firsthand, with home-cooked meals and personalized service. Breakfast is usually included, featuring a spread of traditional Turkish dishes like fresh bread, olives, cheeses, and homemade jams. These guesthouses are ideal for travelers looking for a more authentic and budget-friendly experience, with prices ranging from 500 to 1,500 TRY ($18-$50) per night, depending on the location and amenities offered.

Business Hotels

Istanbul's business hotels are designed to meet the needs of corporate travelers, offering a range of services and facilities that cater to professional requirements. These hotels are commonly located in business districts like Levent, Maslak, and the Asian side's Ataşehir, close to major corporate offices and conference centers. Rooms in business hotels are typically modern and equipped with high-speed internet, work desks, and comfortable seating areas. On-site amenities often include business centers, meeting rooms, and event spaces, as well as fitness facilities and restaurants that provide quick and efficient service. Some business hotels also offer executive lounges and airport shuttle services, ensuring a seamless travel experience. Prices for business hotels range from 2,500 to 5,500 TRY ($90-$190) per night, making them a convenient and practical choice for business travelers.

Chapter 4: Attractions and Landmarks

20 Must-See Sights and Attractions in Istanbul, Turkey

Istanbul is a city rich with history, culture, and stunning architecture. Here are 20 must-see sights and attractions that capture the essence of this fascinating metropolis:

1. Hagia Sophia

Hagia Sophia, originally built in 537 AD as a cathedral by the Byzantine Emperor Justinian I, is an architectural marvel in Istanbul. Renowned for its massive dome, it was the world's largest cathedral for nearly a thousand years. The structure later served as an imperial mosque after the Ottoman conquest in 1453 and was converted into a museum in 1935. In 2020, it was re-opened as a mosque. The interior is adorned with stunning mosaics, calligraphic panels, and marble pillars, reflecting both Byzantine and Ottoman art. The vast space and natural light filtering through the windows create a serene and majestic ambiance. Its historical significance and architectural grandeur make it a must-visit landmark, offering a unique glimpse into Istanbul's rich cultural heritage.

- **Opening Hours:** Daily, 24 hours (limited access during prayer times)
- **Address:** Ayasofya Meydanı, Sultanahmet, Fatih, Istanbul, Turkey

- **How to Get There:** Take the tram to Sultanahmet station and walk a few minutes.
- **Insider Tip:** Visit early in the morning or late in the afternoon to avoid crowds and enjoy a more peaceful experience.

2. Blue Mosque (Sultan Ahmed Mosque)

The Blue Mosque, also known as the Sultan Ahmed Mosque, is one of Istanbul's most iconic landmarks. Constructed between 1609 and 1616 during the rule of Sultan Ahmed I, it is renowned for its stunning architecture, which features a large central dome, six minarets, and a spacious courtyard. The mosque's name derives from the tens of thousands of Iznik tiles that adorn its interior, creating a mesmerizing blue hue. Visitors are captivated by the mosque's intricate designs, grand scale, and serene ambiance. The Blue Mosque is still an active place of worship, and visitors are reminded to dress modestly and remove their shoes before entering. The mosque's strategic location in Sultanahmet makes it easily accessible and a central part of any historical tour of Istanbul.

- **Opening Hours:** 9:00 AM to 6:00 PM (Closed during prayer times)
- **Address:** Sultan Ahmet, Atmeydanı Cd. No:7, 34122 Fatih/Istanbul, Turkey
- **How to Get There:** Easily accessible via tram to Sultanahmet station or by walking from nearby attractions.

- **Insider Tip:** Visit early in the morning or late in the afternoon to avoid crowds, and don't miss the chance to see it illuminated at night.

3. Topkapi Palace

Topkapi Palace, a symbol of the Ottoman Empire's grandeur, served as the main residence of the Sultans for over 400 years. Built-in the 15th century by Sultan Mehmed II, it sprawls over a vast area and comprises four main courtyards and numerous smaller buildings. The palace showcases opulent architecture, intricate tile work, and a stunning collection of treasures, including the famous Topkapi Dagger and the Spoonmaker's Diamond. Visitors can explore the Harem, where the sultan's family lived, the Imperial Treasury, and the Sacred Relics room, which houses items of religious significance. The palace also offers breathtaking views of the Bosphorus and the Golden Horn, making it a must-see attraction in Istanbul.

- **Opening Hours:** Wednesday to Monday, 9:00 AM to 5:00 PM (last entrance at 4:00 PM), Closed on Tuesdays.
- **Address:** Cankurtaran, 34122 Fatih/Istanbul, Turkey
- **How to Get There:** Take the tram to Gülhane or Sultanahmet stations; the palace is a short walk from either stop.
- **Admission Fee:** Approximately $15 for adults (excluding Harem entry, which is an additional $7).

- **Insider Tip:** Visit early in the morning to avoid crowds, and don't miss the Harem for a deeper insight into the lives of the Ottoman royal family.

4. Basilica Cistern

The Basilica Cistern is an ancient underground water reservoir constructed in the 6th century during the reign of Byzantine Emperor Justinian I. Located near the Hagia Sophia in the Sultanahmet district, this massive subterranean structure is supported by 336 marble columns, each nine meters high, arranged in 12 rows. The cistern, known as Yerebatan Sarayi ("Sunken Palace") in Turkish, was designed to store water for the Great Palace of Constantinople and surrounding buildings. Notable features include the two Medusa head columns, whose origins and purpose remain a mystery. The dim lighting, the sound of dripping water, and the reflections in the water create an eerie yet captivating atmosphere, making it a favorite spot for tourists and photographers.

- **Opening Hours:** Daily, 9:00 AM - 6:30 PM
- **Address:** Alemdar, Yerebatan Cd. 1/3, 34110 Fatih/Istanbul, Turkey
- **How to Get There:** Accessible via the Sultanahmet tram stop (T1 line).
- **Admission Fee:** Approximately USD 10
- **Insider Tip:** Visit early in the morning or late in the afternoon to avoid crowds and get the best photo opportunities with the least amount of people.

5. Grand Bazaar

The Grand Bazaar in Istanbul, one of the largest and oldest covered markets in the world, is a vibrant, labyrinthine hub of commerce and culture. Established in the 15th century, it spans over 60 streets and houses more than 4,000 shops. The bazaar offers a rich variety of goods, from intricately designed jewelry, handwoven carpets, and antique furniture to spices, ceramics, and textiles. The atmosphere is a sensory delight, with the sounds of merchants haggling, the scent of exotic spices, and the sight of colorful displays creating an unforgettable experience. The Grand Bazaar is not just a shopping destination; it's a cultural journey through Istanbul's history, reflecting its significance as a major trading hub for centuries. Visitors can also enjoy the charming cafes and restaurants scattered throughout the bazaar, providing a perfect respite amid the bustling activity.

- **Opening Hours:** Monday to Saturday, 9:00 AM to 7:00 PM
- **Address:** Beyazıt, 34126 Fatih/Istanbul, Turkey
- **How to Get There:** Take the tram to Beyazıt-Kapalıçarşı or Vezneciler stations.
- **Insider Tip:** Visit early in the morning or late afternoon to avoid crowds and have a more leisurely shopping experience.

6. Spice Bazaar (Egyptian Bazaar)

The Spice Bazaar, also known as the Egyptian Bazaar, is one of Istanbul's most vibrant and aromatic attractions. Established in the 17th century, it served as a crucial trading center for spices coming from Egypt, hence its name. Today, the bazaar is a sensory delight, filled with the rich scents of saffron, cinnamon, and myriad other spices. In addition to spices, you'll find Turkish delights, dried fruits, nuts, teas, and various souvenirs. The architectural design features vaulted ceilings and narrow alleys, creating an immersive shopping experience that harks back to Ottoman times. The bazaar is located next to the Yeni Cami (New Mosque), adding to its historical charm.

- **Opening Hours:** Monday to Saturday, 8:00 AM to 7:00 PM
- **Address:** Eminönü, Rüstem Paşa, 34116 Fatih/Istanbul, Turkey
- **How to Get There:** Easily accessible by tram; take the T1 line to Eminönü station. It's also a short walk from the Eminönü ferry terminal.
- **Insider Tip:** Visit early in the morning to avoid the crowds and have a more relaxed shopping experience. Don't hesitate to haggle with the vendors for better prices.

7. Dolmabahce Palace

Dolmabahce Palace, situated along the European shore of the Bosphorus, stands as a magnificent symbol of Ottoman grandeur and European architectural influence. Built in the mid-19th century, it served as the main administrative center of the Ottoman Empire, blending elements of Baroque, Rococo, and Neoclassical styles. The palace boasts 285 rooms, including the opulent Ceremonial Hall with its crystal chandeliers and the lavish Harem quarters. Its stunning waterfront location offers panoramic views of the Bosphorus, making it a favorite among visitors seeking to immerse themselves in Istanbul's imperial history.

- **Opening Hours:** Tuesday to Sunday, 9:00 AM to 4:00 PM
- **Address:** Dolmabahce Cd., 34357 Beşiktaş/İstanbul, Turkey
- **How to Get There:** Take the tram T1 line to Kabatas station or use a ferry to Besiktas and walk along the coast.
- **Admission Fee:** Approximately USD 12
- **Insider Tip:** Guided tours are available and highly recommended to fully appreciate the palace's history and intricate details. Arrive early to avoid crowds, especially during peak tourist seasons. Photography is restricted inside, so enjoy the architecture and gardens to the fullest.

8. Galata Tower

The Galata Tower is a medieval stone tower in the Galata district of Istanbul, offering panoramic views of the city and the Bosphorus Strait. Originally built as a defensive tower in the 14th century by the Genoese, it has since served various purposes, including as an observatory for astronomers. Standing tall at 66.9 meters (219 feet), its upper floors provide visitors with breathtaking 360-degree views of Istanbul's skyline, making it a popular spot for both locals and tourists to capture stunning sunset vistas or admire the city lights at night. The tower's cylindrical shape and conical roof make it a distinctive landmark against the city's skyline.

- **Opening Hours:** Daily from 9:00 AM to 8:00 PM
- **Address:** Bereketzade Mahallesi, Galata Kulesi, 34421 Beyoğlu/İstanbul, Turkey
- **How to Get There:** Take the tram to Karaköy or the funicular to Tünel, followed by a short walk uphill to the tower.
- **Admission Fee:** Approximately USD 9
- **Insider Tip:** Visit in the late afternoon to catch the sunset and avoid long queues. The café on the upper floors is a great spot to relax and enjoy the views with a cup of Turkish tea.

9. Suleymaniye Mosque

The Suleymaniye Mosque, situated atop one of Istanbul's seven hills, is a masterpiece of Ottoman architecture and a must-see attraction in Istanbul. Commissioned by Sultan Suleiman the Magnificent and designed by the renowned architect Mimar Sinan, it was completed in 1557. The mosque impresses with its grand scale, featuring a massive dome and four minarets that dominate the city skyline. Inside, intricate tile work, stained glass windows, and calligraphy adorn the spacious prayer hall, creating a serene atmosphere conducive to reflection and prayer. The complex also includes a hospital, Quranic school, and tombs of Sultan Suleiman and his wife, Hurrem Sultan, adding historical depth to its significance.

- **Opening Hours:** Daily from 9:00 AM to 6:00 PM
- **Address:** Prof. Sıddık Sami Onar Cd. No:1, 34116 Fatih/İstanbul, Turkey
- **How to Get There:** Take the tram T1 line to Eminonu or Vezneciler stations, then a short walk uphill to the mosque.
- **Insider Tip:** Visit early in the morning to experience the mosque in a peaceful setting before crowds arrive. Don't forget to explore the gardens and enjoy panoramic views of Istanbul from the mosque's terrace.

10. Ortakoy Mosque

Ortakoy Mosque, formally known as Büyük Mecidiye Camii, is a picturesque gem located on the European shore of the Bosphorus in Istanbul. Constructed in the 19th century in a fusion of Baroque and Neo-Classical Ottoman architecture, it stands out with its elegant domes and slender minarets against the backdrop of the Bosphorus Bridge. The mosque's interior features intricate decorations and stained-glass windows, while its location offers stunning views of the Bosphorus and the waterfront cafes and boutiques that surround it. Ortakoy Mosque is not only a place of worship but also a popular spot for locals and tourists alike, especially during sunset when the sky is painted with hues of orange and purple.

- **Opening Hours:** Daily, from early morning to late evening
- **Address:** Mecidiye Mahallesi, Ortakoy, 34347 Besiktas/Istanbul, Turkey
- **How to Get There:** Take a taxi, bus, or tram to Ortakoy Square; the mosque is a short walk from there.
- **Insider Tip:** Visit during the evening to enjoy the mosque lit up against the Bosphorus, and try local snacks like kumpir (stuffed baked potatoes) from the nearby food stalls for a delightful experience.

11. Chora Church (Kariye Museum)

The Chora Church, now known as the Kariye Museum, is a hidden gem in Istanbul renowned for its stunning Byzantine mosaics and frescoes. Originally built in the 4th century outside the city walls, it underwent several renovations, with the current structure dating back to the 11th century. The interior walls are adorned with intricate mosaics depicting scenes from the life of Christ, the Virgin Mary, and other biblical narratives, characterized by their vibrant colors and detailed craftsmanship. The frescoes, added in the 14th century, further enhance its beauty with scenes from the Last Judgment and the genealogy of Christ.

- **Opening Hours:** Tuesday to Sunday, 9:00 AM to 7:00 PM
- **Address:** Kariye Cami Sk. No:26, 34087 Fatih/İstanbul, Turkey
- **How to Get There:** Take the T4 tram line to Edirnekapi station, then walk about 10 minutes to the museum. Alternatively, taxis and rideshare apps are convenient options.
- **Admission Fee:** Approximately USD 10
- **Insider Tip:** Visit early in the morning or later in the afternoon to avoid crowds and fully appreciate the detailed artwork and serene atmosphere. Audio guides are available for a deeper understanding of the historical and religious significance of the mosaics and frescoes.

12. Bosphorus Bridge

The Bosphorus Bridge, officially known as the 15 July Martyrs Bridge, spans the Bosphorus Strait, connecting Europe and Asia. Completed in 1973, it was the first bridge to link the continents and remains an iconic symbol of Istanbul. The bridge's sleek design and nighttime illumination make it a striking sight, especially when viewed from nearby parks or during a Bosphorus cruise. Its importance isn't just structural; it's a cultural landmark that embodies Istanbul's geographical and historical significance as a bridge between East and West.

- **Opening Hours:** Open 24 hours
- **Address:** Bosphorus Strait, Istanbul, Turkey
- **How to Get There:** Accessible by car, taxi, or public transportation. The nearest metro station is 4. Levent on the European side, and Haciosman on the Asian side.
- **Insider Tip:** For the best views, consider visiting at dusk or night when the bridge is illuminated, offering a spectacular backdrop of Istanbul's skyline. If driving, be mindful of traffic congestion during rush hours, which can affect travel times across the bridge.

13. Istiklal Avenue

Istiklal Avenue is Istanbul's vibrant cultural heart, a bustling pedestrian street stretching from Taksim Square to Galata Tower. Lined with historic buildings, shops, cafes, and galleries, it offers a lively atmosphere day and night. Originally known as Grande Rue de Pera during the Ottoman era, it has retained its cosmopolitan charm, attracting locals and tourists alike. Stroll along cobblestone paths under the shade of historic tram lines, passing by iconic landmarks like St. Anthony of Padua Church and the nostalgic Pera Palace Hotel. The avenue is a hub for fashion, dining, and entertainment, with everything from trendy boutiques to traditional Turkish eateries and lively bars. It's not just a shopping street but a cultural experience that reflects Istanbul's modern identity and historical legacy.

- **Opening Hours:** Open daily, shops generally from 10:00 AM to 8:00 PM
- **Address:** Beyoglu, Istanbul, Turkey
- **How to Get There:** Take the metro to Taksim Square or use the historic tram from Tunel to Taksim.
- **Insider Tip:** Visit in the evening for a more atmospheric experience with street performances and illuminated buildings. Explore side streets for hidden gems like historic bookstores and art galleries.

14. Taksim Square

Taksim Square serves as the vibrant heart of modern Istanbul, known for its bustling atmosphere and historical significance. Surrounded by shops, restaurants, and hotels, it's a cultural hub where locals and tourists converge. At its center stands the Republic Monument, commemorating the foundation of the Turkish Republic. The square is a focal point for celebrations, protests, and events, reflecting its role in Turkish social and political life. Istiklal Avenue, a bustling pedestrian street full of shops and cafes, begins at Taksim Square, making it a starting point for exploring Beyoglu's lively district.

- **Opening Hours:** Open 24/7
- **Address:** Taksim Square, Beyoglu, Istanbul, Turkey
- **How to Get There:** Take the metro to Taksim station (M2 line) or various buses and dolmus services that stop directly at Taksim Square.
- **Insider Tip:** Visit in the evening to experience the square when it's most lively. Explore Istiklal Avenue for shopping, dining, and a taste of Istanbul's contemporary culture.

15. Maiden's Tower

The Maiden's Tower (Kız Kulesi), located on a small islet in the Bosphorus Strait, is a captivating icon of Istanbul's skyline and history. Dating back to ancient times, this tower has served as a lighthouse, customs station, and defense fortification throughout its storied past. Today, it stands as a picturesque landmark with panoramic views of Istanbul and the Bosphorus, offering visitors a tranquil escape from the bustling city. The tower is steeped in myths and legends, including the tragic tale of a princess locked inside to protect her from a prophecy.

- **Opening Hours:** Daily, 9:00 AM to 7:00 PM
- **Address:** Salacak Mahallesi, Üsküdar, Istanbul, Turkey
- **How to Get There:** Reachable by boat from Üsküdar or Kabataş, with regular ferry services available.
- **Admission Fee:** Approximately USD 5
- **Insider Tip:** Visit during sunset for breathtaking views of the cityscape bathed in golden light, and consider dining at the tower's restaurant for a unique dining experience on the Bosphorus.

16. Camlica Hill

Camlica Hill offers panoramic views of Istanbul, making it a must-see attraction for visitors. Located on the Asian side of the city, it is the highest point in Istanbul and provides breathtaking vistas of the Bosphorus Strait, the European skyline, and the Sea of Marmara. The hill is divided into two peaks, Büyük Çamlıca (Big Camlica) and Küçük Çamlıca (Small Camlica), both offering excellent vantage points for sunset and cityscape photography. In addition to its natural beauty, Camlica Hill features landscaped gardens, walking paths, and cafes where visitors can relax and enjoy the scenery.

- **Opening Hours:** Daily from 9:00 AM to 10:00 PM
- **Address:** Çamlıca Tepesi, Üsküdar, Istanbul, Turkey
- **How to Get There:** Take a taxi or public bus to Çamlıca Hill from Üsküdar or Kadıköy.
- **Insider Tip:** Visit during the late afternoon to catch the sunset and see Istanbul illuminated at night. Bring a camera for stunning panoramic shots.

17. Istanbul Archaeological Museums

The Istanbul Archaeological Museums complex consists of three distinct museums: the Archaeological Museum, the Museum of the Ancient Orient, and the Tiled Kiosk Museum.

Together, they house an extensive collection of artifacts from ancient civilizations, including relics from Mesopotamia, Anatolia, and the classical world. Notable exhibits include the Alexander Sarcophagus, a masterpiece of Hellenistic sculpture, and the Sphinx of Babylon, showcasing the grandeur of ancient Mesopotamian art. The museums provide a comprehensive overview of the region's rich historical and cultural heritage.

Address: Alemdar Mahallesi, Osman Hamdi Bey Yokusu, 34122 Fatih/Istanbul, Turkey

Opening Hours:

- Daily: 9:00 AM – 7:00 PM
- Closed: Mondays

How to Get There:

- By Tram: Take the T1 Tram Line and get off at Sultanahmet Station. The museums are a short walk from the tram stop.
- By Metro: Use the M2 Metro Line and get off at Vezneciler Station, then transfer to the T1 Tram Line.

Admission Fee: 200 TRY: Approximately $7.50

Insider Tip: Visit the Istanbul Archaeological Museums early in the day to avoid the crowds, especially during peak tourist seasons. Consider purchasing a museum pass to save on admission fees and gain access to other museums in Istanbul. Don't miss the Museum of the Ancient Orient for its impressive collection of ancient artifacts, including the monumental statues of the Hittite Empire.

18. Bosphorus Cruise

A Bosphorus cruise offers a scenic journey along the strait that separates Europe and Asia, providing breathtaking views of Istanbul's skyline, historic landmarks, and luxurious waterfront mansions. The cruise typically passes iconic sites such as the Dolmabahçe Palace, Rumeli Fortress, and the Bosphorus Bridge. There are various options for cruises, including short tours and longer, more comprehensive excursions. The experience combines stunning vistas with a unique perspective of Istanbul's diverse architecture and natural beauty.

Address: Various departure points, including:

- Eminönü: Galata Bridge, Eminönü, Istanbul
- Kabataş: Kabataş Ferry Terminal, Kabataş, Istanbul

Opening Hours:

- Daily: Cruises typically operate from 10:00 AM to 8:00 PM
- Departure Times: Varies by cruise operator

How to Get There:

- By Tram: Take the T1 Tram Line to Eminönü Station for cruises departing from this area.
- By Metro: Take the M2 Metro Line to Kabataş Station for cruises departing from Kabataş.
- By Ferry: Ferries connect various parts of the city, including Eminönü and Kabataş, with regular services.

Insider Tip: For the best experience, choose a cruise that includes a sunset or evening option to enjoy the city illuminated by night. Book your tickets in advance, especially during peak tourist seasons, to secure your spot.

Consider bringing a light jacket, as it can get breezy on the water. Additionally, some cruises offer meals or refreshments, so check the options available to enhance your experience.

19. Sultanahmet Square

Sultanahmet Square is the historic heart of Istanbul, home to several of the city's most iconic landmarks. This central area features the Hagia Sophia, the Blue Mosque, and the Hippodrome. The square is a vibrant hub where ancient history meets modern life. The Hippodrome, once a Byzantine chariot racing track, now hosts the Egyptian Obelisk and other historical monuments. The surrounding area is lined with cafés and shops, making it a lively spot for visitors to explore Istanbul's rich cultural heritage.

Address: Sultanahmet Mahallesi, 34122 Fatih/Istanbul, Turkey

How to Get There:

- By Tram: Take the T1 Tram Line and get off at Sultanahmet Station. The square is a short walk from the tram stop.
- By Metro: Use the M2 Metro Line and get off at Vezneciler Station, then transfer to the T1 Tram Line to reach Sultanahmet.
- By Bus: Several public buses stop near Sultanahmet Square, including routes 28, 30, 31, and 36.

Admission Fee:

- Hagia Sophia: 200 TRY (approx. $7.50)

- Blue Mosque: Free entry, but donations are welcome
- Hippodrome: Free to visit

Insider Tip: Early mornings or late afternoons are the best times to visit Sultanahmet Square to avoid large crowds and enjoy a more peaceful experience. For a unique perspective, consider taking a walk around the square to capture photographs of the landmarks with different lighting. Be sure to check the opening hours of the individual attractions in advance, as they may vary or be subject to special events.

20. Rüstem Paşa Mosque

The Rüstem Paşa Mosque is a lesser-known gem in Istanbul, renowned for its exquisite İznik tiles that adorn its interior. Commissioned by Rüstem Paşa, the grand vizier of Suleiman the Magnificent, this mosque is a masterpiece of Ottoman architecture. It features a compact yet beautifully decorated prayer hall with intricate tile work in vibrant blues, greens, and reds. The mosque's design includes a stunning courtyard and a charming, serene atmosphere, offering a more intimate experience compared to Istanbul's larger mosques.

Address: Hasırcılar Caddesi, 34116 Eminönü/Fatih, Istanbul, Turkey

Opening Hours: Daily: 9:00 AM – 5:00 PM

How to Get There:

- By Tram: Take the T1 Tram Line and get off at Eminönü Station. The mosque is a short walk from the tram stop.
- By Metro: Use the M2 Metro Line and get off at Vezneciler Station, then transfer to the T1 Tram Line to reach Eminönü.
- By Bus: Several public buses stop near Eminönü, including routes 28, 30, 31, and 36.

Admission Fee: Free (Donations are welcome)

Insider Tip: Visit the Rüstem Paşa Mosque early in the day to enjoy its serene beauty without the crowds. The mosque's compact size makes it an excellent spot for a quiet moment of reflection. Take time to admire the detailed tile work up close, and consider bringing a camera to capture the vibrant colors and intricate patterns. Also, dress modestly and remember to remove your shoes before entering the mosque.

Chapter 5: Getting Around Istanbul

Public Transportation: Metro, Trams, Buses and Ferries

Getting around Istanbul is relatively easy due to its extensive public transportation network and various options suited to different preferences and budgets. Here's a comprehensive guide:

Public Transportation

1. Metro:

The metro system in Istanbul is one of the most efficient and reliable means of transportation, connecting various parts of the city, including the European and Asian sides. Here's a detailed guide to help you understand and make the most of Istanbul's metro network.

Overview of the Metro System

Istanbul's metro system consists of several lines that serve different parts of the city. The system is constantly expanding to accommodate the growing population and to provide better connectivity. The key lines are:

- M1 Line (Aksaray - Atatürk Airport / Kirazlı)
- M2 Line (Yenikapı - Hacıosman)
- M3 Line (Başakşehir - Metrokent / Kirazlı)
- M4 Line (Kadıköy - Tavşantepe)
- M5 Line (Üsküdar - Çekmeköy)
- M6 Line (Levent - Boğaziçi University / Hisarüstü)
- M7 Line (Kabataş - Mahmutbey)
- M9 Line (Bahariye - Olimpiyat)
- Marmaray (Gebze - Halkalı)

Key Metro Lines and Their Significance

a. M1 Line (Yenikapı - Atatürk Airport / Kirazlı)

Stations: Key stations include Yenikapı (connection to M2 and Marmaray), Aksaray, Otogar (main bus terminal), and Atatürk Airport.

Significance: This line is crucial for travelers coming from the old Atatürk Airport (now mostly used for cargo and private jets) and for those connecting to long-distance buses.

b. M2 Line (Yenikapı - Hacıosman)

Stations: Important stops include Yenikapı, Taksim (central hub for tourists), Şişli-Mecidiyeköy (shopping district), and Levent (business district).

Significance: The M2 line is essential for reaching central business districts, popular shopping areas, and tourist attractions.

c. Marmaray Line (Gebze - Halkalı)

Stations: Major stations are Halkalı, Yenikapı, Sirkeci (historical center), Üsküdar, and Gebze.

Significance: This line runs under the Bosphorus, linking the European and Asian sides, making it a critical line for cross-continental commuting.

d. M4 Line (Kadıköy - Tavşantepe)

Stations: Key stations include Kadıköy (ferry port and cultural hub), Ayrılık Çeşmesi (transfer to Marmaray), and Tavşantepe.

Significance: Serving the Asian side, this line connects residential areas to Kadıköy, a major hub for culture, dining, and transportation.

Using the Metro

a. Tickets and Istanbulkart

Istanbulkart: The most convenient way to pay for metro rides is with the Istanbulkart, a rechargeable smart card that can be used across all public transportation systems, including metros, buses, trams, and ferries.

Where to Buy: Istanbulkarts can be purchased at major metro stations, newsstands, and kiosks. They can be topped up at machines located in metro stations and convenience stores.

Fare: Using an Istanbulkart offers a discount compared to single-ride tokens or paper tickets. The fare for a single ride with an Istanbulkart is significantly cheaper, and there are further discounts for transfers within a certain time frame.

b. Navigating the Metro

Maps and Signage: Metro maps are available at all stations and on the trains. Signage in stations is in both Turkish and English, making it easy for non-Turkish speakers to navigate.

Announcements: Announcements on the trains are made in Turkish and English, providing information about upcoming stations and connections.

Apps: Several mobile apps can help with navigating the metro system, providing real-time updates on train schedules and potential delays.

c. Accessibility

Elevators and Escalators: All major stations are equipped with elevators and escalators to assist passengers with mobility issues.

Signage and Assistance: Stations have clear signage for accessible routes, and staff are available to assist if needed.

d. Safety and Security

Security Checks: Most metro stations have security checks at entrances, including bag scanners and metal detectors.

CCTV: The metro system is monitored by CCTV, ensuring passenger safety.

Emergency Assistance: In case of emergencies, there are help points and intercoms throughout the stations and in trains.

Advantages of Using the Metro

Speed and Efficiency: The metro is often faster than surface transportation, especially during peak traffic hours.

Cost-Effective: Using an Istanbulkart makes the metro an affordable option for both residents and tourists.

Connectivity: The metro system connects to other modes of transport, including trams, buses, ferries, and funiculars, making it easy to reach almost any part of the city.

Tips for Metro Travel

Avoid Peak Hours: The metro can get very crowded during rush hours (7:00-9:00 AM and 5:00-7:00 PM). If possible, plan your travels outside these times.

Stay Informed: Keep an eye on electronic displays for real-time updates on train arrivals and potential service disruptions.

Plan Your Route: Use maps and apps to plan your journey, ensuring you take the most efficient route.

2. Trams:

Trams are an integral part of Istanbul's public transportation network, offering a convenient and efficient way to navigate the city's bustling streets. With their extensive coverage of key tourist attractions and central areas, trams are a preferred mode of transport for both locals and visitors. Here's a detailed look at using trams in Istanbul:

Overview of the Tram Network

Istanbul's tram network consists of several lines that serve both the European and Asian sides of the city. The most prominent and useful lines for tourists are:

T1 Kabataş-Bağcılar Line: This is the most famous tram line, connecting key areas such as Sultanahmet, Eminönü, and the Grand Bazaar.

T2 Taksim-Tünel Nostalgic Tram Line: Running along Istiklal Avenue, this line provides a charming ride through one of the city's busiest shopping streets.

T3 Kadıköy-Moda Nostalgic Tram Line: Located on the Asian side, this line offers a scenic route through the Kadıköy district.

T4 Topkapı-Mescid-i Selam Line: This line serves the northern part of the European side, connecting Topkapı to Mescid-i Selam.

Key Stops and Attractions

Sultanahmet: Home to major historical sites such as the Hagia Sophia, Blue Mosque, and Topkapi Palace. The Sultanahmet stop on the T1 line is a must-visit for history enthusiasts.

Eminönü: A bustling area where you can visit the Spice Bazaar and catch ferries to various parts of the city. This stop is also on the T1 line.

Grand Bazaar (Kapalıçarşı): One of the largest and oldest covered markets in the world. Accessible from the Beyazit-Kapalıçarşı stop on the T1 line.

Karaköy: This stop on the T1 line is close to the Galata Bridge and Galata Tower, offering stunning views of the Golden Horn.

Taksim Square: The starting point of the T2 Nostalgic Tram, Taksim Square is a major commercial and entertainment hub.

Kadıköy: The T3 line starts here, taking you through the vibrant Kadıköy district known for its markets, cafes, and shops.

How to Use the Tram

a. Tickets and Istanbulkart:

Istanbulkart: The most convenient way to pay for tram rides. It's a reloadable smart card used across all public transportation in Istanbul, including buses, metros, and ferries. You can purchase and top up the card at major stations, kiosks, and some shops.

Single Ride Tickets: Available at tram stations, but more expensive and less convenient than using an Istanbulkart.

b. Boarding and Exiting:

Trams typically have multiple doors for boarding and exiting. Ensure you board through the designated doors.

Validate your Istanbulkart by tapping it on the card reader at the entrance.

c. Frequency and Operating Hours:

Trams run frequently, with shorter intervals during peak hours. The T1 line operates from around 6:00 AM to midnight.

Check the schedule for the specific line you plan to use, as operating hours may vary.

d. Accessibility:

Most trams are modern and accessible, with low floors and designated spaces for wheelchairs and strollers.

Stations are equipped with ramps or elevators for easy access.

Tips for Riding the Tram

Avoid Peak Hours: Trams can get crowded, especially during morning and evening rush hours. Plan your trips during off-peak times for a more comfortable ride.

Keep Valuables Safe: As with any crowded public transportation, be mindful of your belongings to avoid pickpocketing.

Stand on the Right: When using escalators at tram stations, stand on the right side to allow others to pass on the left.

Observe Local Etiquette: Offer seats to elderly passengers, pregnant women, and those with children. Follow any posted signs and announcements for a smooth journey.

Advantages of Using the Tram

Efficient and Fast: Trams often have dedicated tracks, avoiding traffic congestion and ensuring timely arrivals.

Scenic Routes: Many tram lines pass through scenic and historic parts of the city, offering beautiful views along the way.

Eco-Friendly: Trams are an environmentally friendly option, reducing the city's carbon footprint compared to cars and buses.

3. Buses:

Istanbul's bus system is one of the most extensive and crucial components of the city's public transportation network, connecting virtually every neighborhood and offering a flexible option for residents and tourists alike. Here's a detailed guide to navigating Istanbul by bus.

Coverage: Istanbul's bus network spans the entire city, from the bustling European side to the scenic Asian side.

With thousands of buses operating on hundreds of routes, you can reach almost any destination within the metropolitan area.

Operators: The primary operator of the bus network is the Istanbul Electricity, Tramway, and Tunnel General Management (IETT). Additionally, private operators run some routes under the supervision of IETT, ensuring comprehensive coverage.

Types of Buses

Standard Buses: These are the most common buses, serving regular routes throughout the city. They are typically blue and white and offer a standard level of comfort.

Metrobus: The Metrobus is a rapid transit bus system running on dedicated lanes, significantly reducing travel time, especially during peak hours. It connects the European and Asian sides, with key stops including Zincirlikuyu, Mecidiyekoy, and Avcilar.

Private/Public Partnership Buses: These buses are operated by private companies in collaboration with IETT and usually have different colors but adhere to similar standards and fare systems.

Using the Bus System

Istanbulkart: The most efficient way to pay for bus fares is by using the Istanbulkart, a reloadable smart card. It can be purchased and recharged at kiosks, metro stations, and convenience stores. The card offers discounted fares and can be used on all public transport modes, including buses, trams, metros, and ferries.

Fare: The fare system is straightforward. The Istanbulkart fare for a standard bus ride is usually less than paying with cash. Transfers between buses or other forms of transport within a certain period (usually two hours) also benefit from reduced rates.

Bus Stops and Stations: Bus stops are marked with signposts displaying route numbers and destinations. Major bus stations like Esenler and Harem serve as hubs for long-distance and intercity buses.

Timetables and Schedules: Bus schedules can be found at bus stops, online on the IETT website, or through mobile apps. While buses generally adhere to schedules, traffic conditions can cause delays.

Key Routes and Popular Lines

Route 500T: One of the longest and most popular routes, it connects Tuzla on the Asian side to Cevizlibag on the European side, passing through key districts.

Route 145T: Connects the central district of Taksim with the suburban area of Beylikduzu, offering a scenic journey through various neighborhoods.

Metrobus Line: Running from Beylikduzu in the west to Sogutlucesme in the east, it operates 24/7 and is one of the fastest ways to traverse the city across the Bosphorus.

Tips for Using Buses in Istanbul

Avoid Rush Hours: Buses can be extremely crowded during peak times (7-9 AM and 5-7 PM). If possible, plan your travel outside these hours for a more comfortable journey.

Stay Alert: Keep an eye on your belongings, as buses can get crowded, and be aware of pickpockets.

Ask for Help: Locals are generally friendly and willing to assist with directions or bus information. Basic Turkish phrases or a translation app can be very helpful.

Plan: Use mobile apps like Moovit or the official IETT app to check routes, schedules, and live bus tracking to plan your journey efficiently.

Prepare for Traffic: Istanbul's traffic can be unpredictable. Allocate extra travel time if you have a tight schedule, especially when heading to the airport or important appointments.

Accessibility: Most modern buses are equipped with low floors and ramps for wheelchair access, but older buses may not be as accessible. It's advisable to check in advance if you have mobility concerns.

Advantages of Using Buses

Extensive Coverage: Buses reach areas not serviced by metro or tram lines, making them indispensable for comprehensive city travel.

Cost-Effective: Buses are an economical choice, especially with the discounted rates provided by Istanbulkart.

Scenic Routes: Some bus routes offer scenic views of the city, including coastal roads and historic districts, providing an enjoyable travel experience.

4. Funiculars and Cable Cars:

Istanbul's unique topography, characterized by its hills and valleys, makes funiculars and cable cars essential parts of the city's transportation network. These modes of transport are not only practical for navigating the steep terrain but also provide scenic views and a unique experience for both locals and tourists. Here's a detailed guide to the funiculars and cable cars in Istanbul:

Funiculars

a. Taksim-Kabataş Funicular (F1 Line): The Taksim-Kabataş Funicular connects Taksim Square, the heart of modern Istanbul, with Kabataş, a major transportation hub along the Bosphorus.

Route and Operation: The funicular covers a distance of about 600 meters in approximately 2.5 minutes. It operates from early morning until late at night, with frequent departures every few minutes.

Connections: Taksim, links with the M2 metro line, providing easy access to areas like Levent and Şişli. At Kabataş, it connects with the T1 tram line, which runs to Sultanahmet and Eminönü, and with ferries that cross the Bosphorus.

Usage: The funicular is particularly useful for avoiding the steep climb from Kabataş to Taksim, making it popular among both commuters and tourists.

b. Karaköy-Beyoğlu (Tünel) Funicular (F2 Line): Known as the Tünel, this historic funicular line is one of the oldest in the world, second only to the London Underground. It connects Karaköy near the Galata Bridge to Istiklal Street in Beyoğlu.

Route and Operation: The Tünel covers a distance of about 573 meters and takes around 90 seconds. It operates from early morning until midnight, with departures every 5 minutes during peak times.

Connections: Karaköy, connects with the T1 tram line and ferries to the Asian side. At Beyoğlu, it provides access to the vibrant Istiklal Street, filled with shops, cafes, and cultural sites.

Historical Significance: The Tünel, opened in 1875, is a historical attraction in itself, offering a glimpse into Istanbul's past while providing practical transport.

Cable Cars

a. Eyüp-Pierre Loti Cable Car (TF2 Line): This cable car offers a scenic ride from the Eyüp district up to Pierre Loti Hill, named after the famous French writer who frequented the area.

Route and Operation: The cable car travels a distance of about 400 meters in a few minutes, offering panoramic views of the Golden Horn. It operates daily from morning until evening, with frequent departures.

Connections: At Eyüp, visitors can explore the Eyüp Sultan Mosque and nearby historical sites. At Pierre Loti Hill, there's a popular cafe and viewing terrace with stunning vistas of Istanbul.

Tourist Attraction: The cable car is a favorite among tourists for its picturesque views and convenient access to one of the city's most famous viewpoints.

b. Macka-Taşkışla Cable Car (TF1 Line): This cable car connects the Maçka neighborhood with Taşkışla, near Taksim Square. It is often used by students and visitors to the nearby Istanbul Technical University.

Route and Operation: The route spans about 333 meters and takes around 3 minutes. It operates daily from morning until evening.

Connections: At Maçka, it connects with parks and recreational areas. At Taşkışla, it is close to Taksim Square and provides access to the M2 metro line and numerous bus routes.

Scenic Views: The ride offers beautiful views of the Maçka Park, the Bosphorus, and parts of Istanbul's skyline.

Practical Tips

Istanbulkart: The Istanbulkart, a reloadable smart card, can be used on funiculars and cable cars. It provides a convenient and cost-effective way to pay for rides.

Accessibility: Both funiculars and cable cars are generally accessible to people with disabilities, although it's advisable to check specific facilities and accessibility options beforehand.

Operating Hours: While most funiculars and cable cars operate from early morning to late evening, it's a good idea to check the exact operating hours, especially during holidays or maintenance periods.

Scenic Rides: For the best experience, try to ride the cable cars during daylight hours to enjoy the stunning views.

5. Dolmus:

Dolmuş (pronounced "dole-moosh") is a unique and integral part of Istanbul's public transportation system, providing a flexible and often faster alternative to buses and trams. The word "dolmuş" means "stuffed" or "full" in Turkish, reflecting how these shared minibusses or vans operate: they pick up passengers until they are full and then proceed to their destination.

Overview

Dolmuş services fill the gaps between regular public transportation routes, making them ideal for short to medium distances within the city. They follow specific routes but do not have fixed stops, allowing passengers to get on and off at any point along the way. This flexibility makes dolmuş a convenient option for many locals and tourists alike.

Key Features

a. Routes and Operation:

Dolmuş vehicles have set routes displayed on signs in their front windows. These routes cover various parts of the city, including major neighborhoods, business districts, and suburban areas.

Common routes include Taksim-Besiktas, Kadikoy-Bostanci, and Uskudar-Beykoz. There are also routes connecting European and Asian sides, such as Taksim-Kadikoy.

They operate from early morning until late at night, though exact hours may vary depending on the route.

b. Boarding and Alighting:

To board a dolmuş, simply wave it down from the side of the road. The driver will stop to let you on if there is space available.

To alight, notify the driver by saying "inecek var" (someone wants to get off) or pressing a button if available. The driver will pull over at a safe spot to let you out.

c. Payment:

Payment is made in cash directly to the driver, usually after boarding. Fares are typically fixed based on the route and distance, often ranging from 5 to 15 Turkish Lira. It is advisable to carry small change, as drivers may not have a lot of change for larger bills.

d. Seating:

Dolmuş vehicles are typically minibusses or large vans with seating for around 8 to 15 passengers. Once all seats are occupied, the vehicle is considered full.

Passengers may need to share space with others closely, especially during peak hours when demand is high.

e. Convenience and Speed:

Dolmuş services are generally faster than buses because they do not stop at every official bus stop and can take advantage of more flexible routes.

They can navigate narrow streets and congested areas more easily than larger buses.

f. Popular Dolmuş Hubs:

Major dolmuş hubs in Istanbul include Taksim Square, Besiktas, Kadikoy, and Uskudar. These areas have multiple dolmuş routes converging, making it easy to transfer to other forms of transportation or continue to different parts of the city.

Tips for Using Dolmuş

Understanding Routes: Familiarize yourself with the major routes and destinations by observing the signs on the vehicles or asking locals. Online maps and apps may also provide route information.

Language: While some drivers may understand basic English, knowing a few Turkish phrases can be helpful. "Nereye gidiyorsunuz?" (Where are you going?) can be useful for confirming the route.

Crowds: During peak hours, dolmuş vehicles can be crowded. Be prepared for a tight squeeze and keep personal belongings secure.

Safety: Dolmuş services are generally safe, but as with any crowded transportation, be mindful of your belongings to avoid pickpocketing.

Etiquette: It's customary to pass money from the back to the front if you are seated far from the driver. Passengers will hand it along, and change will be returned in the same manner.

Ferries and Sea Buses

6. Ferries:

Istanbul's ferries are an integral part of the city's transportation network, providing an efficient, scenic, and enjoyable way to travel between the European and Asian sides of the city. The ferries not only offer a practical means of transportation but also provide breathtaking views of the Bosphorus, the Golden Horn, and the city's historic skyline. Here's everything you need to know about using ferries to get around Istanbul:

Types of Ferries

Traditional City Ferries: Operated by Şehir Hatları, these are the most common ferries, servicing various routes between the European and Asian sides. They are known for their reliability and scenic routes.

Sea Buses (Deniz Otobüsleri): These are faster and more modern than traditional ferries, operated by Istanbul Deniz Otobüsleri (IDO). They offer quicker travel times but are generally more expensive.

Private Ferries: Several private companies operate ferries, often offering alternative routes and more flexible schedules. These can be a good option if public ferries are crowded or not available.

Tourist Ferries and Bosphorus Cruises: These ferries offer specific tours, including short cruises, sunset tours, and full-day Bosphorus cruises. They focus on providing a tourist experience with guided tours and refreshments on board.

Major Ferry Routes

Eminönü to Kadıköy: One of the busiest routes, connecting the historic Eminönü district on the European side with Kadıköy, a vibrant neighborhood on the Asian side. The trip takes about 20-30 minutes.

Karaköy to Kadıköy: This route also connects to Kadıköy but starts from Karaköy, near the Galata Tower and the heart of Beyoğlu.

Beşiktaş to Üsküdar: A popular route for those traveling between the European district of Beşiktaş and the Asian district of Üsküdar. The journey takes around 10-20 minutes.

Eminönü to Üsküdar: Another important route linking the historic peninsula with Üsküdar on the Asian side.

Bosphorus Line: Connects various stops along the Bosphorus, including Beşiktaş, Üsküdar, Emirgan, Kanlıca, and Anadolu Kavağı. This route is particularly scenic and popular among tourists.

Golden Horn Line: Travels along the Golden Horn, connecting Eminönü with districts such as Haliç and Eyüp.

Schedules and Frequency

Peak Hours: Ferries are more frequent during morning and evening rush hours, with departures every 15-20 minutes on major routes.

Off-Peak Hours: During midday and late evening, ferries run less frequently, usually every 30-60 minutes.

Weekends and Holidays: Schedules may vary, with some routes having limited services.

Tickets and Payment

Istanbulkart: The most convenient way to pay for ferry rides. The Istanbulkart is a reloadable smart card that can be used across all public transportation modes, including ferries. It offers discounted fares compared to single tickets.

Single Tickets: Available at ferry terminals, but more expensive than using an Istanbulkart.

Round-Trip Tickets: Sometimes available for specific tourist routes and Bosphorus cruises.

Amenities on Board

Seating: Indoor and outdoor seating options are available, allowing passengers to enjoy the views or stay sheltered from the weather.

Cafeterias: Many ferries have onboard cafeterias offering tea, coffee, snacks, and light refreshments.

Restrooms: Available on most traditional city ferries and sea buses.

Wi-Fi: Some modern ferries and sea buses provide free Wi-Fi for passengers.

Tips for Riding the Ferries

Timing: Arrive a few minutes early, especially during peak times, to ensure a good spot on the ferry.

Weather: Consider the weather conditions, as outdoor seating can be chilly and windy during colder months.

Photography: Bring a camera or smartphone to capture the stunning views of Istanbul's landmarks, such as the Hagia Sophia, Topkapi Palace, and the Bosphorus Bridge.

Seating Choice: For the best views, choose outdoor seating at the front or rear of the ferry.

Local Culture: Embrace the local culture by ordering a traditional Turkish tea or simit (sesame bread) from the onboard cafeteria.

Popular Ferry Experiences

Sunset Ferry Ride: Catching a ferry during sunset offers a magical experience with the city's skyline illuminated by the setting sun.

Bosphorus Tour: A dedicated tour that takes you along the Bosphorus, providing detailed insights into the city's history and landmarks.

Princes' Islands Ferry: A longer ferry ride to the Princes' Islands, offering a peaceful escape from the city's hustle and bustle.

7. Sea Buses (Deniz Otobusleri):

Sea Buses, known as "Deniz Otobüsleri" in Turkish, are high-speed catamarans that operate on the waters of Istanbul, providing a fast and efficient mode of transport between various parts of the city, particularly between the European and Asian sides. Managed primarily by Istanbul Sea Buses (IDO), they are an essential part of the city's extensive public transportation network.

Routes and Services

Sea Buses operate on several key routes, offering both intra-city and intercity services. Here are some of the primary routes within Istanbul:

Kabatas to Kadikoy: This route connects the bustling Kabatas district on the European side with Kadikoy, a vibrant neighborhood on the Asian side. It's one of the most popular routes for commuters and tourists alike.

Eminonu to Kadikoy: This service connects Eminonu, a historical district near the Golden Horn, with Kadikoy. It's a scenic route that offers views of the Golden Horn and the Bosphorus.

Bakirkoy to Bostanci: This route links Bakirkoy on the European side with Bostanci on the Asian side. It's especially convenient for travelers heading towards the southern parts of the city.

Yenikapi to Yalova: An intercity route connecting Istanbul with Yalova, a town located to the south of Istanbul across the Sea of Marmara. This service is particularly popular among those looking to travel outside the city.

Timetables and Frequency

Sea Bus services typically operate from early morning until late at night, with frequent departures during peak hours to accommodate commuters. The exact timetables vary depending on the route and season, so it's advisable to check the latest schedules on the IDO website or app before planning your journey.

Tickets and Fares

Istanbulkart: The Istanbulkart, a reloadable smart card used across all public transportation in Istanbul, can be used to pay for Sea Bus fares. It offers a convenient and cost-effective way to travel, with discounted rates compared to single-use tickets.

Single Tickets: For those without an Istanbulkart, single tickets can be purchased at Sea Bus terminals. Prices vary depending on the route and distance.

Facilities and Comfort

Sea Buses are designed to offer a comfortable and fast journey across the waters of Istanbul. Key features include:

Spacious Seating: Comfortable seats with ample legroom, ensure a pleasant ride.

Air Conditioning: Climate-controlled interiors provide a comfortable environment regardless of the weather.

Restrooms: Clean and well-maintained restroom facilities for passenger convenience.

Snack Bars: Some Sea Buses are equipped with snack bars, offering refreshments and light snacks during the journey.

Accessibility: Most Sea Buses are wheelchair accessible, with ramps and designated areas for passengers with disabilities.

Advantages of Using Sea Buses

Speed: Sea Buses are faster than traditional ferries, making them ideal for those looking to save time, especially during peak hours when road traffic can be heavy.

Scenic Views: Traveling by Sea Bus offers spectacular views of Istanbul's skyline, historical landmarks, and the Bosphorus Strait.

Convenience: With multiple routes and frequent departures, Sea Buses provide a convenient option for crossing between the European and Asian sides of the city.

Avoiding Traffic: By traveling on the water, passengers can avoid the notorious traffic congestion of Istanbul's roads.

Tips for Travelers

Check Schedules: Always check the latest schedules and departure times on the IDO website or app, as they can change due to weather conditions or operational reasons.

Arrive Early: It's advisable to arrive at the terminal a bit early, especially during peak hours or if you're unfamiliar with the boarding process.

Use Istanbulkart: For the best fares and ease of use, get an Istanbulkart. It can be used across all modes of public transportation in Istanbul.

Weather Considerations: Sea Bus services may be affected by adverse weather conditions, so plan accordingly and have alternative travel options in mind.

Taxis and Ridesharing

8. Taxis:

Taxis are a convenient and relatively affordable way to get around Istanbul, especially for those who prefer direct, door-to-door transportation. Here's an in-depth look at using taxis in the city:

Availability and Hailing a Taxi

Availability: Taxis are widely available throughout Istanbul. You can find them at taxi stands near major hotels, tourist attractions, shopping centers, and transportation hubs such as airports, ferry terminals, and metro stations. They are also frequently seen cruising the streets, especially in busy areas.

Hailing a Taxi: To hail a taxi, simply stand by the roadside and wave your hand. Taxis with a green or red light on top are available for hire. Alternatively, you can use taxi stands or hotel services to call a taxi for you.

Types of Taxis

Standard Yellow Taxis: These are the most common type of taxis in Istanbul. They are identifiable by their yellow color and taxi signs on the roof. They operate on a metered fare system.

Luxury Taxis: Also known as "Turkuaz" (turquoise) taxis, these are more upscale options offering a higher level of comfort and service. They are slightly more expensive than standard yellow taxis.

Electric Taxis: Recently introduced in Istanbul, these eco-friendly taxis are part of the city's initiative to reduce carbon emissions. They offer the same services as standard taxis but are more environmentally friendly.

Fares and Payment

Metered Fares: All taxis in Istanbul are required to use a meter. The fare starts with a base rate (initial charge) and increases based on distance and time. The meter should be turned on at the beginning of your journey. As of 2023, the base fare is around 9.8 TL with an additional charge per kilometer.

Additional Charges: Be aware of possible additional charges, such as for bridge tolls when crossing between the European and Asian sides of the city, and extra fees for airport trips. It is also customary to round up the fare or leave a small tip, although this is not obligatory.

Payment Methods: Most taxis accept cash (Turkish Lira), and some may accept credit/debit cards. However, it's advisable to confirm with the driver before starting your journey. Mobile payment apps like Istanbulkart and some international payment apps are also becoming more accepted.

Tips for Using Taxis

Ensure the Meter is On Always ensure that the driver starts the meter when you begin your trip. If the driver refuses or claims the meter is broken, it's best to get out and find another taxi.

Agree on a Fare for Long Trips: For longer trips or if you're unsure about the fare, it can be helpful to agree on an approximate fare beforehand. However, this is less common as all taxis are supposed to use the meter.

Carry Small Change: It's useful to have small denominations of Turkish Lira for paying taxi fares, as drivers may not always have change for larger bills.

Language Barrier: Most taxi drivers speak little to no English. Have your destination written down in Turkish or use a map app to show your destination to the driver.

Safety and Scams: While most taxi drivers are honest, some may try to take advantage of tourists. Be cautious of drivers who take unnecessarily long routes or claim the meter is broken. Using rideshare apps like BiTaksi or Uber can provide more transparency.

Rideshare Apps: Apps like Uber and BiTaksi operate in Istanbul and offer a convenient and reliable alternative to hailing a traditional taxi.

These apps provide estimated fares, driver ratings, and the ability to track your journey in real time.

Major Taxi Stands and Hotspots

Airports: Both Istanbul Airport (IST) and Sabiha Gokcen Airport (SAW) have designated taxi stands. Official airport taxis are regulated and should use the meter.

Tourist Areas: Sultanahmet, Taksim Square, and Istiklal Street have numerous taxis available. However, be cautious of taxis in tourist hotspots as they may charge higher fares.

Hotels: Most hotels in Istanbul can call a taxi for you. This service is often more reliable, especially for non-Turkish speakers.

9. Ridesharing Apps:

Ridesharing apps have become a popular mode of transportation in Istanbul, offering convenience, safety, and ease of use. Here's a detailed look at how ridesharing apps function in Istanbul, the options available, and tips for using them effectively.

Overview

Ridesharing apps connect passengers with drivers through a smartphone application. These services offer a convenient alternative to traditional taxis, providing transparent pricing, ease of payment, and the ability to track your ride in real time. In Istanbul, the two primary ridesharing apps are Uber and BiTaksi.

a. Uber in Istanbul

Service Types:

- UberX: The most affordable option, suitable for everyday rides.
- UberXL: Offers larger vehicles for groups or travelers with extra luggage.
- UberBlack: Premium service with luxury vehicles and professional drivers.

Features:

- **Real-time Tracking:** Track your driver's location and estimated arrival time.
- **Cashless Payments:** Pay via the app using a credit card, debit card, or PayPal.

- **Driver Ratings:** Rate drivers and view their ratings to ensure a high-quality experience.
- **Safety Features**: Share your trip details with friends and family, and access emergency assistance if needed.

Availability: Uber operates extensively across Istanbul, covering both the European and Asian sides.

b. BiTaksi

Service Types:

- Standard Taxi: Licensed yellow taxis that you can book through the app.
- Black Taxi: Premium service with higher-end vehicles.

Features:

- **Real-time Tracking:** Similar to Uber, you can track your driver's location and estimated arrival time.
- **Multiple Payment Options:** Pay with cash, credit card, or through the BiTaksi app.
- **Driver Ratings:** Rate drivers and view their ratings.
- **Languages:** The app supports multiple languages, including English, which is helpful for tourists.

Availability: BiTaksi is widely available throughout Istanbul and is particularly popular among locals.

Advantages of Using Ridesharing Apps

Convenience: Easily book a ride with a few taps on your smartphone without the need to hail a taxi on the street.

Transparency: Clear pricing and fare estimates before you book. No need to worry about meter tampering or being overcharged.

Safety: Track your ride in real-time, share trip details with friends or family, and access in-app safety features.

Language Barrier: Many ridesharing drivers speak basic English, and the app interfaces are user-friendly for non-Turkish speakers.

Comfort: Clean and well-maintained vehicles with professional drivers.

Payment Flexibility: Options to pay through the app or in cash.

How to Use Ridesharing Apps

Download the App: Install Uber or BiTaksi from the App Store or Google Play Store.

Create an Account: Sign up with your email address and phone number. For Uber, you'll need to link a payment method.

Set Pickup Location: Allow the app to access your location or manually enter your pickup point.

Choose Ride Type: Select the type of ride you need based on your preferences and the number of passengers.

Confirm Ride: Check the fare estimate and confirm your booking. The app will match you with the nearest available driver.

Track Your Ride: Monitor the driver's arrival and follow the route in real time.

Rate Your Driver: After the ride, rate your driver and provide feedback to help maintain service quality.

Tips for Using Ridesharing Apps in Istanbul

Peak Times: Be aware of peak times (morning and evening rush hours) when demand is high, and fares may be higher.

Traffic: Istanbul's traffic can be heavy, especially during rush hours. Plan extra travel time.

Location Accuracy: Ensure your pickup location is accurately set, especially in busy areas or large landmarks.

Safety: Always check the driver's details and vehicle information before entering the car. Share your trip details with a friend or family member.

Customer Support: Use the app's support features if you encounter any issues or need assistance.

Car Rental

Renting a car in Istanbul can provide flexibility and convenience, especially if you plan to explore beyond the city center or prefer a more independent mode of transportation. Here's a comprehensive guide to car rental in Istanbul, including key information and contacts:

Renting a Car in Istanbul

Rental Companies

a. International Brands: Major international car rental companies operate in Istanbul, including:

- Avis: +90 212 444 28 47
- Budget: +90 212 465 24 60
- Europcar: +90 216 588 58 58
- Hertz: +90 212 465 50 00
- Sixt: +90 212 444 00 00

These companies have offices at Istanbul Airport (IST), Sabiha Gokcen Airport (SAW), and several downtown locations across both the European and Asian sides of Istanbul.

b. Local Companies: There are also local car rental companies that may offer competitive rates. It's advisable to check reviews and compare prices online before booking.

Requirements and Tips

Driver's License: A valid national or international driver's license is required. Some rental companies may require you to have held your license for a minimum period, typically one to two years.

Age Restrictions: Generally, drivers must be at least 21 years old, and there may be additional fees for drivers under 25.

Insurance: Basic insurance coverage is usually included, but it's recommended to check what is covered and consider additional coverage for peace of mind, especially for theft and damage.

Booking in Advance: During peak tourist seasons or holidays, booking your rental car in advance is advisable to secure availability and better rates.

Driving in Istanbul

Traffic: Istanbul is known for heavy traffic, especially during rush hours (morning and late afternoon). Consider traffic conditions when planning your journeys.

Parking: Parking can be challenging in central areas like Sultanahmet and Taksim. Look for paid parking lots (Otopark) or street parking with designated meters (usually blue).

Road Conditions: Roads in Istanbul vary from modern highways to narrower streets in older parts of the city. Be prepared for diverse driving conditions.

Cost and Payment

Rates: Rental rates vary based on the car size, rental duration, and insurance options. Prices can start from around 100-150 TRY per day for economy cars, excluding additional fees and insurance.

Payment: Most rental companies accept major credit cards. Cash payments may also be accepted but check with the rental company beforehand.

Contacts and Resources

Istanbul Airport Car Rental: For rentals at Istanbul Airport (IST), contact the rental desks located in the arrivals hall of both international and domestic terminals.

Sabiha Gokcen Airport Car Rental: For rentals at Sabiha Gokcen Airport (SAW), rental desks are located in the arrivals hall.

Chapter 6: Hidden Gems and Off-the-Beaten-Path

Lesser-known Attractions and Unique Experiences in Istanbul

Istanbul, where East meets West, is full of hidden gems and unique experiences that go beyond the well-trodden tourist paths. Here are some lesser-known attractions and experiences to explore in this vibrant city:

Yıldız Park

Yıldız Park is a serene and expansive green space tucked away between the neighborhoods of Beşiktaş and Ortaköy. Once part of the imperial gardens of Yıldız Palace, this park offers a tranquil escape from the bustling city. It features beautifully landscaped gardens, meandering paths, and stunning views of the Bosphorus. The park is home to a variety of flora, charming pavilions, and a small artificial lake. It's an ideal spot for a stroll, a picnic, or simply to relax amidst nature. Despite its central location, Yıldız Park remains relatively uncrowded, making it a peaceful retreat.

Location: Yıldız, 34349 Beşiktaş/Istanbul, Turkey

Tips: Visit early in the morning or on weekdays for a quieter experience. Bring along some snacks for a picnic and enjoy the Bosphorus views from the higher terraces.

Kariye Museum (Chora Church)

The Kariye Museum, also known as the Chora Church, is a hidden treasure showcasing some of the most exquisite Byzantine mosaics and frescoes in the world. Located in the Edirnekapı neighborhood, this former church-turned-museum offers a glimpse into Istanbul's rich Byzantine past. The detailed artwork, depicting scenes from the New Testament, is remarkably well-preserved and provides insight into the religious and artistic heritage of the era. The building's exterior, though modest, contrasts with the opulence within, making it a must-visit for those interested in history and art.

Location: Kariye Cami Sk. No:8, 34087 Fatih/Istanbul, Turkey

Tips: To avoid crowds, visit early in the day or late in the afternoon. Be sure to spend time appreciating the detailed mosaics and frescoes in the nave and inner narthex.

Süleymaniye Hammam

The Süleymaniye Hammam is a historical Turkish bath built by the renowned Ottoman architect Mimar Sinan in the 16th century. Located near the Süleymaniye Mosque, this hammam offers an authentic and relaxing experience away from the more touristy baths in Istanbul. The bathhouse is separated into private sections, making it ideal for couples or families seeking a more intimate experience.

The original design and ambiance of the hammam have been carefully preserved, providing a unique opportunity to indulge in a centuries-old tradition.

Location: Mimar Sinan Caddesi No:20, 34116 Süleymaniye/Fatih/Istanbul, Turkey

Tips: Reservations are recommended, especially during peak tourist seasons. Bring a change of clothes and enjoy the relaxing bath, followed by a traditional Turkish tea in the lounge area.

Büyük Valide Han

Hidden in the heart of Istanbul's bustling Grand Bazaar district, Büyük Valide Han is a lesser-known historical han (caravanserai) that dates back to the 17th century. Once a key stop for traders traveling the Silk Road, it now offers a glimpse into the city's past. The han features an atmospheric courtyard and crumbling rooms, but its true hidden gem is the rooftop, which provides an incredible panoramic view of Istanbul's skyline, including the domes of the Süleymaniye Mosque and the Bosphorus. The slightly dilapidated state of the han adds to its charm and authenticity.

Location: Çakmakçılar Yokuşu No:48, 34126 Fatih/Istanbul, Turkey

Tips: Access to the rooftop is informal and may require a small tip to the caretaker. The climb can be a bit tricky, so wear sturdy shoes and be cautious while navigating the old stairs.

Rumeli Hisarı

Rumeli Hisarı, a medieval fortress located on the European side of the Bosphorus, is a lesser-known historical site that offers breathtaking views and a fascinating glimpse into Istanbul's past. Built by Sultan Mehmed II in 1452, the fortress played a crucial role in the conquest of Constantinople. Today, it stands as an impressive example of Ottoman military architecture. Visitors can explore the fortress's towers, walls, and courtyard, all while enjoying panoramic views of the Bosphorus and the Asian side of Istanbul. The surrounding area is lush with greenery, making it a great spot for a peaceful stroll or a picnic.

Location: Yahya Kemal Cd., 34470 Sarıyer/Istanbul, Turkey

Tips: Wear comfortable shoes as the fortress grounds include steep stairs and uneven terrain. Early morning or late afternoon visits are ideal for avoiding crowds and enjoying the best lighting for photographs.

Pierre Loti Hill Cemetery

Pierre Loti Hill Cemetery, nestled on the serene Pierre Loti Hill, is a peaceful burial ground with historical and cultural significance. Named after the French novelist Pierre Loti, the cemetery features ornate Ottoman-era tombstones and provides a tranquil retreat from the city's hustle. It offers an evocative atmosphere, where visitors can reflect on Istanbul's rich history amidst beautifully landscaped grounds.

The cemetery is known for its captivating views of the Golden Horn and the surrounding areas, enhancing its historical charm. This site is both a resting place and a quiet, contemplative spot with a unique perspective on the city's past.

Location: İdris Köşkü Cd. No:16, 34087 Eyüp/Istanbul, Turkey

Tips: To reach the cemetery, take the cable car up to Pierre Loti Hill or enjoy a scenic walk. The cemetery is a quiet place, so it's best visited respectfully. Consider visiting early in the morning or late afternoon for the best light and to avoid crowds.

Kuzguncuk Neighborhood

Kuzguncuk is a charming, historic neighborhood on the Asian side of Istanbul, nestled between the Bosphorus and Üsküdar. Known for its well-preserved Ottoman-era houses, narrow cobblestone streets, and vibrant community spirit, Kuzguncuk offers a picturesque escape from the city's hustle and bustle. The neighborhood is renowned for its colorful wooden houses, quaint cafes, and traditional shops. Visitors can explore local landmarks such as the Kuzguncuk Mosque and the historic Jewish cemetery, adding depth to the cultural experience. The area's relaxed atmosphere, combined with its beautiful waterfront views and friendly local vibe, makes it an ideal spot for a stroll or a quiet afternoon café visit.

Location: Kuzguncuk, 34674 Üsküdar/Istanbul, Turkey

Tips: Visit on a weekday to avoid crowds and enjoy a more peaceful experience. Wander around the streets to fully appreciate the traditional architecture and stop by local eateries for authentic Turkish breakfast or lunch. Don't miss the chance to take a walk along the Bosphorus waterfront for stunning views.

Fener and Balat Neighborhoods

The historic neighborhoods of Fener and Balat, situated along the Golden Horn, are a labyrinth of narrow, winding streets filled with colorful Ottoman-era houses, charming cafes, and hidden churches. These neighborhoods were once home to Istanbul's Greek Orthodox and Jewish communities, and the area still retains a rich cultural heritage. Walking through Fener and Balat feels like stepping back in time, with the vibrant facades of old wooden houses and cobblestone streets creating a picturesque setting. Highlights include the impressive Phanar Greek Orthodox College, Ahrida Synagogue, and several small art galleries and antique shops.

Location: Fener, 34087 Fatih/Istanbul, Turkey

Tips: Wear comfortable shoes as the streets are steep and cobblestoned. Allocate at least a few hours to explore at a leisurely pace, stopping at local cafes for tea and snacks.

Yeni Cami (New Mosque) Courtyard

The courtyard of the Yeni Cami, or New Mosque, is a tranquil and lesser-known space offering a peaceful respite amidst the bustling energy of the Eminönü district. Built in the early 17th century, the mosque's courtyard features a stunning mix of Ottoman architecture and serene outdoor spaces. The central fountain, surrounded by intricate tile work and marble colonnades, serves as a focal point, offering a serene atmosphere perfect for reflection or a quiet rest. The mosque's iconic minarets and intricately decorated domes provide a majestic backdrop, making the courtyard a hidden gem for visitors seeking to experience the architectural beauty of Istanbul without the usual crowds.

Location: Emin Ali Paşa, 34116 Fatih/Istanbul, Turkey

Tips: Visit early in the morning or late afternoon to enjoy the courtyard in a quieter setting. Dress modestly, as it is a place of worship, and be respectful of those performing prayers. The courtyard's tranquil ambiance makes it ideal for taking a moment to appreciate the craftsmanship and historical significance of the mosque.

Büyükada Greek Orphanage (Prinkipo Greek Orthodox Orphanage)

The Büyükada Greek Orphanage, also known as the Prinkipo Greek Orthodox Orphanage, is a strikingly atmospheric and historic building located on Büyükada, the largest of the Princes' Islands. Completed in 1898, this abandoned Byzantine-style structure was once one of the largest wooden buildings in Europe and served as an orphanage for Greek Orthodox children. Its grand, turreted facade and expansive wooden interior are shrouded in an air of mystery and decay, making it a fascinating subject for photographers and history enthusiasts. Although it has been closed since the 1960s, the building's imposing presence and intricate architectural details remain a testament to its former grandeur. The orphanage's unique design and its place in the island's history make it a compelling site to visit.

Location: Büyükada, Adalar, Istanbul, Turkey

Tips: Access to the building is restricted, so it's best to view it from the outside. Guided tours are not available, but you can enjoy a walk around the perimeter and take in the impressive structure from various angles. Combine your visit with a tour of Büyükada to fully appreciate the island's historical and cultural context. Respect the property's private status and avoid trespassing.

Yedikule Fortress

Yedikule Fortress, also known as the Fortress of the Seven Towers, is a historic Byzantine and Ottoman fortification situated on the southern edge of the old city. Originally built in the 5th century as part of the city's defensive walls, it was expanded and renovated by the Ottomans. The fortress is renowned for its imposing towers, thick stone walls, and panoramic views of the Marmara Sea and the Golden Horn. Visitors can explore its well-preserved battlements, guard rooms, and the eerie dungeon area known as the "Dungeons of Yedikule." The fortress also features an exhibition on Istanbul's history and the various roles the fortress played over the centuries. Its relatively off-the-beaten-path location provides a quieter, more reflective experience compared to the city's more crowded landmarks.

Location: Yedikule, 34087 Fatih/Istanbul, Turkey

Tips: Wear comfortable shoes for walking on uneven surfaces and climbing stairs. Consider visiting in the morning or late afternoon to avoid the midday heat and large tour groups. Check for any special events or exhibitions that may be taking place during your visit.

Chapter 7: Where to Stay in Istanbul

Guide to Istanbul Neighborhoods and Districts

Istanbul is a sprawling metropolis with a rich history and culture. It can be overwhelming to decide where to stay and what to see. To help you navigate this amazing city, here's a list of 10 districts and neighborhoods that are perfect for tourists:

1. Sultanahmet

Sultanahmet, the heart of historic Istanbul, is a captivating labyrinth of Ottoman grandeur, Byzantine whispers, and bustling bazaars. This district, where continents meet and cultures collide, offers a symphony of experiences for every kind of traveler.

Characters:

History Buff: You'll feel right at home here. Imagine yourself as a Sultan strolling the halls of Topkapi Palace, marveling at the architectural feat of Hagia Sophia, or deciphering the mysteries of the Basilica Cistern.

Art Enthusiast: Immerse yourself in the vibrant Iznik tiles adorning the Blue Mosque, or marvel at the intricate mosaics that adorn the Hagia Sophia Museum. Don't miss the Museum of Turkish and Islamic Arts for a deeper dive into Ottoman artistry.

Foodie: Indulge in the aromatic world of Turkish spices at the Spice Bazaar, savor succulent kebabs at a local restaurant, or sip on fragrant Turkish coffee while people-watching in Hippodrome Square.

Shopaholic: Brace yourself for the Grand Bazaar, a sensory overload of carpets, jewelry, ceramics, and an endless array of souvenirs. Refine your bargaining skills and relish the thrill of the hunt for that perfect treasure.

Top Attractions:

Hagia Sophia: Witness the architectural marvel that has been a church, a mosque, and a museum throughout its long and fascinating history. Be mesmerized by the towering dome and the breathtaking mosaics.

Topkapi Palace: Delve into the opulent world of Ottoman Sultans. Explore the sprawling palace complex, including the Harem, the Treasury, and the breathtaking courtyards.

Blue Mosque: Be captivated by the dazzling Iznik tiles that bathe the interior in an ethereal blue light. Admire the intricate calligraphy and the six minarets that pierce the Istanbul skyline.

Hippodrome Square: Stand on the very ground where chariot races once thrilled Byzantine crowds. See the remnants of ancient monuments like the Obelisk of Theodosius and the Serpentine Column.

Basilica Cistern: Descend into a fascinating underground world. Imagine yourself navigating a maze of ancient columns, illuminated by an eerie, almost otherworldly, light.

Grand Bazaar: Lose yourself in this labyrinthine marketplace, a shopper's paradise with over 4,000 shops. Haggle for treasures ranging from carpets and hand-painted ceramics to spices and Turkish delight.

Hidden Gems:

The Museum of Innocence: Step into the fictional world of Orhan Pamuk's novel and explore a beautifully curated museum that captures the essence of Istanbul life in the early 20th century.

Suleymaniye Mosque: Escape the crowds and admire the architectural prowess of this majestic 16th-century mosque, offering panoramic city views.

The Turkish and Islamic Arts Museum: Delve into the rich tapestry of Islamic art and artifacts, from calligraphy and ceramics to carpets and weaponry.

Arasta Bazaar: Specializes in high-quality handicrafts and carpets, offering a more relaxed shopping experience compared to the Grand Bazaar.

Mosaic Museum: Uncover stunning Byzantine mosaics salvaged from archaeological sites, offering a glimpse into the artistic heritage of the Eastern Roman Empire.

Experiences:

Turkish Bath (Hamam): Indulge in a traditional hammam experience. Cleanse your body and soul with a hot steam, followed by a vigorous scrub and a relaxing massage.

Bosphorus Cruise: Set sail on the Bosphorus Strait, the waterway separating Europe and Asia. Admire the stunning waterfront palaces, mosques, and historical landmarks from a unique perspective.

Turkish Night: Immerse yourself in the vibrant culture with a traditional Turkish night performance. Enjoy belly dancing, folk music, and a delicious Turkish feast.

Carpet Demonstration: Witness the intricate art of carpet weaving firsthand. Learn about the traditional techniques and materials used to create these beautiful works of art.

Calligraphy Workshop: Unleash your inner artist and learn the basics of traditional Ottoman calligraphy.

Beyond the Tourist Trail:

Wander the Arasta Bazaar: Discover a haven for handcrafted souvenirs and unique local finds.

Sip Turkish Coffee: Savor a cup of strong Turkish coffee in a traditional cafe, soaking up the local atmosphere.

Explore Culinary Delights: Venture beyond kebabs and delve into the rich tapestry of Turkish cuisine at hidden cafes and local restaurants.

Take a Cooking Class: Learn how to prepare traditional Turkish dishes alongside a local chef.

People Watch in Sultanahmet Park: Relax in a green oasis, watching locals and tourists mingle amidst historical landmarks.

Staying in Sultanahmet:

This area offers a wide range of hotels, from charming boutique hotels to luxurious accommodations overlooking iconic landmarks.

A Word of Caution:

Sultanahmet can get crowded, especially during peak season. Be prepared for crowds and persistent vendors.

Overall, Sultanahmet offers an unforgettable experience for travelers seeking a glimpse into Istanbul's rich history, vibrant culture, and captivating charm.

2. Beyoglu

Beyoglu, Istanbul's beating heart, pulsates with a vibrant energy that's both modern and historic. This district, particularly the Taksim area, is a must-visit for any tourist seeking a dynamic Istanbul experience. Here's a glimpse into what awaits you in Beyoglu:

Characters:

The Social Butterfly: Beyoglu is a melting pot. You'll find artists, students, young professionals, and international visitors rubbing shoulders in cafes and bars.

The Night Owl: This district comes alive after dark. The streets thrum with live music, laughter spills from rooftop bars, and nightclubs pulsate with energy.

The History Buff: While not as steeped in Ottoman history as Sultanahmet, Beyoglu boasts remnants of a rich European past in its grand architecture.

The Ardent Shopper: From high-street brands on Istiklal Street to hidden vintage stores on side streets, Beyoglu caters to all budgets and styles.

Top Attractions:

Taksim Square: The symbolic heart of modern Istanbul, Taksim Square is a bustling hub, perfect for people-watching and soaking in the city's energy.

Istiklal Street: This iconic pedestrianized avenue is a kilometer-long kaleidoscope of shops, cafes, restaurants, street performers, and historic buildings. Ride the nostalgic red tram for a unique perspective.

Galata Tower: This medieval Genoese tower offers panoramic views of the city and a glimpse into Istanbul's past.

Pera Palace Hotel: A luxurious landmark steeped in history, the Pera Palace has hosted famous figures like Agatha Christie and is a visual feast in itself.

Museums: From the Museum of Innocence, inspired by Orhan Pamuk's novel, to the Pera Museum showcasing Orientalist art, Beyoglu offers diverse cultural experiences.

Hidden Gems:

Passageways (Pasajlar): Duck into the labyrinthine alleyways off Istiklal Street to discover hidden courtyards, independent art galleries, and quirky cafes. The Çiçek Pasajı (Flower Passage) is a particularly charming spot.

Cihangir: This bohemian neighborhood offers a respite from the crowds. Explore its narrow streets, art galleries, and vintage shops.

Independent Theaters: Catch a play at one of Beyoglu's many independent theaters and experience the city's vibrant contemporary art scene.

Rooftop Bars: Ascend to a rooftop bar and be mesmerized by the cityscape as you sip cocktails and enjoy the cool night air.

Experiences:

Indulge in Turkish Coffee: Savor a strong cup of Turkish coffee at a historic cafe like Çukurcuma Kahvesi and soak in the local atmosphere.

Live Music: Catch a live music performance at a jazz bar or a traditional Turkish music venue.

Foodie Paradise: From delicious street food like "döner" (rotating meat kebabs) to upscale restaurants serving Ottoman cuisine, Beyoglu offers endless culinary adventures.

The Grand Bazaar: A short walk from Taksim Square lies the iconic Grand Bazaar for those seeking a quintessential Turkish shopping experience.

The Nightlife: Beyoglu transforms into a party zone after dark. Dance the night away at a nightclub, listen to live music at a bar, or simply wander the lively streets and soak in the energy.

Beyond the Tourist Trail:

Take a Walking Tour: Join a local walking tour to discover hidden gems, learn about Beyoglu's history, and get insider tips from a local guide.

Learn a Few Turkish Phrases: A few basic Turkish phrases will go a long way in connecting with locals and enhancing your experience.

Catch a Local Football Match: Immerse yourself in the passionate atmosphere of a Turkish football match at the Galatasaray Stadium (depending on the season).

A Few Cautions:

Pickpockets: As with any crowded tourist area, be mindful of your belongings in Beyoglu.

Bargaining: While not as prevalent as in the Grand Bazaar, bargaining is still expected in some shops.

Uneven Sidewalks: Be aware of uneven sidewalks and cobblestone streets, especially when wearing heels.

So, if you're looking for a vibrant, energetic, and culturally rich experience in Istanbul, then Beyoglu is the place for you. Come and discover the beating heart of this fascinating city!

3. Karaköy

Karaköy, a district on the northern shore of Istanbul's Golden Horn, pulsates with a unique energy. Once a historic port brimming with warehouses and workshops, it's now a vibrant tapestry woven from tradition and contemporary cool. Here's your guide to experiencing the best of Karaköy:

Characters:

The Art Enthusiast: Karaköy is their haven. Independent art galleries showcasing local and international talent line the streets. Keep an eye out for street art that adds a dynamic touch to old buildings.

The Coffee Connoisseur: Third-wave coffee shops abound, each brewing a perfect cup. Chat with baristas passionate about their craft, and soak in the trendy atmosphere.

The Vintage Hunter: Antique shops and hidden boutiques hold treasures waiting to be discovered. From furniture and jewelry to clothing and quirky finds, there's something for every vintage aficionado.

The Foodie: Karaköy caters to all palates. Sample delicious Turkish cuisine with a modern twist at innovative restaurants. International flavors are also well-represented, with trendy cafes and delis offering global dishes.

Top Attractions:

The Galata Tower: This medieval Genoese tower offers panoramic views of Istanbul. Ascend to the top and be mesmerized by the cityscape sprawling beneath you.

Istanbul Modern: Delve into the world of contemporary art at this prestigious museum. Explore exhibitions showcasing Turkish and international artists, pushing the boundaries of creativity.

The Karaköy Tram: Take a nostalgic ride on the historic Karaköy tram, a funicular railway that shuttles passengers up the steep hill to Beyoglu.

Hidden Gems:

French Passage (French Street): Wander down this charming alley lined with 19th-century French neoclassical buildings. Now home to art galleries and cafes, it retains a distinctly European vibe.

Çukurcuma: This neighborhood bordering Karaköy is a treasure trove of antique shops and vintage stores. Haggle for unique finds and lose yourself in the labyrinthine streets.

Corlulu Ali Pasha Medresesi: Step into this serene Ottoman-era madrasa (Islamic school) and marvel at the peaceful courtyard and traditional architecture.

Experiences:

Street Art Walk: Hire a local guide to lead you on a street art tour, unveiling hidden murals and learning about the city's burgeoning street art scene.

Turkish Coffee Ritual: Indulge in the traditional Turkish coffee ceremony at a historic coffee shop. Savor the rich, strong coffee and learn about its cultural significance.

Bosphorus Cruise: Embark on a scenic cruise along the Bosphorus Strait, departing from Karaköy's docks. Witness Istanbul's magnificent skyline and iconic landmarks from a unique perspective.

Foodie Tour: Join a walking food tour to discover Karaköy's culinary delights. Sample local delicacies, visit hidden restaurants, and learn about Turkish cuisine from a knowledgeable guide.

Karaköy's charm lies in its ability to surprise and delight you around every corner. So, come explore this dynamic district, and let its blend of history, art, and trendy vibes create a lasting impression on your Istanbul adventure.

4. Besiktas

Besiktas, a vibrant district perched on the European shore of the Bosphorus Strait, offers a unique blend of history, culture, and modern energy. While it boasts iconic landmarks, it also pulsates with a local charm that's sure to capture the hearts of tourists.

Characters:

History Buff: Besiktas is a paradise for those who love to delve into the past. The magnificent Dolmabahce Palace, the last residence of Ottoman Sultans, stands as a testament to a bygone era. Explore its opulent halls and imagine the grandeur of the Ottoman court.

Art Enthusiast: Unleash your inner artist in Besiktas. The Yildiz Palace complex houses museums brimming with Ottoman treasures and art collections. For a contemporary touch, head to the vibrant art galleries scattered around the district.

Foodie: Besiktas is a haven for your taste buds. Start your day with a traditional Turkish breakfast by the Bosphorus, then head to the Besiktas Fish Market, a feast for the senses with its colorful displays of fresh seafood. Don't miss the chance to savor succulent balık ekmek (fish bread) – a local favorite.

Sports Fanatic: Feel the electric atmosphere at Vodafone Park, the home stadium of Besiktas JK, one of Turkey's most passionate football clubs. Catch a game and immerse yourself in the roaring cheers of the fans.

Nature Lover: Escape the city buzz and find serenity at Yıldız Park, a sprawling green oasis. Stroll through its manicured gardens, spot hidden pavilions, and enjoy breathtaking views of the Bosphorus.

Top Attractions:

Dolmabahce Palace: Witness the epitome of Ottoman opulence. This extravagant palace boasts a dazzling blend of architectural styles and houses priceless collections.

Ortaköy Mosque: A picturesque gem on the Bosphorus shore, this historic mosque with its white facade and red minaret is a popular landmark and a photographer's delight.

Naval Museum: Dive into Turkey's maritime history at this fascinating museum showcasing naval artifacts, ship models, and historical photographs.

Bosphorus Cruise: Embark on a scenic cruise along the Bosphorus Strait, marveling at the stunning palaces, charming villages, and historic bridges lining the shores.

Vodafone Park: Catch a football game and experience the electrifying energy of Turkish sports fans.

Hidden Gems:

Barbaros Hayrettin Paşa Mosque: A hidden gem tucked away in the backstreets, this 16th-century mosque offers a serene atmosphere and stunning calligraphy.

Yıldız Park: Beyond the Dolmabahce Palace complex lies this sprawling park with hidden pavilions, tranquil ponds, and a glimpse into Ottoman leisure life.

Beşiktaş Bazaar: Discover a treasure trove of local produce, spices, and handcrafted souvenirs at this vibrant market, offering a taste of authentic Turkish life.

Akaretler Row Houses: Wander through this charming neighborhood with its colorful 19th-century Ottoman row houses, now brimming with trendy cafes and art galleries.

Sanatorium: This former Ottoman sanatorium, now a cultural center, hosts art exhibitions, concerts, and workshops, offering a unique glimpse into the city's creative scene.

Experiences:

Savor a Turkish Breakfast by the Bosphorus: Start your day with a leisurely breakfast overlooking the Bosphorus, indulging in a spread of cheeses, olives, menemen (Turkish scrambled eggs), and freshly baked simit (Turkish bagel).

Shop at the Besiktas Fish Market: Immerse yourself in the vibrant atmosphere of this bustling fish market, where vendors display their colorful catch. Enjoy a freshly caught fish sandwich (balık ekmek) – a local delicacy.

Take a Bosphorus Cruise at Sunset: Witness the magical transformation of the Bosphorus as the sun dips below the horizon, casting golden hues on the city skyline and historical landmarks.

Cheer at a Besiktas JK Football Game: Experience the electrifying atmosphere of a football match at Vodafone Park, surrounded by passionate Besiktas fans cheering on their team.

Explore the Backstreets of Besiktas: Wander through the charming backstreets, discover hidden mosques and historical gems, and get a glimpse into the local way of life.

5. Kadiköy

Kadiköy, the vibrant heart of Istanbul on the Asian side, pulsates with a unique energy that sets it apart from the historic grandeur of Sultanahmet. Here, you'll find a captivating blend of trendy cafes, independent art galleries, bustling markets, and a relaxed local vibe, making it a haven for off-the-beaten-path explorers.

Characters:

The Young and Trendy: Kadiköy is a magnet for Istanbul's young, creative crowd. Expect to see university students sipping Turkish coffee at sidewalk cafes, artists showcasing their work in quirky galleries, and musicians jamming in hidden bars.

The Local Foodies: Kadiköy is a paradise for gourmands. You'll find friendly shopkeepers selling fresh produce at the Kadiköy Pazarı, families savoring steaming bowls of "mantı" (Turkish dumplings) at cozy restaurants, and passionate chefs experimenting with innovative cuisine.

The Laid-Back Bohemians: Artists, writers, and musicians have long called Kadiköy home. The district hums with creative energy, evident in the vibrant street art that adorns many buildings and the independent bookstores overflowing with local literature.

Top Attractions:

Kadiköy Bazaar (Kadiköy Pazarı): Immerse yourself in the sights, sounds, and smells of this sprawling market. Browse through aisles overflowing with fresh produce, fragrant spices, and unique Turkish handicrafts. Don't miss the chance to grab a delicious "simit" (Turkish bagel) for breakfast.

Barış Manço Museum: Pay homage to the legendary Turkish rock star Barış Manço at his former home turned museum. Explore his flamboyant costumes, quirky instruments, and personal effects, offering a glimpse into the life of this beloved musician.

Moda Promenade: Take a stroll along the beautiful Moda Promenade, a scenic seafront path lined with cafes and restaurants. Enjoy breathtaking views of the Bosphorus Strait, watch local fishermen casting their lines, or simply relax and soak up the sunshine.

Caddebostan Culture Center: This impressive cultural center hosts a variety of exhibitions, concerts, and theater performances throughout the year. Explore contemporary Turkish art, catch a captivating play, or enjoy a classical music concert.

Hidden Gems:

Kadife Street: Venture off the beaten path and explore Kadife Street, a charming alleyway lined with independent art galleries and vintage clothing stores. Discover hidden courtyards brimming with creativity and find unique souvenirs to treasure.

Yeldeğirmeni: Explore the up-and-coming neighborhood of Yeldeğirmeni, a haven for local artists and musicians. Wander through converted warehouses showcasing contemporary art installations, grab a craft beer at a trendy microbrewery, or catch a live music performance at a hidden bar.

Osmanlı Bankası Museum: Delve into the history of finance at the Osmanlı Bankası Museum, housed in a magnificent Ottoman-era building. Learn about the evolution of banking in Turkey, admire the ornate architecture, and discover hidden treasures within the museum's vaults.

Haydarpaşa Train Station: While not operational, the magnificent Haydarpaşa Train Station is a sight to behold. Admire its neo-Renaissance architecture, capture stunning photos of its grand facade, and imagine the bustling atmosphere when trains once chugged through its halls.

Experiences:

Catch a ferry across the Bosphorus: Enjoy a scenic ferry ride across the Bosphorus Strait, the waterway separating Europe from Asia. Watch the Istanbul skyline shimmer in the sunlight, capture breathtaking photos of iconic landmarks, and experience the thrill of traveling between continents.

Indulge in Turkish street food: Explore the endless street food options available in Kadiköy. Savor savory "kokoreç" (grilled intestines), indulge in crispy "lahmacun" (flatbread pizza), or tantalize your taste buds with a sweet "künefe" (cheese pastry drenched in syrup).

Shop for unique treasures: From traditional Turkish handicrafts at the Kadiköy Bazaar to vintage clothing finds on Kadife Street, Kadiköy offers something for every shopper. Explore the bustling streets, support local businesses, and discover unique souvenirs to bring home.

Enjoy the nightlife: Kadiköy comes alive at night with a vibrant bar and music scene. Catch a live jazz performance at a cozy bar, dance the night away at a trendy club, or sip cocktails on a rooftop bar with stunning views of the city.

Overall, Kadiköy offers a genuine glimpse into the heart of modern Istanbul. Embrace the laid-back local vibe, explore hidden gems, indulge in delicious food, and create unforgettable memories in this dynamic and ever-evolving district.

6. Uskudar

Üsküdar, bathed in the golden glow of the Asian sunrise, offers a unique perspective on Istanbul. While Sultanahmet boasts grand palaces and iconic mosques, Üsküdar beckons with a slower pace, deep-rooted traditions, and a local charm that unveils a different side of the city.

Characters You'll Meet:

The Tea Seller (Çaycı): A friendly face you'll encounter at almost every corner. Grab a steaming glass of çay (Turkish tea) for a refreshing break and a chance to chat with a local.

The Mosque Caretaker: Often an elderly gentleman with a warm smile, he'll be happy to answer questions about the mosque's history and traditions. Dress modestly and be respectful when entering a mosque.

The Market Vendors: From fresh produce at the bazaar (market) to handcrafted souvenirs at the Çarşı (bazaar), the vendors add a vibrant energy to Üsküdar. Be prepared to bargain for the best price!

Top Attractions Unveiled:

Çamlıca Mosque: Ascend the city's highest hill for breathtaking panoramic views and a marvel of modern architecture. Witness the grandeur of this colossal mosque, one of the largest in Turkey.

Yeni Valide Mosque (Mosque of the New Valide): Admire the intricate tilework and calligraphy adorning this 17th-century Ottoman masterpiece.

Mihrimah Sultan Mosque: Nicknamed "The Mosque with the Balcony," this charming structure offers a unique vantage point overlooking the Bosphorus.

Hidden Gems Uncovered:

Kuzguncuk: Wander the narrow cobbled streets of this historic Armenian neighborhood. Admire colorful houses with flower-laden balconies and peek into hidden courtyards.

Fıstık (Pistachio) Museum: A quirky and delightful museum dedicated to the humble pistachio nut. Learn about its history, cultivation, and unique varieties found in Turkey.

Büyük Haydar Paşa Hamam: Indulge in a traditional Turkish bath experience at this historic hammam. Unwind and rejuvenate in the steamy chambers and experience the centuries-old ritual of cleansing.

Beyond the Tourist Trail:

Ferry Ride Magic: Take a scenic ferry ride across the Bosphorus from Üsküdar to Eminönü or Karaköy. Enjoy the cool breeze on your face and capture stunning photos of the Istanbul skyline.

Hilltop Picnic: Pack a picnic basket and head to the green slopes of Büyük Çamlıca Hill. Spread out a blanket, enjoy delicious Turkish treats, and take in the panoramic views of the city.

Sunset by the Sea: Stroll along the Üsküdar coast at sunset. Witness the sky ablaze with vibrant colors and soak in the peaceful atmosphere as the city lights begin to twinkle.

Experiencing the Local Side:

Friday Prayer at the Mosque: Witness the vibrant Friday prayer ceremony at one of Üsküdar's many mosques. Observe the traditions and respectful silence, soaking in the spiritual atmosphere.

Turkish Coffee Ritual: Savor a strong cup of Turkish coffee at a traditional kahve (coffee shop). Watch the locals play backgammon and lose yourself in the authentic Turkish social scene.

Street Food Delights: Venture beyond restaurants and indulge in delicious street food like "kokoreç" (grilled intestines) or "lahmacun" (Turkish pizza). It's a truly local experience for the adventurous foodie!

7. Balat

Balat, a captivating neighborhood nestled within the Fatih district of Istanbul, offers a unique blend of history, charm, and artistic energy. Once a center for the Greek and Jewish communities, Balat boasts a rich heritage reflected in its colorful architecture, narrow cobbled streets, and hidden gems waiting to be discovered.

Characters:

The Local Artisans: Balat is experiencing a creative renaissance. Independent artists, antique dealers, and skilled craftspeople have set up shop here, breathing new life into the historic buildings. You might encounter a friendly woodcarver restoring a piece of furniture, a potter meticulously shaping clay, or a young painter showcasing their latest work.

The Storytellers: The older residents of Balat hold the key to the neighborhood's past. Engage in conversation with a shopkeeper or a local enjoying Turkish tea in a quaint cafe. They might share stories of their families history and the vibrant life of Balat in bygone eras.

The Cats: Feline companions are a ubiquitous presence in Istanbul, and Balat is no exception. Keep an eye out for these furry locals basking in the sun or napping in doorways, adding to the neighborhood's laid-back charm.

Top Attractions:

The Rainbow Houses: Balat's most iconic sight is undoubtedly its rows of colorful houses. These beautifully restored Ottoman-era wooden structures, painted in vibrant hues of pink, blue, yellow, and green, create a picture-perfect backdrop for your Istanbul photos.

St. Mary of the Mongols Church: This magnificent Greek Orthodox church, dating back to the 18th century, boasts stunning frescoes and a tranquil atmosphere.

The Synagogues: Balat's rich Jewish heritage is evident in its three active synagogues: Ahrida Synagogue, Yanik Synagogue, and the Ahyion Synagogue. Admire their unique architecture and learn about the history of the Jewish community in Istanbul (respectful dress code required when entering).

Hidden Gems:

Balat Antique Shops: Delve into the labyrinthine streets and discover a treasure trove of antique shops brimming with hidden gems. Unearth unique Turkish rugs, vintage jewelry, Ottoman ceramics, and other fascinating finds.

Studio Homes: Balat is home to numerous art studios housed in beautifully restored historic buildings. Keep an eye out for open studio days or galleries showcasing local talent.

Küçük Ayasofya Camii (The Little Hagia Sophia): This lesser-known mosque, built in the 16th century, offers a glimpse into Ottoman architecture and a serene escape from the crowds.

Experiences:

Wander the Cobblestone Streets: The best way to experience Balat's magic is to get lost in its maze-like streets. Around every corner, you'll discover hidden courtyards, charming cafes, and architectural details that whisper stories of the past.

Savor Turkish Delights: Indulge in a traditional Turkish breakfast or a refreshing glass of çay (Turkish tea) at a local cafe. Many cafes have outdoor seating, allowing you to soak up the neighborhood atmosphere.

Take a Turkish Calligraphy Class: Immerse yourself in Turkish culture by learning the art of calligraphy from a local artist. This unique experience will provide a lasting souvenir and a deeper appreciation for Turkish craftsmanship.

Attend a Local Festival: Throughout the year, Balat comes alive with vibrant festivals celebrating art, music, and culture. Participating in one of these events is a fantastic way to connect with the local community and experience Balat's unique energy.

Beyond the Tourist Trail:

Balat offers an escape from the bustling tourist areas of Istanbul. Here, you'll find a slower pace of life, allowing you to truly connect with the city's soul. By exploring the hidden gems, engaging with the locals, and immersing yourself in the creative energy, you'll discover the true magic of Balat.

8. Ortaköy

Ortaköy, nestled on the European shore of the Bosphorus Strait in Istanbul's Beşiktaş district, is a captivating neighborhood that enthralls visitors with its rich history, vibrant atmosphere, and stunning waterfront location. Here's a deeper dive into what makes Ortaköy a must-visit for any Istanbul itinerary:

Characters:

The Locals: Ortaköy boasts a friendly and welcoming community. You'll find a mix of young professionals, families, and older residents who take pride in their neighborhood's unique character.

Street Vendors: The lively Ortaköy Square is a haven for street vendors selling an array of delicious treats. From the iconic "dondurma" (Turkish ice cream) vendors with their theatrical flair to the aroma of freshly baked "kumru" (stuffed bread), these vendors add to the lively energy of the neighborhood.

Fishermen: Early mornings witness local fishermen casting their nets from the pier, a reminder of Ortaköy's maritime heritage.

Top Attractions:

Ortaköy Mosque: This iconic neo-Baroque-style mosque is the heart of Ortaköy. Its beautiful white facade and minarets stand out majestically against the Bosphorus backdrop. Take a moment to admire the intricate details and the peaceful atmosphere inside (remember to dress modestly).

Sunday Market: Every Sunday, a vibrant market explodes across Ortaköy Square. Browse through a delightful assortment of handmade crafts, souvenirs, clothes, and local delicacies.

Bosphorus Cruise: Hop on a ferry or a private boat tour from the Ortaköy pier and experience the magic of the Bosphorus Strait. Marvel at the stunning Dolmabahçe Palace, the ancient Rumeli Fortress, and the charming neighborhoods lining the shores.

Hidden Gems:

Etz Hayim Synagogue and Hagia Fokas Church: A testament to Ortaköy's historical tolerance, these beautifully preserved places of worship stand within walking distance of the mosque.

Backstreets and Local Cafes: Wander through the charming backstreets and discover hidden cafes with water views. Enjoy a leisurely Turkish coffee or sip on some freshly squeezed apple tea (elma çayı) while soaking in the local atmosphere.

Çırağan Palace Kempinski: Indulge in a luxurious experience by having lunch or afternoon tea at the Çırağan Palace Kempinski, a former Ottoman palace transformed into a stunning hotel. The breathtaking Bosphorus views and opulent setting are unforgettable.

Experiences:

Street Food Extravaganza: Savor the diverse street food scene. From the melt-in-your-mouth "dondurma" to crispy "balik ekmek" (fish sandwich) and savory "kokoreç" (grilled intestines - for the adventurous!), Ortaköy offers a delicious adventure for your taste buds.

Sunset on the Bosphorus: Find a spot along the Ortaköy waterfront and witness the mesmerizing sunset over the Bosphorus. The sky explodes with vibrant colors as the sun dips below the horizon, creating a picture-perfect moment.

People Watching: Grab a seat at a waterfront cafe and enjoy the lively scene. Watch locals playing backgammon, families enjoying a stroll, and street performers entertaining the crowds.

Beyond the Tourist Trail:

Bomonti Beer District: Venture a little further and explore the trendy Bomonti Beer District. Sample locally brewed craft beers at historical buildings converted into breweries and restaurants.

Yıldız Park: Escape the crowds and discover Yıldız Park, a sprawling green oasis offering a peaceful escape with historical landmarks and beautiful gardens.

Tips:

- Ortaköy gets crowded, especially on weekends. Consider visiting during weekdays for a more relaxed experience.
- Bargaining is expected at the Sunday market. Have fun with it, but be respectful.
- Comfortable shoes are recommended as you'll likely be doing a lot of walking and exploring the charming streets.

9. Bebek

Bebek, nestled on the European shore of the Bosphorus Strait, offers a unique blend of tranquility, upscale charm, and stunning water views. While not bursting with historical landmarks, Bebek provides a delightful escape from the bustling heart of Istanbul, perfect for travelers seeking a relaxed and scenic experience.

Characters:

Affluent Istanbulis: Bebek is a popular neighborhood for Istanbul's wealthy residents. Expect to see families strolling along the waterfront, young professionals enjoying a leisurely coffee, and perhaps even a local celebrity or two.

Yachting Enthusiasts: The Bebek bay is a haven for yachts, adding a touch of nautical flair to the neighborhood. You might see people sailing, tinkering with their boats, or simply enjoying the view from their decks.

Nature Lovers: Bebek boasts several green spaces, including parks and the sprawling Belgrade Forest nearby. These areas offer a respite from the urban environment and a chance to breathe in some fresh air.

Top Attractions:

Bosphorus Waterfront: The star attraction of Bebek is undoubtedly the Bosphorus Strait. Take a stroll along the well-maintained corniche, watch the boats glide by, and soak in the breathtaking panorama.

Upscale Restaurants and Cafes: Bebek is renowned for its vibrant cafe and restaurant scene. Choose from a variety of options, from trendy cafes serving specialty coffee and pastries to upscale restaurants with international cuisine and breathtaking Bosphorus views. Indulge in a long lunch on a terrace overlooking the water, or grab a refreshing drink and people-watch in the afternoon sun.

Bar Scene: Bebek transforms into a lively spot in the evenings. Upscale bars with outdoor seating offer a sophisticated ambiance to enjoy a drink and conversation while taking in the night lights of the Bosphorus.

Hidden Gems:

Yildiz Park: Located just north of Bebek, Yildiz Park is a sprawling green oasis. Explore the former hunting grounds of Ottoman sultans, admire the neoclassical Çadır Kiosk, and enjoy the peaceful atmosphere away from the crowds.

Bebek Mosque: This 19th-century mosque, with its elegant minaret, is a charming example of Ottoman architecture. While smaller than the grand mosques of Sultanahmet, it offers a glimpse into the local religious life and a peaceful retreat.

Snake Mansion (Yılanlı Yalı): This historic wooden mansion, dating back to the 19th century, gets its name from the decorative snake motifs on its facade. Though not open to the public, it's a captivating piece of Bebek's architectural heritage.

Experiences:

Bosphorus Cruise: Embark on a scenic cruise from Bebek and sail along the Bosphorus, marveling at the architectural wonders lining the shores, from opulent palaces to grand Ottoman mansions.

Kayaking or Stand-Up Paddling: Rent a kayak or stand-up paddleboard and explore the Bebek bay from a different perspective. Enjoy the tranquility of being on the water surrounded by the beautiful scenery.

People-Watching: Grab a seat at a waterfront cafe and simply observe the local life unfold. Watch families enjoying picnics, dog walkers strolling by, and the overall relaxed vibe of the neighborhood.

Shopping at Boutiques: Explore the charming boutiques scattered around Bebek. Find unique souvenirs, handcrafted items, and stylish clothing from local designers.

Beyond Bebek:

Ortaköy: Take a short walk south to Ortaköy, another charming neighborhood known for its picturesque Ortaköy Mosque and delicious street food, especially the famous "dondurma" (Turkish ice cream).

Rumeli Fortress: Venture further north and explore the imposing Rumeli Fortress, a historical landmark guarding the Bosphorus Strait. This impressive structure offers stunning views of the waterway and a glimpse into Istanbul's Ottoman past.

10. Arnavutköy

Arnavutköy, tucked away on the European shore of the Black Sea, offers a delightful escape from the bustling heart of Istanbul. Unlike the grand mosques and palaces of the city center, Arnavutköy exudes a charming village atmosphere, perfect for a relaxing and authentic Istanbul experience.

Characters:

Local Fishermen: The heart of Arnavutköy beats with the rhythm of the fishing community. You'll see friendly fishermen mending their nets, casting lines from the piers, and sharing stories over cups of çay (Turkish tea).

Artsy Residents: In recent years, Arnavutköy has attracted artists, photographers, and writers seeking a peaceful haven with stunning scenery. You might encounter them strolling the narrow streets, capturing the essence of the neighborhood in their works.

Warm Community: Arnavutköy retains a strong sense of community. Residents greet each other with friendly smiles, and the atmosphere is welcoming and relaxed.

Top Attractions:

Bosphorus Views: While technically on the Black Sea, Arnavutköy boasts breathtaking vistas of the Bosphorus Strait where Europe and Asia meet. Take a stroll along the waterfront promenade and admire the sparkling water dotted with ferries and yachts.

Historical Yalis: Dotting the coastline are stunning Ottoman-era wooden mansions called "yalis." These architectural gems, some intricately restored, serve as elegant restaurants or private residences.

19th-Century Church: The charming 19th-century Agia Marina Greek Orthodox Church, with its whitewashed facade and bell tower, stands as a testament to Arnavutköy's multicultural heritage.

Hidden Gems:

Narrow Backstreets: Venture beyond the waterfront and explore Arnavutköy's labyrinthine backstreets. Discover hidden courtyards adorned with colorful flowers, stumble upon quaint cafes tucked away in corners, and find unique shops selling local crafts.

Art Galleries: Keep an eye out for the small art galleries showcasing the works of local and regional artists. You might find the perfect souvenir or simply appreciate the creative energy of the neighborhood.

Sunset Spot: Head to a waterfront restaurant or cafe as the sun dips below the horizon. The sky explodes with vibrant colors, casting a magical glow over the Bosphorus and creating a truly unforgettable scene.

Unforgettable Experiences:

Seafood Feast: Indulge in the freshest seafood at Arnavutköy's many waterfront restaurants. Sample succulent grilled fish, savory meze platters, and traditional Turkish dishes while enjoying the breathtaking sea views.

Bosphorus Cruise: Embark on a scenic Bosphorus cruise from Arnavutköy, offering a unique perspective of the city's iconic landmarks like Dolmabahçe Palace and the Blue Mosque from the water.

Turkish Bath Ritual: Pamper yourself at a traditional Turkish bath (hamam) located in Arnavutköy. Experience the cleansing heat, invigorating massage, and a sense of rejuvenation in this historic Turkish tradition.

Shopping for Local Crafts: Browse the charming shops lining the narrow streets. Find unique souvenirs like hand-painted ceramics, colorful textiles, and traditional Turkish delights as mementos of your time in Arnavutköy.

Overall, Arnavutköy offers a unique blend of history, charm, and natural beauty, making it a perfect destination for travelers seeking a tranquil and authentic Istanbul experience.

Best Places to Stay Based on Interests

Budget Travelers

For budget travelers visiting Istanbul, several neighborhoods offer affordable accommodations, easy access to public transportation, and proximity to key attractions. Here are some of the best neighborhoods to stay in Istanbul for budget travelers:

1. Sultanahmet

Sultanahmet is Istanbul's historic heart, home to iconic landmarks like the Blue Mosque, Hagia Sophia, and Topkapi Palace. Budget hotels, hostels, and guesthouses abound here, catering to tourists who wish to explore the city's rich history on foot. You'll find budget-friendly eateries, souvenir shops, and easy access to tram lines for exploring other parts of the city.

2. Beyoğlu (Taksim)

Beyoğlu centered around the lively Taksim Square, is known for its vibrant atmosphere, bustling nightlife, and cultural diversity.

Budget accommodations range from hostels to budget hotels, particularly around Istiklal Avenue. This area offers an array of dining options, from street food to local cafes, and is well-connected by metro, tram, and bus networks.

3. Kadıköy

Located on the Asian side of Istanbul, Kadıköy offers a more relaxed vibe compared to the European side. Budget travelers will find affordable hotels, hostels, and guesthouses here, along with a variety of budget-friendly eateries, markets, and local shops. Kadıköy is well-connected to the European side via ferry, making it easy to explore both sides of Istanbul.

4. Sirkeci

Sirkeci, near Sultanahmet, is another excellent option for budget travelers seeking proximity to Istanbul's historic sites and easy access to transportation hubs like Sirkeci Train Station. Budget hotels and guesthouses are plentiful here, offering convenience for exploring attractions like the Grand Bazaar and Spice Bazaar on foot.

5. Fatih (Aksaray)

Fatih, particularly around Aksaray and Laleli, offers budget-friendly accommodations and a bustling local atmosphere. This area is known for its textile shops, budget eateries serving delicious Turkish cuisine, and proximity to historical sites like the Valens Aqueduct. Aksaray is well-connected by tram and metro, providing easy access to other parts of Istanbul.

6. Şişli (Osmanbey)

Şişli, especially around Osmanbey and Bomonti, offers a mix of budget hotels, hostels, and guesthouses. This area is known for its shopping opportunities at Istanbul Cevahir Mall and Nişantaşı's boutiques. Şişli is well-served by metro and bus lines, making it convenient for budget travelers to explore both the historic and modern sides of Istanbul.

7. Eminönü

Eminönü, situated near the Golden Horn, offers budget accommodations close to the waterfront and major attractions like the Spice Bazaar and Galata Bridge. Budget hotels and guesthouses cater to travelers interested in exploring

Istanbul's vibrant markets, historic mosques, and waterfront promenades. Eminönü is well-connected by tram and ferry services.

Backpackers and Solo Travelers

For backpackers and solo travelers visiting Istanbul, choosing the right neighborhood can significantly enhance the travel experience, offering proximity to attractions, affordability, and a vibrant atmosphere conducive to meeting fellow travelers. Here are some of the best neighborhoods to consider:

1. Sultanahmet

Sultanahmet is Istanbul's historic heart, home to iconic landmarks like the Blue Mosque, Hagia Sophia, and Topkapi Palace. Staying here puts you within walking distance of these attractions, making it convenient for exploring on foot. The area has a range of budget accommodations, hostels, and guesthouses catering to backpackers. You'll also find bustling markets, cozy cafés, and restaurants serving traditional Turkish cuisine.

2. Beyoğlu (Taksim)

Beyoğlu centered around the lively Taksim Square, is known for its vibrant nightlife, art galleries, and shopping streets like Istiklal Avenue. It's a hub for budget-friendly hostels and boutique hotels, making it ideal for solo travelers looking to explore the city's modern side. From Taksim, you can easily access cultural sites like the Galata Tower and Dolmabahçe Palace, as well as trendy cafes and rooftop bars.

3. Kadıköy

Located on Istanbul's Asian side, Kadıköy offers a more relaxed and local vibe compared to the European side. It's known for its bustling markets, waterfront promenade, and vibrant food scene. Kadıköy is popular among backpackers for its affordable hostels and guesthouses, as well as its bohemian cafes and artsy atmosphere. Ferries to the European side are frequent, offering easy access to Sultanahmet and other attractions.

4. Galata

Galata, situated near Beyoğlu, is characterized by its historic tower, narrow cobblestone streets, and trendy boutiques. It's a great neighborhood for solo travelers interested in art, music, and nightlife.

Accommodation options range from budget hostels to boutique hotels with rooftop views of the Golden Horn. You can explore nearby attractions like the Galata Bridge, Galata Tower, and the vibrant Karaköy district.

5. Karaköy

Karaköy, once a bustling port area, has transformed into a trendy neighborhood with art galleries, hip cafes, and stylish bars. It's known for its mix of historic architecture and contemporary culture. Solo travelers will find a variety of budget accommodations here, along with easy access to the Galata Bridge and ferry terminals for exploring both sides of Istanbul. The area is lively during the day and night, offering plenty of opportunities to mingle with locals and fellow travelers.

6. Eminönü

Eminönü, located at the southern end of the Galata Bridge, is a bustling district known for its historic spice market (Egyptian Bazaar) and ferry docks. It's a convenient base for exploring Sultanahmet's attractions on foot and accessing public transportation hubs. Accommodations in Eminönü range from budget hotels to hostels, catering to backpackers looking to immerse themselves in Istanbul's vibrant street life and culinary delights.

7. Üsküdar

Üsküdar, on Istanbul's Asian side, offers a quieter and more residential atmosphere compared to the bustling European side. It's known for its historic mosques, waterfront parks, and local markets. Solo travelers can find affordable guesthouses and hostels here, enjoying panoramic views of the Bosphorus and easy access to attractions like Maiden's Tower and Çamlıca Hill for stunning city views.

Families and Leisure Travelers

Istanbul offers several neighborhoods that are ideal for families and leisure travelers, providing a blend of comfort, convenience, and attractions suitable for all ages.

1. Sultanahmet

Sultanahmet is Istanbul's historic heart, home to iconic landmarks such as the Blue Mosque, Hagia Sophia, and Topkapi Palace. Staying here puts you within walking distance of these architectural marvels, making it convenient for families to explore Istanbul's rich history. The area also offers charming streets, traditional restaurants, and easy access to tram lines for exploring other parts of the city.

- **Accommodation:** There are a variety of hotels ranging from boutique options to luxury accommodations, many with views of historic sites.
- **Attractions:** Blue Mosque, Hagia Sophia, Topkapi Palace, Basilica Cistern.
- **Activities:** Guided tours, cultural experiences, Turkish cuisine.

2. Taksim

Taksim Square and its surrounding area offer a vibrant atmosphere with bustling streets, shops, and a variety of restaurants. Families can enjoy leisurely walks along Istiklal Avenue, known for its historic tram and diverse dining options. Taksim is also a hub for nightlife and cultural events, offering a lively atmosphere day and night.

- **Accommodation:** Hotels range from budget-friendly options to upscale boutique hotels.
- **Attractions:** Istiklal Avenue, Taksim Square, Galata Tower (nearby).
- **Activities:** Shopping, dining, nightlife, visiting art galleries.

3. Beyoglu (Galata)

Beyoglu, particularly around the Galata Tower area, offers a mix of historic charm and modern amenities. Families will appreciate the neighborhood's artistic vibe, with galleries, trendy cafes, and panoramic views from the Galata Tower. The area also hosts family-friendly attractions like the Istanbul Modern Art Museum and the historic Pera Palace Hotel.

- **Accommodation:** Boutique hotels, guesthouses, and apartments with views of the Bosphorus.
- **Attractions:** Galata Tower, Istanbul Modern Art Museum, Pera Museum.
- **Activities:** Exploring art galleries, scenic walks, enjoying panoramic views.

4. Besiktas

Besiktas is a lively district situated along the Bosphorus, offering a mix of residential charm and local culture.

Families will find plenty of parks, cafes, and seafood restaurants along the waterfront promenade. The area is also home to Dolmabahce Palace, ideal for history buffs, and lively markets like Besiktas Fish Market.

- **Accommodation:** Hotels range from budget-friendly options to upscale accommodations with views of the Bosphorus.
- **Attractions:** Dolmabahce Palace, Besiktas Fish Market, Yildiz Park.
- **Activities:** Bosphorus cruises, visiting historic sites, enjoying local cuisine.

5. Ortakoy

Ortakoy is known for its picturesque setting along the Bosphorus, offering stunning views of the Bosphorus Bridge and lively markets. Families will enjoy exploring the neighborhood's art galleries, boutiques, and waterfront cafes. The area is famous for its Ortakoy Mosque and vibrant street food scene, making it a delightful spot for strolls and cultural experiences.

- **Accommodation:** Boutique hotels and guesthouses with views of the Bosphorus.
- **Attractions:** Ortakoy Mosque, Bosphorus Bridge views, local markets.
- **Activities:** Sampling street food, visiting art galleries, Bosphorus boat tours.

6. Kadikoy

Kadikoy, located on Istanbul's Asian side, offers a more relaxed atmosphere with a blend of modern amenities and local culture. Families will appreciate the neighborhood's parks, historic buildings, and bustling markets like Kadikoy Market. The area also boasts a vibrant dining scene, with numerous restaurants serving traditional Turkish cuisine.

- **Accommodation:** Hotels range from budget-friendly options to boutique hotels.
- **Attractions:** Kadikoy Market, Moda neighborhood, Haydarpasa Train Station.
- **Activities:** Exploring local markets, visiting historic sites, and sampling Turkish cuisine.

For Couples

Istanbul is a city of contrasts, where history meets modernity and diverse cultures blend seamlessly. For couples, it offers an enchanting mix of romantic experiences, from intimate dinners with views of the Bosphorus to serene strolls through ancient streets. Here are the best neighborhoods in Istanbul for couples, each with its unique charm and appeal:

1. Sultanahmet

Sultanahmet is the historic heart of Istanbul, home to some of the city's most iconic landmarks, including the Hagia Sophia, Blue Mosque, and Topkapi Palace. Staying in Sultanahmet allows couples to immerse themselves in Istanbul's rich history and vibrant culture. The neighborhood's narrow, cobbled streets, charming Ottoman-era houses, and atmospheric cafes make it a romantic choice.

Highlights for Couples:

- Visiting the Hagia Sophia and Blue Mosque at sunrise or sunset.
- Strolling through the peaceful gardens of Topkapi Palace.
- Enjoying a traditional Turkish breakfast in a cozy café.
- Experiencing a Turkish bath at one of the historical hammams.

Best Time to Visit: Spring and autumn for pleasant weather and fewer crowds.

Recommended Hotels:

- Four Seasons Hotel Istanbul at Sultanahmet (Luxury)
- White House Hotel Istanbul (Boutique)
- Sirkeci Mansion (Mid-range)

2. Beyoğlu

Beyoğlu, encompassing areas like Taksim and Galata, is known for its lively atmosphere, eclectic mix of shops, restaurants, and bars, and rich artistic heritage. The neighborhood offers a blend of modernity and history, with bustling streets, vibrant nightlife, and stunning views from the Galata Tower.

Highlights for Couples:

- Taking a romantic stroll along Istiklal Avenue.
- Enjoying a sunset view from the Galata Tower.
- Exploring the quaint streets and artisan shops of Galata.
- Dining at rooftop restaurants with panoramic views of the Bosphorus.

Best Time to Visit: Year-round, but spring and autumn are particularly pleasant.

Recommended Hotels:

- The Marmara Taksim (Luxury)
- Georges Hotel Galata (Boutique)
- Pera Palace Hotel (Historic)

3. Kadıköy

Kadıköy, located on the Asian side of Istanbul, offers a more laid-back and authentic local experience. Known for its vibrant street life, bustling markets, and lively waterfront, Kadıköy is perfect for couples looking to explore the lesser-known parts of Istanbul while enjoying the city's dynamic atmosphere.

Highlights for Couples:

- Wandering through the colorful Kadıköy Market.
- Enjoying a ferry ride across the Bosphorus.
- Dining at waterfront seafood restaurants in the Moda neighborhood.
- Relaxing at cozy cafes and sampling local delicacies.

Best Time to Visit: Spring and summer for pleasant outdoor activities.

Recommended Hotels:

- DoubleTree by Hilton Istanbul Moda (Luxury)
- Riva's Moda (Boutique)
- Juliet Rooms & Kitchen (Mid-range)

4. Ortaköy

Ortaköy is a picturesque neighborhood along the Bosphorus, known for its stunning views, historic mosque, and lively waterfront. It offers a romantic setting with its charming streets, vibrant art scene, and diverse dining options. Couples can enjoy the serene ambiance and beautiful scenery.

Highlights for Couples:

- Visiting the Ortaköy Mosque and enjoying its stunning Bosphorus views.
- Browsing through the weekend art and crafts market.
- Savoring street food like kumpir (stuffed baked potatoes) along the waterfront.
- Taking a Bosphorus cruise from the nearby piers.

Best Time to Visit: Spring and summer for outdoor enjoyment.

Recommended Hotels:

- Radisson Blu Bosphorus Hotel, Istanbul (Luxury)
- The Stay Bosphorus (Boutique)
- Ortaköy Princess Hotel (Mid-range)

5. Cihangir

Cihangir is a bohemian neighborhood known for its artistic vibe, cozy cafes, and vintage shops. It's a favorite among artists, writers, and expats, offering a relaxed and romantic atmosphere. The narrow streets, beautiful old buildings, and vibrant street art make it a charming place to explore.

Highlights for Couples:

- Enjoy a leisurely breakfast at one of the many quaint cafes.
- Exploring the local art galleries and antique shops.
- Taking a romantic walk through the leafy streets and enjoying the city views.
- Relaxing at a cozy tea house or patisserie.

Best Time to Visit: Spring and autumn for the best weather.

Recommended Hotels:

- Witt Istanbul Suites (Boutique)
- Nuru Ziya Suites (Mid-range)
- Cihangir Hotel (Budget-friendly)

6. Arnavutköy

Arnavutköy is a charming and peaceful neighborhood along the Bosphorus, known for its historic wooden houses, picturesque streets, and excellent seafood restaurants. It offers a tranquil setting for couples seeking a romantic getaway with beautiful views and a slower pace of life.

Highlights for Couples:

- Strolling along the Bosphorus and admiring the historic wooden mansions.
- Dining at one of the renowned seafood restaurants with Bosphorus views.
- Enjoying a leisurely coffee at a waterfront café.

- Taking a boat ride to explore the Bosphorus.

Best Time to Visit: Spring and summer for the best outdoor experience.

Recommended Hotels:

- Sumahan on the Water (Luxury Boutique)
- Ajia Hotel (Boutique)
- Arnavutköy Hotel (Mid-range)

7. Bebek

Bebek is an upscale neighborhood on the European side of Istanbul, famous for its beautiful waterfront, lush green parks, and trendy cafes and restaurants. It's an ideal spot for couples looking to enjoy luxurious amenities and scenic walks along the Bosphorus.

Highlights for Couples:

- Walking hand-in-hand along the Bebek waterfront promenade.
- Enjoy a romantic dinner at one of the elegant restaurants with Bosphorus views.
- Relaxing in Bebek Park with a picnic.
- Taking a private yacht tour from the marina.

Best Time to Visit: Spring and summer for the best outdoor activities.

Recommended Hotels:

- The Stay Bosphorus (Luxury Boutique)
- Bebek Hotel by The Stay Collection (Boutique)
- Bosphorus Palace Hotel (Historic)

8. Balat

Balat is a historic neighborhood known for its colorful houses, cobblestone streets, and rich cultural heritage. It offers a unique and romantic experience for couples who enjoy exploring off-the-beaten-path locations and discovering the city's hidden gems.

Highlights for Couples:

- Exploring the narrow, winding streets lined with colorful houses.

- Visiting historic churches and synagogues.
- Enjoying a coffee at one of the charming, vintage-style cafes.
- Taking photographs of the vibrant street art and historic architecture.

Best Time to Visit: Year-round, but spring and autumn are particularly pleasant.

Recommended Hotels:

- Hotel Troya Balat (Boutique)
- Balat Residence (Mid-range)
- Cheers Hostel Balat (Budget-friendly)

9. Karaköy

Karaköy is a trendy neighborhood that has undergone significant transformation in recent years, becoming a hub for art, cuisine, and nightlife. Its mix of modern and historic elements, along with its vibrant atmosphere, makes it a great place for couples to stay.

Highlights for Couples:

- Visiting contemporary art galleries and exhibitions.
- Dining at chic restaurants and rooftop bars with stunning views.
- Strolling through the historic streets and discovering boutique shops.
- Enjoying the lively nightlife with trendy bars and cafes.

Best Time to Visit: Year-round, but spring and autumn are particularly pleasant.

Recommended Hotels:

- 10 Karaköy Istanbul (Luxury Boutique)
- Vault Karaköy House Hotel (Boutique)
- Portus House Istanbul (Mid-range)

10. Üsküdar

Üsküdar, located on the Asian side of Istanbul, offers a more traditional and serene experience. It is known for its historic mosques, tranquil waterfront, and beautiful parks. Couples can enjoy a more relaxed pace of life and stunning views of the Bosphorus and the historic peninsula.

Highlights for Couples:

- Visiting the beautiful Mihrimah Sultan Mosque and other historic landmarks.
- Strolling along the Bosphorus promenade and watching the sunset.
- Enjoying a peaceful afternoon in the expansive Fethi Pasha Grove.
- Taking a ferry ride to the European side for a day trip.

Best Time to Visit: Spring and summer for the best outdoor experiences.

Recommended Hotels:

- Sumahan on the Water (Luxury Boutique)
- Boscolo Palace Hotel (Boutique)
- Harem Hotel (Mid-range)

Luxury Travelers

Istanbul offers a variety of neighborhoods that cater to luxury travelers, each providing unique experiences and amenities. Here are the best neighborhoods to stay in Istanbul for those seeking a luxurious visit:

1. Nişantaşı

Nişantaşı is Istanbul's premier upscale neighborhood, often compared to New York's Upper East Side or Paris's Champs-Élysées. It is known for its high-end boutiques, designer stores, and luxury hotels. The streets are lined with chic cafés, gourmet restaurants, and vibrant nightlife venues. The architecture here is a mix of historic buildings and modern structures, giving it a sophisticated urban feel. Abdi İpekçi Street, the heart of Nişantaşı, is where you'll find the flagship stores of world-renowned brands.

- **Best Luxury Hotels:** The St. Regis Istanbul, Park Hyatt Istanbul - Maçka Palas
- **Notable Attractions:** City's Nişantaşı Shopping Mall, Maçka Park, and numerous art galleries.
- **Dining:** Vogue Restaurant, Brasserie Nişantaşı, and Spago by Wolfgang Puck.

2. Beşiktaş

Beşiktaş is a vibrant neighborhood that seamlessly blends the old and the new. It is home to some of Istanbul's most iconic landmarks, such as the Dolmabahçe Palace and the Bosphorus waterfront.

Beşiktaş is known for its lively atmosphere, upscale hotels, and fine dining establishments. The neighborhood is also a hub for nightlife with its trendy bars and clubs.

- **Best Luxury Hotels:** Four Seasons Hotel Istanbul at the Bosphorus, Shangri-La Bosphorus
- **Notable Attractions:** Dolmabahçe Palace, Yıldız Park, and the Maritime Museum.
- **Dining:** Ulus 29, Sunset Grill & Bar, and Çırağan Palace Kempinski's Tugra Restaurant.

3. Sultanahmet

Sultanahmet is the historic heart of Istanbul, home to many of the city's most famous landmarks, including the Hagia Sophia, Blue Mosque, and Topkapi Palace. While it is a major tourist area, it also offers luxurious accommodations that provide a blend of modern comfort and historical charm. Staying in Sultanahmet allows luxury travelers to immerse themselves in Istanbul's rich history while enjoying top-notch amenities.

- **Best Luxury Hotels:** Four Seasons Hotel Istanbul at Sultanahmet, Ajwa Hotel Sultanahmet
- **Notable Attractions:** Hagia Sophia, Blue Mosque, Topkapi Palace, and Basilica Cistern.
- **Dining:** Matbah Ottoman Palace Cuisine, Seven Hills Restaurant, and Deraliye Ottoman Cuisine Restaurant.

4. Beyoğlu

Beyoğlu is a bustling, cosmopolitan district known for its vibrant nightlife, historic landmarks, and cultural institutions. It encompasses areas like Taksim Square and İstiklal Avenue, which are filled with luxury boutiques, gourmet restaurants, and upscale hotels. The neighborhood is also home to many art galleries, theaters, and historical sites, making it a cultural hotspot.

- **Best Luxury Hotels:** The Marmara Taksim, Pera Palace Hotel
- **Notable Attractions:** İstiklal Avenue, Galata Tower, and the Museum of Innocence.
- **Dining:** 360 Istanbul, Mikla Restaurant, and Meze by Lemon Tree.

5. Kadıköy

Kadıköy, located on the Asian side of Istanbul, offers a blend of modernity and tradition with its bustling markets, vibrant arts scene, and scenic waterfront. This neighborhood is known for its relaxed atmosphere, high-end boutiques, and luxurious accommodations. It provides a unique perspective on Istanbul, away from the more tourist-heavy European side.

- **Best Luxury Hotels:** Wyndham Grand Istanbul Kalamış Marina Hotel, DoubleTree by Hilton Hotel Istanbul - Moda
- **Notable Attractions:** Kadıköy Market, Moda Park, and the historic Haydarpaşa Railway Station.
- **Dining:** Ciya Sofrasi, Viktor Levi Wine House, and Moda Teras.

6. Ortaköy

Ortaköy is a picturesque neighborhood along the Bosphorus, known for its charming cobblestone streets, boutique shops, and vibrant nightlife. The area is famous for the Ortaköy Mosque, which sits right on the waterfront. This neighborhood is perfect for luxury travelers seeking scenic views, fine dining, and a lively atmosphere.

- **Best Luxury Hotels:** Radisson Blu Bosphorus Hotel, Istanbul; The House Hotel Bosphorus
- **Notable Attractions:** Ortaköy Mosque, Bosphorus cruises, and weekend markets.
- **Dining:** Feriye Palace, Banyan Restaurant, and The House Café Ortaköy.

7. Galata

Galata is a historic neighborhood known for its iconic Galata Tower, narrow winding streets, and bohemian atmosphere. It has become a trendy area with a mix of luxury boutique hotels, art galleries, and upscale restaurants. Staying in Galata provides a unique blend of history, culture, and luxury.

- **Best Luxury Hotels:** Georges Hotel Galata, The House Hotel Karaköy
- **Notable Attractions:** Galata Tower, Istanbul Modern Art Museum, and the vibrant Karaköy area.
- **Dining:** Neolokal, Nola Istanbul, and Karaköy Lokantası.

8. Levent

Levent is a modern business district that also caters to luxury travelers with its high-end shopping centers, skyscrapers, and upscale hotels. The area is home to some of Istanbul's most prestigious shopping malls, such as Kanyon and Zorlu Center, offering an array of designer stores and gourmet restaurants. Levent provides a sleek, contemporary stay for those who prefer a modern luxury experience.

- **Best Luxury Hotels:** Hyatt Centric Levent Istanbul, Wyndham Grand Istanbul Levent
- **Notable Attractions:** Kanyon Shopping Mall, Zorlu Center, and the Sapphire Observation Deck.
- **Dining:** Morini Istanbul, Tom's Kitchen Istanbul, and Serafina Istanbul.

9. Etiler

Etiler is an affluent residential and commercial neighborhood known for its upscale lifestyle, luxury boutiques, and gourmet dining options. It is home to several high-end hotels and is close to the vibrant nightlife of Bebek and the scenic Bosphorus. Etiler is ideal for luxury travelers seeking a mix of relaxation and excitement.

- **Best Luxury Hotels:** Le Meridien Istanbul Etiler, Renaissance Istanbul Polat Bosphorus Hotel
- **Notable Attractions:** Akmerkez Shopping Mall, Bebek Park, and nearby Bosphorus cruises.
- **Dining:** Nusret Etiler Steakhouse, Sunset Grill & Bar, and La Boom Istanbul.

10. Bebek

Bebek is a prestigious waterfront neighborhood along the Bosphorus, known for its beautiful views, elegant cafés, and upscale residences. The area is popular among Istanbul's elite and offers luxurious hotels, fine dining, and a peaceful, scenic environment. Bebek is perfect for luxury travelers who want to enjoy the best of Istanbul's coastal charm.

- **Best Luxury Hotels:** Bebek Hotel by The Stay Collection

Recommended Areas and Hotels

1. Sultanahmet

Luxury Hotels

Four Seasons Hotel Istanbul at Sultanahmet (5 stars): Housed in a century-old neoclassical Turkish prison, the Four Seasons Hotel Istanbul at Sultanahmet offers an extraordinary blend of historical charm and modern luxury. The hotel features spacious, elegantly decorated rooms with Ottoman-inspired decor. Guests can enjoy amenities like a luxurious spa, a rooftop terrace with stunning views of the Hagia Sophia and Blue Mosque, and a beautiful courtyard garden. The dining options include fine Turkish and international cuisine. Phone Number: +90 212 402 30 00

Ajwa Hotel Sultanahmet (5 stars): Ajwa Hotel Sultanahmet combines traditional Ottoman elegance with modern comforts. Each room is uniquely decorated with handcrafted furniture, silk Tabriz carpets, and marble bathrooms. The hotel offers a lavish spa, fitness center, and an indoor pool. Zeferan Restaurant serves Azerbaijani and Turkish cuisine with panoramic views of the Sea of Marmara. Personalized service and attention to detail make this hotel a top choice for luxury travelers. Phone Number: +90 212 638 22 00

Boutique Hotels

Sirkeci Mansion (4 stars): Sirkeci Mansion is a family-run boutique hotel that provides a warm and inviting atmosphere with a touch of Ottoman elegance. The rooms are tastefully decorated with traditional furnishings and modern amenities. The hotel features an indoor swimming pool, a sauna, and a rooftop terrace with breathtaking views of the Bosphorus. The Neyzade Restaurant offers delicious Turkish cuisine made with fresh, local ingredients. Phone Number: +90 212 528 43 44

Hotel Amira Istanbul (4 stars): Hotel Amira Istanbul is a charming boutique hotel that combines modern amenities with classic Ottoman design. The rooms are spacious and well-appointed, featuring plush bedding, marble bathrooms, and free Wi-Fi. Guests can relax on the rooftop terrace, which offers stunning views of the Marmara Sea and the Blue Mosque. The hotel provides a complimentary breakfast buffet and afternoon tea. Phone Number: +90 212 516 16 00

Budget-Friendly Hotels

Antique Hostel & Guesthouse (3 stars): Antique Hostel & Guesthouse offers clean and comfortable accommodations, including private rooms and dormitories. The hostel provides free breakfast, and Wi-Fi, and has a rooftop terrace with panoramic views of the Bosphorus and the Blue Mosque. The friendly staff is always ready to assist with travel arrangements and recommendations. Its prime location makes it a perfect base for exploring Istanbul's historical sites. Phone Number: +90 212 638 36 00

Cheers Hostel (3 stars: Cheers Hostel is known for its lively atmosphere and excellent location in Sultanahmet. The hostel offers a range of accommodation options, from dormitory beds to private rooms. Guests can enjoy a complimentary breakfast, free Wi-Fi, and a cozy common area. The highlight is the rooftop bar, offering stunning views of the Hagia Sophia. The staff is friendly and knowledgeable, ensuring a memorable stay. Phone Number: +90 212 518 23 43

Hotel Fehmi Bey (3 stars: Hotel Fehmi Bey is a family-owned budget hotel that offers clean and comfortable accommodations with a friendly atmosphere. The rooms are simply furnished but equipped with all necessary amenities, including free Wi-Fi and air conditioning. The hotel features a rooftop terrace where guests can enjoy their breakfast with views of the Blue Mosque and the Sea of Marmara. Phone Number: +90 212 518 10 25

2. Beyoglu

Luxury Hotels

The Marmara Taksim (5 stars): The Marmara Taksim is a landmark luxury hotel located in the heart of Istanbul's vibrant Beyoğlu district. It offers spectacular views of the Bosphorus and Taksim Square. The elegantly designed rooms and suites feature contemporary decor, plush furnishings, and state-of-the-art amenities. Guests can indulge in the hotel's fine dining options, relax in the rooftop pool, or rejuvenate at the spa and fitness center. The hotel's central location makes it a perfect base for exploring Istanbul's cultural and historical attractions. Phone Number: +90 212 334 83 00

Pera Palace Hotel (5 stars): Pera Palace Hotel is an iconic and historic luxury hotel that has hosted many famous guests since its opening in 1895. The hotel exudes old-world charm with its opulent interiors, antique furnishings, and elegant rooms. Each room is uniquely decorated, blending classical style with modern amenities. Guests can enjoy afternoon tea in the Kubbeli Lounge, dine at Agatha Restaurant, or unwind at the spa and indoor pool. The hotel's rich history and prime location near Istiklal Avenue make it a unique luxury experience. Phone Number: +90 212 377 40 00

Boutique Hotels

Tomtom Suites (5 stars): Tomtom Suites is a boutique hotel housed in a historic building that dates back to the early 1900s. It offers a luxurious and intimate stay with its spacious suites, each uniquely designed with modern decor and antique touches. The hotel features a rooftop terrace with stunning views of the city and the Bosphorus, where guests can enjoy a gourmet breakfast or evening cocktails. Personalized service and attention to detail make Tomtom Suites a top choice for discerning travelers. Phone Number: +90 212 292 49 49

The House Hotel Karaköy (4 stars): The House Hotel Karaköy is a chic boutique hotel located in the up-and-coming Karaköy district of Beyoğlu. The hotel occupies a beautifully restored bank building, blending neoclassical architecture with contemporary design. The stylish rooms and suites feature high ceilings, luxurious bedding, and modern amenities. Guests can enjoy the rooftop bar and restaurant, which offers panoramic views of the Golden Horn and the Old City. The hotel's trendy location is perfect for exploring Istanbul's vibrant arts and nightlife scene. Phone Number: +90 212 244 34 34

Budget-Friendly Hotels

Cheers Midtown Hostel (3 stars): Cheers Midtown Hostel is a budget-friendly option located in the heart of Beyoğlu, offering a range of accommodations from private rooms to dormitory beds. The hostel is known for its friendly atmosphere, clean facilities, and central location. Guests can enjoy free breakfast, Wi-Fi, and a cozy common area. The rooftop terrace offers views of the city and is a great place to socialize with fellow travelers. Its proximity to Istiklal Avenue and public transportation makes it an ideal base for exploring Istanbul. Phone Number: +90 212 251 12 96

Hotel The Public (4 stars): Hotel The Public is a boutique hotel that offers affordable luxury in the lively Beyoğlu district. The hotel features modern, well-appointed rooms with unique design elements and comfortable amenities.

Guests can enjoy a complimentary breakfast, free Wi-Fi, and a friendly, attentive staff. The hotel's prime location on Istiklal Avenue provides easy access to shopping, dining, and cultural attractions. Its stylish ambiance and reasonable rates make it a popular choice for budget-conscious travelers. Phone Number: +90 212 293 00 53

Hotel Monopol (3 stars): Hotel Monopol is a budget-friendly hotel located just a short walk from Istiklal Avenue and Taksim Square. The hotel offers clean and comfortable rooms with basic amenities, including free Wi-Fi, air conditioning, and en-suite bathrooms. Guests can enjoy a complimentary breakfast each morning and the convenience of a 24-hour front desk. The hotel's central location makes it easy to explore the vibrant nightlife, shopping, and historical sites of Beyoğlu. Phone Number: +90 212 293 91 10

3. Karaköy

Luxury Hotels

The House Hotel Karaköy (5 stars): The House Hotel Karaköy is a luxurious hotel housed in a historic neoclassical building, offering an exquisite blend of history and modern elegance. The hotel features stylish rooms with high ceilings, marble bathrooms, and bespoke furnishings. Guests can enjoy the rooftop terrace with stunning views of the Golden Horn, a state-of-the-art fitness center, and the in-house restaurant serving gourmet cuisine. The House Hotel Karaköy is perfect for luxury travelers seeking comfort and sophistication in the heart of Istanbul. Phone Number: +90 212 244 34 34

10 Karaköy Istanbul (5 stars): 10 Karaköy Istanbul is a member of the Morgans Hotel Group, located in a historic and meticulously restored neoclassical building. The hotel offers luxurious accommodations with contemporary design, high-end amenities, and personalized service. The property features a rooftop bar with breathtaking views of the city, a fitness center, and an elegant restaurant offering a diverse menu. Its central location makes it an ideal choice for luxury travelers who want to explore Istanbul's vibrant Karaköy neighborhood. Phone Number: +90 212 703 33 33

Boutique Hotels

Karaköy Rooms (4 stars): Karaköy Rooms is a charming boutique hotel offering a blend of modern comforts and historic charm. The hotel features spacious rooms with stylish decor, wooden floors, and large windows providing plenty of natural light. Some rooms offer stunning views of the Bosphorus. Guests can enjoy a delicious breakfast in the cozy dining area and explore the vibrant Karaköy area with its trendy cafés and art galleries. The friendly staff ensures a personalized and comfortable stay. Phone Number: +90 212 252 56 56

Vault Karaköy House Hotel (4 stars): Vault Karaköy House Hotel, located in a former bank building, is a boutique hotel that combines historical elegance with contemporary design. The hotel offers well-appointed rooms with high ceilings, luxurious linens, and modern amenities. Guests can enjoy a range of facilities, including a spa, fitness center, and a rooftop terrace with panoramic views of the Bosphorus. The hotel's restaurant serves gourmet Turkish and international cuisine. Vault Karaköy House Hotel is ideal for travelers seeking a unique and stylish experience. Phone Number: +90 212 244 64 64

Budget-Friendly Hotels

Cheers Porthouse (3 stars): Cheers Porthouse is a budget-friendly hotel located in the lively Karaköy neighborhood. The hotel offers clean and comfortable rooms with basic amenities, including free Wi-Fi and air conditioning. The décor is simple yet tasteful, providing a cozy atmosphere for guests. The hotel's central location makes it easy to explore nearby attractions and enjoy the vibrant nightlife of Karaköy. The friendly staff is always ready to assist with travel tips and recommendations. Phone Number: +90 212 243 26 50

Portus House Istanbul (3 stars): Portus House Istanbul is a budget-friendly hotel offering a comfortable stay in the heart of Karaköy. The hotel features well-maintained rooms with modern amenities, including free Wi-Fi and air conditioning. Guests can enjoy a complimentary breakfast each morning and relax in the communal lounge area. The hotel's central location provides easy access to popular attractions, restaurants, and cafés. The friendly and helpful staff ensures a pleasant and hassle-free stay. Phone Number: +90 212 243 42 43

Karaköy VAV Suites (3 stars): Karaköy VAV Suites is a budget-friendly option that provides comfortable accommodations with a modern touch. The rooms are equipped with essential amenities, including free Wi-Fi, air conditioning, and flat-screen TVs. The hotel is located in a prime area, close to many of Karaköy's trendy cafés, bars, and historical sites. Guests can enjoy a convenient and affordable stay while exploring the vibrant Karaköy district. Phone Number: +90 212 249 52 55

4. Besiktas

Luxury Hotels

Four Seasons Hotel Istanbul at the Bosphorus (5 stars): Housed in a beautifully restored 19th-century Ottoman palace, the Four Seasons Hotel Istanbul at the Bosphorus offers an unparalleled luxury experience. The hotel features elegantly appointed rooms with contemporary decor and Ottoman touches, offering stunning views of the Bosphorus. Guests can enjoy world-class amenities, including a lavish spa, a heated outdoor pool, and exquisite dining options at the in-house restaurants. The hotel's impeccable service ensures a memorable stay for discerning travelers. Phone Number: +90 212 381 40 00

Shangri-La Bosphorus, Istanbul (5 stars): Shangri-La Bosphorus, Istanbul is synonymous with luxury and elegance. Nestled along the European shore of the Bosphorus, this hotel offers spacious rooms with chic decor, floor-to-ceiling windows, and marble bathrooms. The property boasts a luxurious spa, an indoor pool, and multiple dining venues, including Shang Palace, which serves authentic Chinese cuisine. The hotel's prime location and exceptional service make it a top choice for luxury travelers. Phone Number: +90 212 275 88 88

Boutique Hotels

House Hotel Bosphorus (4 stars): The House Hotel Bosphorus is a stylish boutique hotel located in the heart of Ortaköy, a vibrant part of Beşiktaş. The hotel combines historical architecture with modern design, offering rooms that feature elegant furnishings and stunning views of the Bosphorus. Guests can enjoy the hotel's chic rooftop bar and restaurant, which serves a fusion of Turkish and international cuisine. The hotel's intimate atmosphere and personalized service make it a perfect choice for boutique luxury. Phone Number: +90 212 327 77 77

Sumahan on the Water (4 stars): Sumahan on the Water is a unique boutique hotel set in a restored 19th-century distillery on the Bosphorus. Each of its rooms and suites offers a contemporary design with large windows overlooking the water. The hotel features a cozy library, a waterside restaurant serving Turkish and Mediterranean dishes, and a private boat service for exploring the Bosphorus. Its serene location and distinctive charm make it a hidden gem for luxury travelers. Phone Number: +90 216 422 80 00

Budget-Friendly Hotels

Besiktas Otel (3 stars): Besiktas Otel is a budget-friendly hotel offering comfortable accommodations in a convenient location. The rooms are simply decorated but equipped with essential amenities, including free Wi-Fi, air conditioning, and en-suite bathrooms. The hotel provides a complimentary breakfast each morning and has a 24-hour front desk to assist guests with their needs. Its central location in Beşiktaş makes it easy to explore nearby attractions and enjoy the local dining scene. Phone Number: +90 212 260 19 19

Nidya Hotel Galataport (3 stars): Nidya Hotel Galataport offers budget-conscious travelers a comfortable stay with modern amenities. The hotel features clean and well-appointed rooms with flat-screen TVs, free Wi-Fi, and minibars. Guests can enjoy a complimentary breakfast buffet and relax at the rooftop terrace with panoramic views of the Bosphorus. Its location near the Galataport and Dolmabahçe Palace makes it a convenient base for exploring Istanbul. Phone Number: +90 212 243 49 49

Valide Sultan Konagi (3 stars): Valide Sultan Konagi provides budget-friendly accommodations with a touch of Ottoman charm. The rooms are decorated with traditional furnishings and offer modern amenities such as free Wi-Fi, air conditioning, and satellite TV. The hotel features a rooftop terrace with stunning views of the Bosphorus and serves a complimentary Turkish breakfast. Its central location in Beşiktaş allows easy access to major attractions and public transportation. Phone Number: +90 212 528 12 24

5. Kadiköy

Luxury Hotels

Wyndham Grand Istanbul Kalamış Marina Hotel (5 stars): Wyndham Grand Istanbul Kalamış Marina Hotel offers luxurious accommodations with stunning views of the Kalamış Marina and the Sea of Marmara. The hotel features elegant rooms and suites with contemporary design and modern amenities, including free Wi-Fi and flat-screen TVs.Guests can enjoy various facilities such as a rooftop pool, a state-of-the-art fitness center, and a lavish spa. The hotel also boasts several dining options, including fine-dining restaurants and stylish bars. Phone Number: +90 216 400 00 33

DoubleTree by Hilton Hotel Istanbul - Moda (5 stars): DoubleTree by Hilton Hotel Istanbul - Moda is a luxurious hotel located in the trendy Moda district.

It offers spacious, well-appointed rooms with panoramic views of the Bosphorus and the city skyline. The hotel features a rooftop pool, a fitness center, and a spa. Dining options include a rooftop restaurant and bar, serving international and Turkish cuisine. The hotel's prime location makes it convenient for exploring Kadıköy's vibrant nightlife and cultural attractions. Phone Number: +90 216 542 43 44

Boutique Hotels

Juliet Rooms & Kitchen (4 stars): Juliet Rooms & Kitchen is a charming boutique hotel located in the heart of Moda, Kadıköy. It offers a cozy and intimate atmosphere with individually decorated rooms featuring modern amenities such as free Wi-Fi and flat-screen TVs. The hotel has a lovely garden and a trendy café serving delicious breakfast and a variety of international dishes. The warm and welcoming staff ensures a personalized experience for each guest. Phone Number: +90 216 550 04 10

Khalkedon Hotel Istanbul (4 stars): Khalkedon Hotel Istanbul is a stylish boutique hotel situated in the lively Kadıköy district. The hotel offers elegantly decorated rooms with contemporary furnishings and modern amenities like free Wi-Fi and flat-screen TVs. Guests can enjoy a complimentary breakfast on the rooftop terrace, which offers stunning views of the Bosphorus. The hotel's central location makes it easy to explore Kadıköy's bustling markets, cafes, and cultural landmarks. Phone Number: +90 216 414 15 31

Budget-Friendly Hotels

Hush Hostel Lounge (3 stars): Hush Hostel Lounge is a popular budget-friendly option located in the heart of Kadıköy. It offers clean and comfortable dormitory and private rooms with free Wi-Fi. The hostel features a spacious common area, a fully equipped kitchen, and a rooftop terrace with panoramic views of the city. Guests can enjoy a complimentary breakfast and participate in various social events organized by the hostel. The friendly staff provides excellent service and local tips. Phone Number: +90 216 449 12 23

Kadıköy Port Hotel (3 stars): Kadıköy Port Hotel offers budget-friendly accommodations with easy access to Kadıköy's bustling center. The hotel provides clean, simply furnished rooms with modern amenities like free Wi-Fi, air conditioning, and flat-screen TVs. Guests can enjoy a complimentary breakfast buffet each morning.

The hotel's convenient location makes it a great base for exploring the local markets, cafes, and nightlife of Kadıköy. Phone Number: +90 216 349 30 41

MyKent Hotel (3 stars): MyKent Hotel is a budget-friendly hotel situated in the heart of Kadıköy. It offers comfortable rooms with modern amenities, including free Wi-Fi, air conditioning, and flat-screen TVs. Guests can enjoy a complimentary breakfast and relax in the hotel's cozy lounge area. The hotel's prime location allows easy access to Kadıköy's vibrant shops, cafes, and cultural sites. The friendly staff is always ready to assist with any needs or travel arrangements. Phone Number: +90 216 349 14 20

6. Uskudar

Luxury Hotels

Sumahan on the Water (5 stars): Sumahan on the Water is a luxurious boutique hotel set in a renovated 19th-century Ottoman distillery right on the Bosphorus. Each room offers breathtaking views of the water and features modern amenities combined with unique architectural details. Guests can enjoy the serene atmosphere, a private dock, and a well-equipped spa. The hotel's restaurant serves a delightful mix of Turkish and international cuisine with a stunning backdrop of the Bosphorus. Phone Number: +90 216 422 80 00

Bosphorus Palace Hotel (5 stars): Bosphorus Palace Hotel offers a luxurious stay in a restored Ottoman mansion, blending historical charm with modern comfort. Located right on the Bosphorus, this hotel features elegantly decorated rooms with antique furnishings and modern amenities. Guests can dine at the on-site restaurant, which serves gourmet Turkish cuisine, and enjoy the beautiful garden and terrace with stunning views of the Bosphorus. Phone Number: +90 216 422 00 03

Boutique Hotels

My Dora Hotel (3 stars): My Dora Hotel is a stylish boutique hotel offering contemporary comfort and design. Located conveniently near the ferry docks in Üsküdar, the hotel features modern rooms with chic decor and all necessary amenities, including free Wi-Fi, flat-screen TVs, and minibars. Guests can start their day with a rich breakfast buffet and enjoy the hotel's friendly and attentive service. Phone Number: +90 216 418 17 00

The Bosphorus House (4 stars): The Bosphorus House provides a cozy boutique hotel experience with its spacious, apartment-style accommodations. Each suite is tastefully decorated and comes with a fully equipped kitchenette, living area, and modern amenities. The hotel is situated close to the Bosphorus, offering easy access to waterfront attractions and ferry services. Guests appreciate the homely atmosphere and personalized service. Phone Number: +90 216 553 00 24

Budget-Friendly Hotels

Hush Hostel Lounge (2 stars): Hush Hostel Lounge is a budget-friendly option offering a vibrant and social atmosphere. It features a variety of accommodation types, from dormitory beds to private rooms. Guests can enjoy a communal kitchen, a lively bar, and a rooftop terrace with panoramic views of Istanbul. The hostel is located in the heart of Kadıköy, near Üsküdar, making it a convenient base for exploring the area. Phone Number: +90 216 450 00 82

Üsküdar Hotel (3 stars): Üsküdar Hotel offers budget-friendly accommodations with clean and comfortable rooms. Each room is equipped with basic amenities, including free Wi-Fi, air conditioning, and a private bathroom. The hotel's location in the heart of Üsküdar provides easy access to public transportation and nearby attractions. Guests appreciate the friendly staff and the value for money. Phone Number: +90 216 391 13 92

The Marist Hotel Kadıköy (3 stars): The Marist Hotel Kadıköy is a budget-friendly hotel located near Üsküdar, offering simple yet comfortable accommodations. The rooms are equipped with modern amenities, including free Wi-Fi, air conditioning, and flat-screen TVs. Guests can enjoy a complimentary breakfast and appreciate the hotel's proximity to public transportation, making it easy to explore both the Asian and European sides of Istanbul. Phone Number: +90 216 338 11 55

7. Balat

Luxury Hotel

Georges Hotel Galata (5 stars): Georges Hotel Galata offers luxurious accommodations with stunning views over the Golden Horn and the historic city skyline. This boutique hotel features elegantly designed rooms with modern amenities, including marble bathrooms and designer furnishings.

Guests can enjoy gourmet Mediterranean cuisine at the rooftop restaurant, along with panoramic views of Istanbul. The hotel also includes a spa and wellness center for relaxation. Phone Number: +90 212 244 24 23

Boutique Hotels

Kılıç Ali Paşa Hamam Suites (4 stars): Kılıç Ali Paşa Hamam Suites provides boutique-style accommodations in a historic building near the Galata Tower. The suites are elegantly decorated with a blend of Ottoman and contemporary design, offering spacious living areas and luxurious amenities. Guests can relax at the Kılıç Ali Paşa Hamam next door, a traditional Turkish bathhouse, and enjoy personalized service and a sense of heritage. Phone Number: +90 212 393 80 10

The Bank Hotel Istanbul (4 stars): The Bank Hotel Istanbul is a boutique hotel housed in a renovated 19th-century bank building in Karaköy, adjacent to Balat. It features stylish rooms with modern décor and amenities, including free Wi-Fi and flat-screen TVs. The hotel's restaurant offers a fusion of Turkish and international cuisine, and guests can unwind with a cocktail at the rooftop bar overlooking the Golden Horn. Phone Number: +90 212 243 16 85

Budget-Friendly Hotels

Skalion Hotel & Spa (3 stars): Skalion Hotel & Spa offers comfortable and affordable accommodations in Balat. The rooms are well-equipped with modern amenities, including air conditioning, free Wi-Fi, and satellite TV. The hotel features a spa and wellness center where guests can relax with various treatments. It also offers a buffet breakfast and has a convenient location for exploring Balat's historic streets and colorful houses. Phone Number: +90 212 526 72 00

The Pashas House Istanbul (3 stars): The Pashas House Istanbul provides budget-friendly accommodations in a traditional Ottoman-style guesthouse. The rooms are cozy and decorated with Turkish carpets and wooden furnishings, offering a glimpse into Istanbul's cultural heritage. Guests can enjoy a complimentary Turkish breakfast in the courtyard and relax in the serene atmosphere of this historic neighborhood. Phone Number: +90 533 231 82 53

8. Ortaköy

Luxury Hotels

Radisson Blu Bosphorus Hotel, Istanbul (5 stars): Radisson Blu Bosphorus Hotel in Ortaköy offers luxury accommodations with breathtaking views of the Bosphorus. The rooms are elegantly furnished and equipped with modern amenities, including free Wi-Fi and flat-screen TVs. Guests can indulge in gourmet cuisine at the hotel's fine dining restaurant or relax with a cocktail at the stylish bar. The hotel also features a spa, fitness center, and a terrace overlooking the Bosphorus, perfect for unwinding after a day of exploring Istanbul. Phone Number: +90 212 310 15 00

The House Hotel Bosphorus (5 stars): The House Hotel Bosphorus is a luxurious boutique hotel located in a restored 19th-century mansion in Ortaköy. The hotel combines historical charm with contemporary elegance, offering spacious rooms with stunning views of the Bosphorus or the garden. Guests can enjoy Turkish and international cuisine at the hotel's restaurant or relax in the chic lounge bar. The hotel also features a spa, fitness center, and a private pier for guests arriving by boat. Phone Number: +90 212 327 77 77

Boutique Hotels

Ortaköy Aparts (4 stars): Ortaköy Aparts offers boutique-style accommodations with a cozy and intimate atmosphere. Each apartment is tastefully decorated and equipped with modern amenities, including kitchenettes and free Wi-Fi. Guests can enjoy the convenience of having their own space while exploring Ortaköy's vibrant neighborhood. The hotel's central location allows easy access to local attractions, including the iconic Ortaköy Mosque and the lively waterfront. Phone Number: +90 212 227 22 44

Ortaköy Princess Hotel (4 stars): Ortaköy Princess Hotel offers boutique accommodations with panoramic views of the Bosphorus. The rooms are elegantly designed with luxurious furnishings and modern amenities. Guests can unwind at the hotel's rooftop terrace, which features a bar and stunning views of the Bosphorus Bridge. The hotel's location in Ortaköy allows guests to explore the neighborhood's charming streets, trendy cafés, and bustling markets. Phone Number: +90 212 227 40 10

Budget-Friendly Hotels

Villa Denise Hotel (3 stars): Villa Denise Hotel provides budget-friendly accommodations in Ortaköy, just a short walk from the waterfront. The rooms are simple yet comfortable, offering amenities such as free Wi-Fi and air conditioning. Guests can enjoy a complimentary breakfast served in the hotel's cozy dining area. The hotel's friendly staff is available to assist with travel arrangements and recommendations for exploring Ortaköy and beyond. Phone Number: +90 212 227 33 66

Feri Suites (3 stars): Feri Suites offers budget-friendly apartments in Ortaköy, ideal for travelers seeking self-catering accommodations. Each suite features a kitchenette, living area, and private bathroom, providing guests with the comforts of home. The hotel is centrally located near Ortaköy's main attractions, including the mosque and waterfront promenade. It's a great choice for those looking to explore Istanbul on a budget without sacrificing comfort. Phone Number: +90 212 227 44 88

Ortaköy Aysem Sultan Hotel (3 stars): Ortaköy Aysem Sultan Hotel offers affordable accommodations with a convenient location in Ortaköy. The rooms are simply furnished and equipped with essential amenities such as free Wi-Fi and air conditioning. Guests can enjoy a complimentary breakfast each morning in the hotel's dining area. The hotel's friendly staff provides personalized service and can offer recommendations for exploring Ortaköy's sights and dining options. Phone Number: +90 212 227 36 07

9. Bebek

Luxury Hotel

Bebek Hotel by The Stay Collection (5 stars): Bebek Hotel by The Stay Collection offers luxurious accommodations with stunning views of the Bosphorus. The rooms are elegantly designed, featuring modern amenities and stylish décor. Guests can enjoy a relaxing spa, fitness center, and an outdoor pool with panoramic views. The hotel's restaurant serves gourmet Turkish and international cuisine. Its prime location in Bebek allows easy access to upscale boutiques, trendy cafés, and the vibrant waterfront promenade. Phone Number: +90 212 358 63 00

Boutique Hotel

Ajia Hotel (5 stars): Ajia Hotel is a luxurious boutique hotel housed in a historic waterfront mansion. Each room is uniquely decorated with a blend of modern and Ottoman-inspired design, offering breathtaking views of the Bosphorus. Guests can relax in the hotel's spa, enjoy gourmet meals at the restaurant, or unwind in the garden overlooking the sea. Ajia Hotel provides personalized service and a tranquil atmosphere, perfect for discerning travelers seeking a unique experience in Bebek. Phone Number: +90 212 265 66 00

Budget-Friendly Hotel

Bosphorus Houses (3 stars): Bosphorus Houses offers affordable accommodations in Bebek, providing comfortable rooms with basic amenities such as free Wi-Fi and air conditioning. The hotel has a cozy atmosphere and a friendly staff that ensures a pleasant stay. Guests can enjoy a continental breakfast served daily. Bosphorus Houses are ideally located near Bebek Park and the Bosphorus waterfront, making it convenient for exploring the scenic surroundings and local attractions. Phone Number: +90 212 263 84 50

10. Arnavutköy

Luxury Hotels

Radisson Blu Bosphorus Hotel, Istanbul (5 stars): Radisson Blu Bosphorus Hotel in Arnavutköy offers luxurious accommodations with panoramic views of the Bosphorus. The rooms are elegantly decorated with modern amenities, including free Wi-Fi, flat-screen TVs, and marble bathrooms. Guests can relax at the hotel’s spa, which features a sauna, Turkish bath, and fitness center. Dining options include traditional Turkish cuisine at StarBoard Restaurant and cocktails at the Terrace Bar overlooking the water. Phone Number: +90 212 310 15 00

The Grand Tarabya Hotel (5 stars): The Grand Tarabya Hotel is a luxurious retreat in Arnavutköy, boasting spacious rooms with Bosphorus views, marble bathrooms, and elegant furnishings. The hotel features a private marina, a spa offering a range of treatments, and several outdoor pools. Guests can dine at a variety of restaurants serving international and Turkish cuisine, or enjoy drinks at the chic bar with live music in the evenings. Phone Number: +90 212 363 33 00

Boutique Hotels

Sumahan on the Water (5 stars): Sumahan on the Water is a boutique hotel located on the Bosphorus shore in Arnavutköy, housed in a renovated Ottoman-era distillery. The rooms and suites feature contemporary decor with touches of Turkish artistry, offering views of the water and the city. Guests can enjoy a private boat service, a waterfront restaurant serving Turkish and Mediterranean cuisine, and a serene spa with traditional hammam treatments. Phone Number: +90 216 422 80 00

Huseyin Bey Konagi (4 stars): Huseyin Bey Konagi is a charming boutique hotel in Arnavutköy, offering a cozy atmosphere and personalized service. The rooms are individually decorated with antique furnishings and modern amenities, providing a comfortable retreat. Guests can relax in the garden courtyard or enjoy Turkish breakfast in the traditional dining area. The hotel's location allows easy access to nearby attractions and waterfront cafes. Phone Number: +90 212 287 71 50

Budget-Friendly Hotels

Fuat Pasa Yalisi - Special Class (3 stars): Fuat Pasa Yalisi offers budget-friendly accommodations in a historic mansion by the Bosphorus in Arnavutköy. The rooms are simply furnished but comfortable, featuring free Wi-Fi and air conditioning. Guests can enjoy breakfast on the terrace overlooking the water or relax in the garden. The hotel's location provides a peaceful environment away from the city's hustle, with easy access to waterfront dining and local shops. Phone Number: +90 212 287 89 00

Sahil Butik Hotel (3 stars): Sahil Butik Hotel offers affordable accommodations with a charming ambiance near the Bosphorus in Arnavutköy. The rooms are cozy and equipped with modern amenities, including free Wi-Fi and satellite TV. Guests can enjoy a complimentary breakfast in the garden courtyard or explore nearby cafes and restaurants along the waterfront. The hotel's friendly staff ensures a pleasant stay with personalized service. Phone Number: +90 212 287 88 00.

Chapter 8: Cultural Experiences

Art Galleries and Museums in Istanbul

Here are top museums and art galleries in Istanbul, each with detailed descriptions, practical information, and insider tips:

Istanbul Archaeology Museums

The Istanbul Archaeology Museums are a complex of three museums: the Archaeology Museum, the Museum of the Ancient Orient, and the Tiled Kiosk Museum. Established in 1891, this museum complex houses over one million artifacts from various civilizations, including ancient Greek, Roman, Byzantine, and Ottoman eras. The Archaeology Museum features the Alexander Sarcophagus, one of the most significant artifacts, and many other sculptures, mosaics, and reliefs. The Museum of the Ancient Orient showcases items from Mesopotamia, Egypt, and Anatolia, while the Tiled Kiosk Museum, dating back to 1472, exhibits an extensive collection of Turkish ceramics and tiles.

- **Opening Hours:** 9:00 AM - 6:00 PM (Closed on Mondays)
- **Address:** Osman Hamdi Bey Yokusu Sokak, Sultanahmet, 34122 Fatih, Istanbul, Turkey
- **Entrance Fee:** 250 TRY ($9.20)

- **How to Get There:** The museums are located in the Sultanahmet district, a short walk from the Sultanahmet Tram Station (T1 line).

Tips:

- **Plan Your Visit:** Allocate at least 2-3 hours to explore all three museums.
- **Audio Guide:** Consider renting an audio guide to get detailed information about the exhibits.
- **Photography:** Photography is allowed in most areas, but be mindful of the flash restrictions.

Istanbul Modern

Istanbul Modern is Turkey's first museum of modern and contemporary art, established in 2004. The museum is located in a striking waterfront building along the Bosphorus, offering breathtaking views of the city. Istanbul Modern showcases a rich collection of paintings, sculptures, installations, and photography from Turkish and international artists. The museum also hosts temporary exhibitions, film screenings, and educational programs. The architecture of the building itself is worth noting, with its sleek, minimalist design harmonizing with its industrial past.

- **Opening Hours:** 10:00 AM - 6:00 PM (Closed on Mondays)
- **Address:** Meclis-i Mebusan Caddesi, Liman İşletmeleri Sahası No:4, Karaköy, Beyoğlu, Istanbul, Turkey

- **Entrance Fee:** 150 TRY ($5.50)
- **How to Get There:** The museum is easily accessible via the Karaköy Tram Station (T1 line) or by ferry to the Karaköy dock.

Tips:

- **Take a Guided Tour:** Guided tours are available and provide insightful commentary on the artworks.
- **Cafe with a View:** Don't miss the museum's cafe, which offers stunning views of the Bosphorus.
- **Visit the Gift Shop:** The museum shop offers unique art-related souvenirs and books.

Topkapi Palace Museum

Topkapi Palace, once the primary residence of the Ottoman sultans, is now a museum that showcases the grandeur and opulence of the Ottoman Empire. The palace, built in the 15th century, is a sprawling complex of courtyards, pavilions, and gardens. Highlights of the museum include the Imperial Treasury, which displays an astonishing collection of jewels, including the famous Topkapi Dagger and the 86-carat Spoonmaker's Diamond. The Harem, with its intricate tilework and lavishly decorated rooms, offers a glimpse into the private lives of the sultans and their families.

- **Opening Hours:** 9:00 AM - 6:00 PM (Closed on Tuesdays)

- **Address:** Cankurtaran, 34122 Fatih, Istanbul, Turkey
- **Entrance Fee:** 500 TRY ($18.40) for the palace; an additional 200 TRY ($7.40) for the Harem
- **How to Get There:** The palace is situated in the Sultanahmet area, a short walk from the Sultanahmet Tram Station (T1 line).

Tips:

- **Early Visit:** Arrive early to avoid long lines, especially for the Harem section.
- **Dress Appropriately:** As a historical site, modest clothing is recommended.
- **Photography Restrictions:** Photography is not allowed in some sections, particularly in the Treasury.

Sakıp Sabancı Museum

Sakıp Sabancı Museum, housed in a 19th-century mansion in the affluent Emirgan district, offers a unique blend of fine arts, history, and cultural heritage. The museum's permanent collection includes a remarkable array of calligraphic art, religious manuscripts, and paintings from the Ottoman and Turkish Republic eras. The museum also hosts temporary exhibitions featuring works from international artists, covering a wide range of art forms. The beautifully landscaped gardens, with views of the Bosphorus, enhance the museum experience, making it a perfect spot for art lovers and those interested in Turkish culture.

- **Opening Hours:** 10:00 AM - 6:00 PM (Closed on Mondays)
- **Address:** Sakıp Sabancı Caddesi No:42, Emirgan, 34467 Sarıyer, Istanbul, Turkey
- **Entrance Fee:** 120 TRY ($4.40)
- **How to Get There:** The museum is accessible by taking the M2 metro line to İstinye or Hacıosman stations, followed by a short taxi ride.

Tips:

- **Enjoy the Gardens:** Spend some time in the museum's gardens, which offer a peaceful retreat and stunning views of the Bosphorus.
- **Check for Temporary Exhibitions:** The museum frequently hosts temporary exhibitions, so check the schedule before your visit.
- **Cafe Recommendation:** The museum's cafe, located in a serene setting, is ideal for a relaxing break.

Pera Museum

Pera Museum, located in the historic Tepebaşı district, is known for its extensive collection of Orientalist paintings, Ottoman-era artworks, and Anatolian weights and measures. The museum, housed in a beautifully restored 19th-century building, combines traditional and contemporary art in its exhibitions.

One of the highlights is the collection of works by Osman Hamdi Bey, a prominent Ottoman artist and archaeologist. The museum also offers a range of temporary exhibitions, film screenings, and cultural events that appeal to both art enthusiasts and general visitors.

- **Opening Hours:** 10:00 AM - 7:00 PM (Closed on Mondays)
- **Address:** Meşrutiyet Caddesi No:65, Tepebaşı, Beyoğlu, 34430 Istanbul, Turkey
- **Entrance Fee:** 75 TRY ($2.75)
- **How to Get There:** The museum is a short walk from the Şişhane Metro Station (M2 line) or the Tünel funicular.

Tips:

- **Free Admission:** The museum offers free entry on Fridays between 6:00 PM and 10:00 PM.
- **Plan Your Visit:** Allocate time to explore the museum's permanent and temporary exhibitions.
- **Photography:** Photography is allowed in most areas, but check for restrictions on temporary exhibitions.

Chora Museum (Kariye Museum)

The Chora Museum, also known as the Kariye Museum, is a stunning example of Byzantine art and architecture. Originally built as a church in the 4th century, it was later converted into a mosque and then a museum. The Chora Museum is renowned for its breathtaking mosaics and frescoes, which depict scenes from the life of Christ and the Virgin Mary. These works of art, dating back to the 14th century, are considered some of the finest examples of Byzantine Christian art in the world. The museum's intimate size allows visitors to appreciate the intricate details of the artwork up close, making it a must-visit for art lovers and history enthusiasts alike.

- **Opening Hours:** 9:00 AM - 5:00 PM (Closed on Wednesdays)
- **Address:** Kariye Cami Sokak No:26, Edirnekapı, Fatih, 34087 Istanbul, Turkey
- **Entrance Fee:** 200 TRY ($7.40)
- **How to Get There:** The museum is located in the Fatih district, accessible by taking the M1B metro line to Topkapı-Ulubatlı station, followed by a short walk or taxi ride.

Tips:

- **Early Visit:** Arrive early in the day to avoid crowds, as the museum's small size can get crowded during peak hours.
- **Photography:** Photography without flash is allowed, but be respectful of the delicate nature of the mosaics and frescoes.
- **Explore the Surroundings:** The area around the museum is rich in history, with several other historic churches and the ancient city walls nearby.

Rahmi M. Koç Museum

The Rahmi M. Koç Museum, located along the Golden Horn, is Turkey's first museum dedicated to the history of transport, industry, and communications. Housed in a beautifully restored Ottoman-era shipyard and an adjacent historic building, the museum offers a fascinating journey through the history of engineering and industry. The collection includes vintage cars, classic boats, locomotives, aircraft, and even a real submarine that visitors can explore. The museum also features hands-on exhibits, making it an engaging experience for visitors of all ages, particularly families with children.

- **Opening Hours:** 10:00 AM - 6:00 PM (Closed on Mondays)
- **Address:** Hasköy Caddesi No:5, Beyoğlu, 34445 Istanbul, Turkey

- **Entrance Fee:** 200 TRY ($7.40); Submarine tour requires an additional fee
- **How to Get There:** The museum is accessible by taking the T1 tram line to the Sütlüce station or by ferry to the nearby dock.

Tips:

- **Submarine Tour:** Don't miss the chance to tour the real submarine, but be aware that it may require an additional fee and has specific tour times.
- **Interactive Exhibits:** Allocate extra time for the interactive exhibits, which are especially enjoyable for children.
- **Museum Cafe:** The museum has a charming cafe with views of the Golden Horn, perfect for a break during your visit.

Istanbul Museum of Turkish and Islamic Arts

The Istanbul Museum of Turkish and Islamic Arts is housed in the historic Ibrahim Pasha Palace, a grand building dating back to the 16th century. The museum's extensive collection includes carpets, calligraphy, woodwork, ceramics, and metalwork from various periods of Islamic art, ranging from the 7th to the 20th century. The collection of carpets is particularly noteworthy, featuring some of the oldest and most exquisite examples in the world. The museum also provides insights into Islamic cultural and religious practices, making it a rich educational experience.

- **Opening Hours:** 9:00 AM - 7:00 PM (Closed on Mondays)
- **Address:** Sultanahmet Square, Fatih, 34122 Istanbul, Turkey
- **Entrance Fee:** 200 TRY ($7.40)
- **How to Get There:** The museum is located in the heart of Sultanahmet, easily accessible by the Sultanahmet Tram Station (T1 line).

Tips:

- **Carpet Collection:** Spend time exploring the carpet collection, as it's one of the most significant parts of the museum.
- **Historical Context:** Take advantage of the informative displays and descriptions that provide context to the artifacts.
- **Combine Visits:** The museum is close to other major attractions like the Blue Mosque and Hagia Sophia, making it easy to combine visits.

Museum of Innocence

The Museum of Innocence is a unique and deeply personal museum created by the Nobel Prize-winning Turkish author Orhan Pamuk. The museum is based on Pamuk's novel of the same name and presents a fictional story set in 1970s and 1980s Istanbul. The exhibits include everyday objects, photographs, and memorabilia that reflect the novel's themes of love, memory, and loss. Each item is meticulously arranged to create a sense of nostalgia and intimacy, making it a compelling experience for fans of Pamuk's work and those interested in Turkish culture and history.

- **Opening Hours:** 10:00 AM - 6:00 PM (Closed on Mondays)
- **Address:** Çukurcuma Caddesi No:24, Çukurcuma, Beyoğlu, 34425 Istanbul, Turkey
- **Entrance Fee:** 150 TRY ($5.50); Free entry for those who bring a copy of the novel
- **How to Get There:** The museum is located in the Beyoğlu district, a short walk from the Tophane Tram Station (T1 line) or the Istiklal Avenue.

Tips:

- **Read the Novel:** If possible, read "The Museum of Innocence" before visiting, as it enhances the experience.
- **Personal Experience:** The museum offers an intimate and personal experience, so take your time to absorb the details.
- **Quiet Hours:** Visit during quieter hours to fully immerse yourself in the atmosphere of the museum.

Istanbul Military Museum (Askeri Müze)

The Istanbul Military Museum is one of the most important military museums in the world, offering a comprehensive look at Turkey's military history. The museum's extensive collection spans over 1,000 years, from the early Turkish states to the Ottoman Empire and modern Turkey. Exhibits include weapons, armor, uniforms, banners, and dioramas depicting famous battles.

One of the museum's highlights is the Mehter Band, an Ottoman military band that performs traditional music daily, providing a lively and authentic experience of Ottoman military culture.

- **Opening Hours:** 9:00 AM - 5:00 PM (Closed on Mondays and Tuesdays)
- **Address:** Harbiye, Vali Konağı Caddesi, 34367 Şişli, Istanbul, Turkey
- **Entrance Fee:** 100 TRY ($3.70)
- **How to Get There:** The museum is located in the Harbiye district, accessible by taking the M2 metro line to Osmanbey station, followed by a short walk.

Tips:

- **Mehter Band Performance:** Time your visit to catch the Mehter Band performance, typically held at 3:00 PM daily.
- **Plan Your Visit:** The museum is large, so allocate at least a couple of hours to explore it fully.
- **Photography:** Photography is allowed, but be mindful of any restrictions in certain sections.

Istanbul Ceramic Museum

The Istanbul Ceramic Museum, housed in a charming 19th-century mansion in the historic Cihangir district, is dedicated to showcasing Turkey's rich tradition of ceramics and tile art. The museum's collection spans from ancient Anatolian pottery to Ottoman and contemporary ceramic works. Highlights include exquisite Iznik tiles, which feature intricate floral and geometric patterns, as well as Ottoman-era ceramic wares. The museum provides insights into the techniques and cultural significance of Turkish ceramics, offering a visual and educational journey through Turkey's ceramic heritage.

- **Opening Hours:** 10:00 AM - 6:00 PM (Closed on Mondays)
- **Address:** Cihangir Mahallesi, Tomtom Kaptan Sokak No:14, Beyoğlu, 34433 Istanbul, Turkey
- **Entrance Fee:** 100 TRY ($3.70)
- **How to Get There:** The museum is a short walk from the Taksim Metro Station (M2 line) or the Galata Tower area.

Tips:

- **Guided Tours:** Consider joining a guided tour for a deeper understanding of the ceramic techniques and history.
- **Explore Nearby:** Cihangir is a vibrant neighborhood with cafes and shops, making it a pleasant area to explore before or after your visit.
- **Check for Workshops:** The museum occasionally hosts workshops on ceramic art, which can be an engaging addition to your visit.

Istanbul Toy Museum

The Istanbul Toy Museum, located in a historic mansion in the Göztepe district, offers a nostalgic journey through the history of toys. Founded by Turkish poet and writer Sunay Akın, the museum houses a vast collection of toys from the 19th century to the present day. Exhibits include vintage dolls, model trains, and action figures, showcasing the evolution of toys and play. The museum's playful and whimsical atmosphere makes it an excellent destination for families and anyone with an interest in the cultural history of toys.

- **Opening Hours:** 9:30 AM - 6:00 PM (Closed on Mondays)
- **Address:** Ömer Paşa Caddesi No:17, Göztepe, Kadıköy, 34730 Istanbul, Turkey

- **Entrance Fee:** 150 TRY ($5.50)
- **How to Get There:** The museum is accessible by taking the M4 metro line to Kadıköy station, followed by a short bus or taxi ride.

Tips:

- **Family-Friendly:** The museum is ideal for families with children, who will enjoy the interactive exhibits and diverse toy collections.
- **Special Events:** Check the museum's schedule for special events, such as toy-making workshops and themed exhibitions.
- **Gift Shop:** The museum's gift shop offers unique toy-related souvenirs and collectibles.

Istanbul Research Institute Museum

The Istanbul Research Institute Museum, part of the Istanbul University, is dedicated to the study and preservation of Istanbul's cultural and historical heritage. The museum's collection includes artifacts from various periods, including ancient, Byzantine, and Ottoman times. Highlights include archaeological finds, historical documents, and art pieces related to Istanbul's development over the centuries. The museum also serves as a research center, contributing to the scholarly study of Istanbul's rich history.

- **Opening Hours:** 10:00 AM - 5:00 PM (Closed on Sundays)
- **Address:** Beyazıt, 34130 Fatih, Istanbul, Turkey
- **Entrance Fee:** Free
- **How to Get There:** The museum is located near Istanbul University in the Beyazıt district, accessible by taking the T1 tram line to Beyazıt-Kapalıçarşı station.

Tips:

- **Educational Value:** Ideal for those interested in academic research and historical study, as the museum provides in-depth information on Istanbul's past.
- **Library Access:** Inquire about access to the museum's library, which contains valuable research materials.
- **Visit During Weekdays:** The museum can be less crowded during weekdays, providing a more peaceful experience.

Istanbul Naval Museum

The Istanbul Naval Museum, located in the Beşiktaş district, offers a comprehensive look at Turkey's naval history. The museum's collection includes historic naval ships, maritime artifacts, and models of famous ships. Highlights include the ceremonial boat of the Ottoman sultans and various naval uniforms and equipment from different eras. The museum provides insight into Turkey's naval heritage and the role of the sea in shaping its history.

- **Opening Hours: 9**:00 AM - 5:00 PM (Closed on Mondays)
- **Address:** Beşiktaş, Muallim Naci Caddesi, No:45, 34353 Istanbul, Turkey
- **Entrance Fee:** 100 TRY ($3.70)
- **How to Get There:** The museum is easily accessible by taking the M2 metro line to Levent station, followed by a short taxi or bus ride.

Tips:

- **Naval Enthusiasts:** Perfect for those interested in maritime history and naval technology.
- **Guided Tours:** Consider a guided tour to gain deeper insights into the exhibits and their historical significance.
- **Explore Beşiktaş:** The Beşiktaş district has a lively atmosphere with many cafes and shops, making it a pleasant area to explore before or after your visit.

Cultural Events and Festivals

Istanbul is a city rich in cultural diversity, reflected in its vibrant calendar of events and festivals throughout the year. Here are cultural events and festivals that showcase Istanbul's heritage, arts, and traditions:

Istanbul International Film Festival

The Istanbul International Film Festival is one of the oldest and most prestigious film festivals in Turkey, showcasing a diverse range of international and Turkish films. Held annually since 1982, the festival takes place in various venues across the city, including historic theaters like Atlas and Beyoğlu. It features screenings, panel discussions, and awards ceremonies, attracting filmmakers, actors, and cinephiles from around the world.

Date: April-May

Istanbul Biennial

The Istanbul Biennial is a contemporary art exhibition held every two years since 1987, organized by the Istanbul Foundation for Culture and Arts. It showcases works by Turkish and international artists, exploring current themes and issues through various mediums such as installations, performances, and multimedia. The biennial takes place at multiple venues, including historic buildings, museums, and public spaces, creating a dialogue between art, culture, and the city's urban fabric.

Date: Biennial years (typically September-November)

Istanbul Music Festival

Organized by the Istanbul Foundation for Culture and Arts since 1973, the Istanbul Music Festival is a celebration of classical music featuring renowned orchestras, soloists, and ensembles from around the world. The festival showcases performances in historic venues such as Hagia Irene and Süreyya Opera House, presenting a diverse program that includes symphonies, chamber music, and operatic productions.

Date: June

Istanbul Jazz Festival

The Istanbul Jazz Festival, launched in 1994, is one of the largest jazz festivals in the region, attracting jazz enthusiasts and musicians from across the globe. Held in various venues throughout the city, including open-air stages, concert halls, and jazz clubs, the festival features performances ranging from traditional jazz to avant-garde and fusion. Alongside concerts, it includes workshops, jam sessions, and street performances, contributing to Istanbul's reputation as a thriving hub for jazz music.

Date: July

Istanbul Tulip Festival

The Istanbul Tulip Festival, held annually since 2005, celebrates the arrival of spring with the blooming of millions of tulips across the city's parks, gardens, and historic sites. Organized by the Istanbul Metropolitan Municipality, the festival showcases colorful displays of tulips in various hues, creating picturesque scenes against the backdrop of Istanbul's landmarks like Emirgan Park and Gulhane Park. Visitors can enjoy cultural events, tulip-themed exhibitions, and photography contests during this vibrant festival.

Date: April

Istanbul International Puppet Festival

The Istanbul International Puppet Festival is a biennial event that celebrates the art of puppetry from around the world. Established in 1994, the festival features performances by puppeteers and theater companies showcasing traditional and contemporary puppetry techniques. Venues such as Istanbul City Theaters and cultural centers host puppet shows, workshops, and exhibitions, offering a magical experience for audiences of all ages.

Date: Biennial years (typically May-June)

Istanbul Coffee Festival

The Istanbul Coffee Festival, held annually since 2014, celebrates Turkey's rich coffee culture and heritage. Taking place at venues like KüçükÇiftlik Park, the festival brings together coffee enthusiasts, baristas, and coffee roasters from Turkey and beyond. Visitors can participate in coffee tastings, and workshops on brewing techniques, and learn about the history and traditions of Turkish coffee. The festival also features live music performances, art exhibitions, and gourmet food stalls, making it a sensory delight for coffee lovers.

Date: September-October

Istanbul International Arts and Culture Festival

The Istanbul International Arts and Culture Festival, known as Istanbuliyye, is a month-long celebration of diverse cultural expressions from around the world. Organized by the Istanbul Metropolitan Municipality, the festival features performances, exhibitions, and workshops showcasing music, dance, theater, and visual arts. Venues such as Atatürk Cultural Center and outdoor stages host international artists and cultural groups, fostering cultural exchange and appreciation among local and international audiences.

Date: July-August

Istanbul International Literature Festival

The Istanbul International Literature Festival, established in 2009, celebrates literature in all its forms through readings, panel discussions, and literary events. Held at venues like Istanbul University and cultural centers, the festival invites writers, poets, and literary figures from Turkey and abroad to explore themes of literature, language, and storytelling. Audiences can engage with authors, attend book signings, and participate in literary workshops, creating a dynamic platform for literary dialogue and exchange.

Date: November

Istanbul Design Biennial

The Istanbul Design Biennial, organized by the Istanbul Foundation for Culture and Arts, showcases innovative design concepts and projects that address social, environmental, and technological challenges.

Held biennially since 2012, the biennial explores themes such as urbanism, sustainability, and digital innovation through exhibitions, installations, and workshops. Venues like Galata Greek Primary School and Istanbul Museum of Modern Art host the biennial, attracting designers, architects, and creatives from around the world.

Date: Biennial years (typically September-November)

Traditional Turkish Tea Ceremony

Turkish tea, or "çay," is a staple of Turkish culture and daily life. Served in tulip-shaped glasses, it is known for its deep red color and robust flavor. Here's a comprehensive look at traditional Turkish tea in Istanbul:

Preparation and Serving

Turkish tea is prepared using a double-stacked teapot called a "çaydanlık." The lower pot contains boiling water, while the upper pot holds a concentrated tea brew. To serve, a small amount of the concentrated tea is poured into a glass, followed by hot water to dilute it to the desired strength. It is usually served strong, but each person can adjust the concentration by adding more hot water.

Tea Types: The most common type of tea used is Rize tea, grown in the Black Sea region of Turkey.

Serving: It is traditionally served in small, tulip-shaped glasses to showcase its color and to keep it hot. Sugar is added to taste, but milk is rarely used.

Etiquette: In Turkey, offering tea is a sign of hospitality. It is common to drink several small glasses of tea throughout the day, especially during social gatherings and business meetings.

Best Places to Enjoy Turkish Tea in Istanbul

Pierre Loti Café: Located on a hill overlooking the Golden Horn, Pierre Loti Café offers stunning views and a relaxing atmosphere. It's a popular spot for both locals and tourists to enjoy a glass of tea while taking in the panoramic vistas of Istanbul.

- **Location:** Eyüp Sultan
- **Phone Number:** +90 212 497 13 13

Çorlulu Ali Pasha Medresesi: This historical tea house, nestled in the bustling Grand Bazaar area, offers an authentic experience with its traditional setting and décor. Visitors can enjoy tea in a serene courtyard surrounded by ancient stone walls.

- **Location:** Beyazıt
- **Phone Number:** +90 212 518 12 34

Mısır Çarşısı (Spice Bazaar): The Spice Bazaar is a great place to experience traditional Turkish tea. Many shops offer free samples of various tea blends, allowing visitors to taste and purchase their favorites.

- **Location:** Eminönü
- **Phone Number:** +90 212 513 65 97

Traditional Turkish Coffee (Türk Kahvesi)

Turkish coffee, known for its strong flavor and unique preparation method, is an integral part of Turkish culture and heritage. Here is a detailed exploration of traditional Turkish coffee in Istanbul:

Preparation and Serving

Turkish coffee is made from finely ground coffee beans that are simmered, not boiled, in a special pot called a "cezve." The process is as follows:

Ingredients: Finely ground coffee, water, and sugar (optional).

Preparation: Coffee and cold water are added to the cezve. Sugar can be added to taste. The mixture is then heated slowly over a low flame. Just before it begins to boil, it is removed from the heat to let the grounds settle. This process can be repeated two or three times to create a thick froth.

Serving: The coffee is served in small cups, with the grounds allowed to settle at the bottom. It is accompanied by a glass of water and sometimes a piece of Turkish delight.

Best Places to Enjoy Turkish Coffee in Istanbul

Mandabatmaz: Renowned for its thick and rich coffee, Mandabatmaz is a small café that has earned legendary status among coffee enthusiasts.

The name "Mandabatmaz" means "so thick that even a buffalo wouldn't sink in it," reflecting the coffee's dense texture.

- **Location:** Beyoğlu
- **Phone Number:** +90 212 243 76 60

Fazıl Bey's Turkish Coffee: Established in 1923, Fazıl Bey's Turkish Coffee in Kadıköy is one of the oldest coffee shops in Istanbul. It offers a traditional ambiance and expertly prepared coffee, making it a favorite among locals.

- **Location:** Kadıköy
- **Phone Number:** +90 216 336 03 32

Sade Kahve: Located in the picturesque neighborhood of Arnavutköy, Sade Kahve offers a tranquil setting with Bosphorus views. It's an excellent spot to enjoy a cup of Turkish coffee while watching the boats pass by.

- **Location:** Arnavutköy
- **Phone Number:** +90 212 265 48 85

Cultural Significance

Both Turkish tea and coffee play vital roles in Turkish culture and social interactions. Tea is often consumed throughout the day, whether at home, work, or in tea houses. It is an essential part of Turkish hospitality, and it's common to be offered tea when visiting someone's home or shop.

Turkish coffee, on the other hand, has a more ceremonial aspect. It's often associated with special occasions, such as engagements and social gatherings. The phrase "a cup of coffee commits one to forty years of friendship" (bir fincan kahvenin kırk yıl hatırı vardır) underscores its importance in forging long-lasting relationships.

Tips for Enjoyment

Traditional Preparation: Embrace the traditional methods of brewing and serving Turkish tea and coffee for an authentic experience.

Accompaniments: Enjoy Turkish tea with a slice of lemon or a cube of sugar, while Turkish coffee pairs well with a small sweet treat like Turkish delight.

Social Experience: Engage with locals at tea gardens or coffeehouses to experience these beverages in their cultural context.

Music and Performing Arts

Traditional Turkish Music and Dance

Traditional Turkish music and dance are rich cultural expressions that have been cultivated over centuries, reflecting the diverse influences and history of Turkey. These forms of art are deeply embedded in Turkish culture and offer insight into the nation's heritage and social customs.

Traditional Turkish Music

a. Classical Turkish Music (Türk Sanat Müziği)

Classical Turkish Music, also known as Türk Sanat Müziği, is an important genre that developed in the Ottoman courts and has roots that go back to the 9th century. It is characterized by intricate melodic patterns and modal systems called makams. Each makam provides a framework for improvisation and composition, often evoking specific emotions or times of the day.

Instruments: Key instruments include the oud (a lute-like instrument), kanun (a type of zither), ney (an end-blown flute), tanbur (a long-necked lute), and kemençe (a small, bowed string instrument).

Composers and Performers: Prominent composers include Dede Efendi and Sultan Selim III. Renowned contemporary performers are Münir Nurettin Selçuk and Zeki Müren.

Structure: Classical pieces often start with a peşrev (instrumental prelude) and are followed by a series of vocal and instrumental compositions. Improvisational sections, known as Taksim, are integral to performances.

b. Folk Music (Türk Halk Müziği)

Folk music, or Türk Halk Müziği, is deeply rooted in the rural traditions and daily lives of Turkish people. It varies significantly across different regions of Turkey, reflecting local cultures and histories.

Instruments: Common instruments include the bağlama (a stringed instrument), zurna (a double-reed woodwind), davul (a large drum), kaval (a shepherd's flute), and saz (a stringed musical instrument).

Regional Styles:

Aegean and Mediterranean: Known for vibrant rhythms and melodies, often performed during celebrations.

Black Sea: Features rapid, lively tunes and is heavily influenced by the kemençe.

Central Anatolia: Characterized by melancholic melodies played on the bağlama.

Southeast Anatolia: Influenced by Kurdish and Arabic music, featuring the darbuka (goblet drum) and zurna.

c. Sufi Music (Tasavvuf Müziği)

Sufi music, or Tasavvuf Müziği, is a form of devotional music associated with the mystical Islamic tradition of Sufism. It is intended to facilitate spiritual contemplation and connection with the divine.

Instruments: The ney is prominently featured, alongside the rebab (a bowed string instrument) and the bendir (a frame drum).

Mevlevi Sema: One of the most famous Sufi practices is the Whirling Dervishes of the Mevlevi order, where music and dance combine to induce a state of spiritual ecstasy. The ceremony includes a sequence of musical pieces, hymns, and dances, culminating in the whirling dance.

Structure: Sufi music typically includes ilahi (hymns) and nefes (poems) sung to the accompaniment of instruments, often structured to mirror spiritual progression.

Traditional Turkish Dance

a. Halay

Halay is a popular folk dance performed in many regions of Turkey, particularly in Central and Eastern Anatolia. It is a group dance that involves holding hands or shoulders and moving in a circular or semi-circular formation.

Music and Instruments: The dance is accompanied by lively music played on the davul and zurna. The rhythm is crucial, often accelerating as the dance progresses.

Dance Structure: Dancers follow a leader, executing steps that include hops, kicks, and shuffles. The movements can be vigorous and energetic, reflecting the communal spirit of the dance.

b. Zeybek

Zeybek is a traditional dance from the Aegean region, often associated with bravery and heroism. It is performed solo or in pairs, characterized by slow, deliberate movements that mimic the actions of eagles.

Music and Instruments: The dance is accompanied by the bağlama, zurna, and sometimes the clarinet. The music has a distinct, dramatic tempo.

Dance Structure: Dancers perform with bent knees and open arms, making grand, sweeping gestures. The movements are symbolic and reflect the tales of the heroic Zeybeks.

c. Kılıç-Kalkan (Sword and Shield Dance)

Kılıç-Kalkan is a traditional dance that originates from Bursa and commemorates the bravery of Ottoman warriors. It is performed with real swords and shields, adding an element of danger and excitement.

Music and Instruments: The dance is performed without musical instruments; instead, the rhythm is created by the clashing of swords and shields.

Dance Structure: Dancers engage in choreographed combat, showcasing agility and skill. The movements are precise and synchronized, reflecting military discipline.

d. Çiftetelli

Çiftetelli is a lively dance performed at weddings and celebrations, commonly in the Marmara and Aegean regions. It is known for its energetic and flirtatious movements.

Music and Instruments: The dance is accompanied by fast-paced music played on the clarinet, drum, and other traditional instruments.

Dance Structure: Dancers often perform in pairs or groups, incorporating quick steps, spins, and shoulder shimmies. It is a joyful and expressive dance, emphasizing rhythm and coordination.

Influence on Modern Turkish Music and Dance

While traditional music and dance are deeply rooted in history, they continue to influence contemporary Turkish culture. Modern Turkish music often incorporates traditional instruments and melodies, blending them with genres like pop, rock, and jazz. Similarly, contemporary dance performances may include elements of folk dances, creating a fusion that resonates with younger audiences.

Experiencing Traditional Turkish Music and Dance

Visitors to Turkey can experience traditional music and dance in various settings:

Cultural Festivals: Festivals like the International Istanbul Music Festival and the Aspendos International Opera and Ballet Festival feature performances of traditional music and dance.

Live Performances: Many restaurants and venues in Istanbul and other cities offer live performances, such as the Hodjapasha Cultural Center and the Galata Mevlevi Museum.

Weddings and Celebrations: Traditional dances are an integral part of Turkish weddings and local celebrations, providing an authentic glimpse into the culture.

Contemporary Performances

Istanbul is a vibrant city that boasts a rich cultural heritage and a thriving contemporary arts scene. The city's contemporary performances encompass a wide range of artistic expressions, including theater, dance, music, and multimedia art. Here's a detailed look at the contemporary performances you can experience in Istanbul:

Theater

1. İstanbul Modern Theatre

İstanbul Modern Theatre is known for its avant-garde productions and innovative performances. The theater showcases a mix of contemporary Turkish plays and international works, often incorporating multimedia elements and experimental techniques. The venue attracts a diverse audience, from local theater enthusiasts to international visitors, and is a hub for new and emerging talent in Istanbul's theater scene.

- **Notable Productions:** "A Doll's House" by Henrik Ibsen, "The Cherry Orchard" by Anton Chekhov, and original works by Turkish playwrights.
- **Location:** Meclis-i Mebusan Cd. No:4, Karaköy, Istanbul

2. Dot Theatre

Dot Theatre is a leading contemporary theater in Istanbul, renowned for its bold and provocative productions. The theater focuses on modern and experimental works, often addressing social and political issues. Dot Theatre is known for its intimate settings and immersive experiences, where the audience becomes part of the performance.

- **Notable Productions:** "Shopping and F***ing" by Mark Ravenhill, "4:48 Psychosis" by Sarah Kane, and various original contemporary Turkish plays.
- **Location:** Harbiye Mh. Halaskargazi Cd. No:40, Şişli, Istanbul

Dance

3. Istanbul State Opera and Ballet

The Istanbul State Opera and Ballet is a premier institution for classical and contemporary ballet performances. While it primarily focuses on traditional ballet, the company also stages contemporary dance pieces that push the boundaries of the art form. The performances often feature international choreographers and guest dancers, bringing a global perspective to Istanbul's dance scene.

- **Notable Productions:** "Giselle," "Swan Lake," and contemporary pieces by choreographers such as William Forsythe and Jiří Kylián.
- **Location:** Atatürk Kültür Merkezi, Taksim, Istanbul

4. Zorlu Performing Arts Center

Zorlu Performing Arts Center is a state-of-the-art venue that hosts a wide array of contemporary dance performances. The center collaborates with international dance companies and choreographers, offering a platform for cutting-edge and innovative dance works. The diverse program includes contemporary ballet, modern dance, and interdisciplinary performances that combine dance with other art forms.

Notable Performances: Performances by companies such as Nederlands Dans Theater, Alvin Ailey American Dance Theater, and Akram Khan Company.

Location: Levazım, Koru Sokağı No:2, Beşiktaş, Istanbul

Music

5. Istanbul Jazz Festival

The Istanbul Jazz Festival is an annual event that brings together a mix of international and Turkish jazz musicians. The festival features a variety of contemporary jazz styles, from traditional and modern jazz to fusion and experimental genres. Concerts are held in various venues across the city, offering both intimate club settings and grand concert halls.

- **Notable Artists:** Past performers include Herbie Hancock, Diana Krall, Kamasi Washington, and Turkish jazz legends like Kerem Görsev and Fahir Atakoğlu.
- **Location:** Various venues across Istanbul

6. Babylon

Babylon is one of Istanbul's most iconic live music venues, known for its eclectic and contemporary music programming. The venue hosts a wide range of performances, including indie rock, electronic music, world music, and jazz. Babylon is a favorite spot for both local and international artists, providing an intimate setting with excellent acoustics.

- **Notable Performances:** Artists such as Bonobo, Alt-J, and Sevdaliza, and local acts like Gaye Su Akyol and Islandman.
- **Location:** Şehbender Sk. No:3, Asmalımescit, Beyoğlu, Istanbul

Multimedia and Experimental Art

7. SALT

SALT is an innovative cultural institution that explores contemporary art, architecture, design, and social issues through exhibitions, screenings, and performances. The institution frequently hosts multimedia performances that blend visual art, sound, and digital media, creating immersive and thought-provoking experiences.

- **Notable Events:** Multimedia installations, performance art pieces, and interdisciplinary projects by artists like Kutluğ Ataman and Ali Kazma.

- **Location:** SALT Beyoğlu, İstiklal Cd. No:136, Beyoğlu, Istanbul; SALT Galata, Bankalar Cd. No:11, Karaköy, Istanbul

8. Borusan Contemporary

Borusan Contemporary is a unique space dedicated to contemporary art and new media. Located in Perili Köşk, a historic mansion, the institution offers a dynamic program of exhibitions and performances that explore the intersections of art and technology. Borusan Contemporary regularly hosts experimental performances that incorporate digital art, interactive installations, and sound art.

- **Notable Events:** Performances by artists like Rafael Lozano-Hemmer, Candas Sisman, and various international new media artists.
- **Location:** Baltalimanı Hisar Cd. No:5, Rumeli Hisarı, Istanbul

Festivals

9. Istanbul Theatre Festival

The Istanbul Theatre Festival is a biennial event that celebrates contemporary theater and performance art. The festival features a diverse program of international and Turkish productions, ranging from experimental theater and multimedia performances to dance and site-specific works. It provides a platform for innovative and cutting-edge performances, attracting artists and audiences from around the world.

- **Notable Productions:** Works by renowned theater companies such as The Wooster Group, Forced Entertainment, and prominent Turkish theater groups.
- **Location:** Various venues across Istanbul

10. IKSV International Performance Series

Organized by the Istanbul Foundation for Culture and Arts (IKSV), the International Performance Series brings global contemporary performance artists to Istanbul. The series includes a variety of genres, from contemporary dance and theater to experimental music and multimedia performances. The events are held in different cultural venues across the city, showcasing the latest trends in contemporary performing arts.

Notable Performances: Artists such as Pina Bausch Tanztheater, Anne Teresa De Keersmaeker, and Robert Lepage.

Location: Various venues across Istanbul

Theater and Opera

Istanbul is a vibrant cultural hub that boasts a rich tradition in theater and opera. The city offers a variety of venues, from grand opera houses to intimate theaters, each contributing to Istanbul's dynamic performing arts scene. Here is a comprehensive look at the major theaters and opera houses in Istanbul:

Major Theaters and Opera Houses in Istanbul

1. Süreyya Opera House

Süreyya Opera House, located in the Kadıköy district on the Asian side of Istanbul, is a stunning example of early 20th-century architecture. Originally built in 1927 by Süreyya İlmen Pasha, it was designed to be an opera house and concert hall but initially served as a movie theater due to financial constraints. After extensive renovations, it was reopened in 2007 as a dedicated opera house. The interior is adorned with beautiful frescoes and crystal chandeliers, reflecting a blend of European styles.

Highlights:

- Hosts performances by the Istanbul State Opera and Ballet.
- Regularly features opera, ballet, and classical music concerts.
- Known for its excellent acoustics and elegant decor.

Location: Kadıköy, Istanbul

Best Time to Visit: Year-round, with a peak season during the winter months when the opera and ballet seasons are in full swing.

Opening Hours: Typically, open for performances in the evenings. Box office hours may vary.

Contact: +90 216 346 15 31

2. Atatürk Cultural Center (AKM)

Located in Taksim Square, the Atatürk Cultural Center (AKM) is one of Istanbul's most iconic cultural venues. The building, originally opened in 1969, underwent extensive renovations and was reopened in 2021. AKM is a multifunctional arts complex that houses a large opera house, a theater, a concert hall, and exhibition spaces. The modern architecture and state-of-the-art facilities make it a centerpiece of Istanbul's cultural life.

Highlights:

- Home to the Istanbul State Opera and Ballet.
- Hosts a wide range of performances, including opera, ballet, theater, and concerts.
- Features modern amenities and cutting-edge stage technology.

Location: Taksim, Istanbul

Best Time to Visit: Year-round, with numerous events scheduled throughout the year.

Opening Hours: Open for performances, with box office hours typically in the afternoon and early evening.

Contact: +90 212 245 10 00

3. Zorlu Performing Arts Center (Zorlu PSM)

Zorlu PSM is a contemporary performing arts center located in the Zorlu Center, one of Istanbul's most luxurious shopping and entertainment complexes. Opened in 2013, Zorlu PSM quickly became a leading venue for high-profile performances. The center boasts multiple theaters, including a large concert hall and a drama stage, equipped with advanced acoustic and visual technologies.

Highlights:

- Hosts international and local productions, including musicals, operas, concerts, and plays.
- Known for staging Broadway and West End productions.
- Features world-class facilities and a vibrant cultural program.

Location: Beşiktaş, Istanbul

Best Time to Visit: Year-round, with a particularly busy schedule during the winter and spring seasons.

Opening Hours: Open for performances, with box office hours typically from late morning to evening.

Contact: +90 212 912 28 28

4. Harbiye Cemil Topuzlu Open-Air Theatre

Harbiye Cemil Topuzlu Open-Air Theatre is one of Istanbul's most beloved outdoor venues. Located in Harbiye, the theater is named after Cemil Topuzlu, a prominent Turkish politician and surgeon. It is renowned for its picturesque setting and excellent acoustics, making it a favorite spot for concerts and theatrical performances during the warmer months.

Highlights:

- Hosts a variety of performances, including concerts, theater, and dance.
- Popular venue for summer events and festivals.
- Known for its beautiful natural surroundings and relaxed atmosphere.

Location: Harbiye, Istanbul

Best Time to Visit: Late spring to early autumn, during the outdoor performance season.

Opening Hours: Performances typically in the evening.

Contact: +90 212 343 77 00

5. Kenter Theater

Founded by the renowned Turkish actors Yıldız and Müşfik Kenter, the Kenter Theater is an intimate venue located in the Şişli district. The theater has been a significant part of Istanbul's cultural scene since its opening in 1968. It is known for its high-quality productions, ranging from classic plays to contemporary works.

Highlights:

- Hosts a variety of theatrical performances, including plays, monologues, and experimental theater.

- Known for its excellent acting and innovative productions.
- Features a cozy and intimate atmosphere, allowing for a close connection between the audience and performers.

Location: Şişli, Istanbul

Best Time to Visit: Year-round, with a diverse program throughout the seasons.

Opening Hours: Performances typically in the evening.

Contact: +90 212 246 35 89

6. Kadıköy Haldun Taner Stage

Kadıköy Haldun Taner Stage is a well-known theater located in the bustling Kadıköy district on the Asian side of Istanbul. Named after the famous Turkish playwright Haldun Taner, the venue is part of the Istanbul Metropolitan Municipality City Theatre. It offers a wide range of theatrical performances and is a key cultural hub in Kadıköy.

Highlights:

- Hosts various theatrical productions, including classical and contemporary plays.
- Known for its commitment to promoting Turkish theater and local artists.
- Features a modern auditorium with comfortable seating and good acoustics.

Location: Kadıköy, Istanbul

Best Time to Visit: Year-round, with a particularly active schedule during the theater season from fall to spring.

Opening Hours: Performances typically in the evening.

Contact: +90 216 348 89 21

7. Moda Sahnesi

Moda Sahnesi is a contemporary theater and cultural venue located in the Moda neighborhood of Kadıköy. Opened in 2013, it has quickly become a popular spot for innovative and experimental performances. The theater is known for its diverse program, which includes plays, dance performances, concerts, and film screenings.

Highlights:

- Hosts a variety of performances, with a focus on contemporary and experimental works.
- Features a modern and flexible performance space.
- Known for its vibrant cultural atmosphere and commitment to artistic innovation.

Location: Kadıköy, Istanbul

Best Time to Visit: Year-round, with a particularly dynamic schedule during the theater season from fall to spring.

Opening Hours: Performances typically in the evening.

Contact: +90 216 330 58 00

Other Notable Venues

8. Bakırköy Municipal Theatres

Bakırköy Municipal Theatres is one of Istanbul's important cultural institutions, offering a range of theatrical performances in various venues throughout the Bakırköy district. It is dedicated to promoting Turkish theater and providing a platform for local artists.

Highlights:

- Hosts a wide variety of theatrical productions, including classic and contemporary plays.
- Known for its support of Turkish playwrights and actors.
- Features multiple performance spaces with modern amenities.

Location: Bakırköy, Istanbul

Best Time to Visit: Year-round, with a full schedule during the theater season from fall to spring.

Opening Hours: Performances typically in the evening.

Contact: +90 212 571 17 17

9. DasDas

DasDas is a contemporary arts and performance venue located in the Ataşehir district. Known for its cutting-edge productions and innovative approach to the performing arts, DasDas offers a diverse program that includes theater, concerts, and workshops.

Highlights:

- Hosts a variety of contemporary and experimental performances.
- Features a modern, flexible performance space.
- Known for its vibrant cultural atmosphere and commitment to artistic innovation.

Location: Ataşehir, Istanbul

Best Time to Visit: Year-round, with a particularly dynamic schedule during the theater season from fall to spring.

Opening Hours: Performances typically in the evening.

Contact: +90 216 504 22 00

10. State Theatres, Istanbul Branch

The State Theatre, Istanbul Branch, is part of Turkey's national theater network, offering high-quality productions of classic and contemporary plays. With several venues across the city, it is dedicated to bringing theater to a wide audience and promoting Turkish cultural heritage.

Highlights:

- Hosts a wide variety of theatrical productions, including classic and contemporary plays.
- Known for its high production standards and professional performances.
- Features multiple performance spaces with modern amenities.

Architectural and Historical Walking Tours

1. Sultanahmet Old City Walking Tour

This tour covers the heart of Istanbul's historical Sultanahmet district, where you can explore some of the city's most iconic landmarks.

You'll start at the majestic Hagia Sophia, an architectural marvel that has served as a church, mosque, and now a museum. The tour continues with a visit to the Blue Mosque, known for its stunning blue tiles and grand dome. You'll also explore the ancient Hippodrome, which was the center of Byzantine public life, and the Basilica Cistern, an underground water reservoir with a mysterious ambiance.

- **Meeting Point:** Sultanahmet Square, Istanbul
- **Highlights:** Hagia Sophia, Blue Mosque, Hippodrome, Basilica Cistern
- **Tour Provider:** Istanbul Walks
- **Duration:** 3 hours
- **Contact:** +90 212 518 18 68

2. Byzantine Heritage Walking Tour

This tour takes you back to the time when Istanbul was known as Byzantium and later Constantinople. You'll visit the Chora Church, famous for its exquisite Byzantine mosaics and frescoes. The tour also includes a walk along the ancient Theodosian Walls, which protected the city for centuries. You'll finish with a visit to the Hagia Sophia, where the guide will delve deep into its history as the largest cathedral of its time.

- **Meeting Point:** Chora Church, Edirnekapı, Istanbul
- **Highlights:** Chora Church, Theodosian Walls, Hagia Sophia, Byzantine architecture
- **Tour Provider:** Byzantine Istanbul Tours
- **Duration:** 4 hours
- **Contact:** +90 212 527 77 12

3. Ottoman Empire Architecture Tour

Discover the grandeur of the Ottoman Empire through its architecture on this walking tour. Starting at the Topkapi Palace, the primary residence of Ottoman sultans, you'll explore its courtyards, chambers, and the Harem section. The tour also takes you to the Süleymaniye Mosque, a masterpiece designed by the famous architect Mimar Sinan. You'll also visit the Rustem Pasha Mosque, known for its intricate Iznik tiles. The guide provides detailed explanations of the architectural styles and historical significance of these landmarks.

- **Meeting Point:** Topkapi Palace, Cankurtaran, Istanbul

- **Highlights:** Topkapi Palace, Süleymaniye Mosque, Rustem Pasha Mosque, Ottoman architecture
- **Tour Provider:** Ottoman Istanbul Tours
- **Duration:** 3.5 hours
- **Contact:** +90 212 512 04 80

4. Galata and Pera: Istanbul's Bohemian Past

This tour explores the historical Galata district and the once cosmopolitan neighborhood of Pera, now known as Beyoğlu. You'll start at the Galata Tower, offering panoramic views of the city. The tour continues along Istiklal Avenue, where you'll see a mix of Art Nouveau buildings and old embassies. The guide provides insights into the area's transformation from a Genoese colony to a vibrant district known for its cultural diversity.

- **Meeting Point:** Galata Tower, Bereketzade, Istanbul
- **Highlights:** Galata Tower, Istiklal Avenue, Pera, Art Nouveau architecture
- **Tour Provider:** Pera Heritage Tours
- **Duration:** 3 hours
- **Contact:** +90 212 243 20 70

5. Hidden Istanbul Walking Tour

For those interested in exploring lesser-known historical sites, this tour takes you off the beaten path. You'll visit the Zeyrek Mosque, formerly the Church of the Pantocrator, one of the best-preserved examples of Byzantine architecture. The tour also includes a visit to the Valens Aqueduct, a Roman-era water system still standing today. The guide will take you through the Fener and Balat neighborhoods, known for their colorful Ottoman-era houses and churches, offering a unique glimpse into the city's diverse history.

- **Meeting Point:** Zeyrek Mosque, Fatih, Istanbul
- **Highlights:** Zeyrek Mosque, Valens Aqueduct, Fener and Balat neighborhoods, hidden gems
- **Tour Provider:** Hidden Istanbul Tours
- **Duration:** 4 hours
- **Contact:** +90 212 444 32 00

6. Bosphorus Waterfront Palaces Walking Tour

This tour takes you along the Bosphorus Strait, where you can explore the opulent palaces and mansions that line its shores, showcasing the splendor of the Ottoman Empire. The tour begins at Dolmabahçe Palace, the largest palace in Turkey, known for its European-style architecture and lavish interiors. You'll also visit the Beylerbeyi Palace on the Asian side, a summer residence for the sultans, and the waterfront mansions, or "yalıs," that demonstrate the elite lifestyle of Ottoman nobility. As you walk along the Bosphorus, the guide shares stories of the city's maritime history and the significance of these palaces.

- **Meeting Point:** Dolmabahçe Palace, Beşiktaş, Istanbul
- **Highlights:** Dolmabahçe Palace, Beylerbeyi Palace, Bosphorus yalıs, Ottoman luxury
- **Tour Provider:** Bosphorus Heritage Tours
- **Duration:** 4 hours
- **Contact:** +90 212 236 90 00

7. Istanbul's Jewish Heritage Walking Tour

This tour offers a unique perspective on Istanbul's Jewish history, which dates back to the Byzantine period. The journey starts in the Karaköy neighborhood, where you will visit the Ashkenazi Synagogue, one of the few remaining active synagogues in Istanbul. The tour then moves to the Galata district, home to the Neve Shalom Synagogue and the Jewish Museum of Turkey. You will also explore Balat, a historic neighborhood that once housed a significant Jewish population, with its old synagogues and Jewish homes. The guide provides in-depth information about the Jewish community's contributions to the city's culture and history.

- **Meeting Point:** Karaköy, Istanbul
- **Highlights:** Ashkenazi Synagogue, Neve Shalom Synagogue, Jewish Museum of Turkey, Balat neighborhood
- **Tour Provider:** Jewish Heritage Istanbul
- **Duration:** 3.5 hours
- **Contact:** +90 212 243 69 98

8. Ottoman Sultans and the Grand Bazaar Tour

This tour combines a visit to the historical residences of Ottoman sultans with a shopping experience in the Grand Bazaar. You'll begin at the Topkapi Palace, the center of the Ottoman Empire for over 400 years, exploring its courtyards, gardens, and the Imperial Harem. The tour then leads you to the Grand Bazaar, one of the world's oldest and largest covered markets, where you can wander through its maze of shops selling everything from jewelry to spices. The guide shares the history of the bazaar and offers tips on bargaining and finding authentic goods.

- **Meeting Point:** Topkapi Palace, Cankurtaran, Istanbul
- **Highlights:** Topkapi Palace, Grand Bazaar, Ottoman sultans, traditional shopping
- **Tour Provider:** Sultan Tours Istanbul
- **Duration:** 4 hours
- **Contact:** +90 212 512 04 80

9. Byzantine and Ottoman Relics Walking Tour

This tour provides a comprehensive overview of Istanbul's history by exploring relics from both the Byzantine and Ottoman periods. You'll start at the Hippodrome, once the sporting and social center of Constantinople, followed by a visit to the Blue Mosque, an Ottoman-era masterpiece. The tour includes a visit to the Hagia Sophia, a symbol of the city's Byzantine heritage, and concludes at the Topkapi Palace, where you can explore the museum's extensive collection of relics. Throughout the tour, the guide explains the historical significance of each site and the transition from Byzantine to Ottoman rule.

- **Meeting Point:** Hippodrome, Sultanahmet Square, Istanbul
- **Highlights:** Hippodrome, Blue Mosque, Hagia Sophia, Topkapi Palace, Byzantine and Ottoman history
- **Tour Provider:** Relics of Istanbul
- **Duration:** 5 hours
- **Contact:** +90 212 527 90 00

These tours offer a deep dive into Istanbul's rich architectural heritage, providing a unique opportunity to experience the city's historical layers through its buildings and streets.

Chapter 9: Cuisine and Dining Choices

Overview of Local Cuisine

Turkish cuisine is a vibrant tapestry of flavors, textures, and aromas that reflect the country's diverse cultural heritage and geographical landscape. It has been influenced by a myriad of cultures and empires, from the ancient Greeks and Romans to the Byzantines and Ottomans. This fusion of influences has created a culinary tradition that is both unique and deeply rooted in history.

Historical Influences

Turkish cuisine has evolved over thousands of years, incorporating elements from various civilizations that have left their mark on the region. The Ottoman Empire, in particular, played a significant role in shaping Turkish culinary traditions. The vast empire, which stretched from Eastern Europe to North Africa and the Middle East, brought together a multitude of culinary practices and ingredients, enriching Turkish cuisine with a wide variety of flavors.

Key Ingredients

The foundation of Turkish cuisine is built on fresh, high-quality ingredients. Commonly used ingredients include:

Olive Oil: Used extensively in cooking, particularly in mezes (appetizers) and vegetable dishes.

Tomatoes, Peppers, and Eggplants: Staples in many Turkish dishes, from stews to salads.

Lamb and Beef: Primary sources of meat, often used in kebabs and stews.

Yogurt: A key component in many dishes, used as a sauce, marinade, or side dish.

Spices and Herbs: Such as cumin, sumac, mint, oregano, and paprika, which add depth and complexity to dishes.

Regional Variations

Turkey's diverse geography contributes to regional variations in its cuisine. Each region has its own specialties and unique culinary traditions:

Aegean Region: Known for its use of olive oil, fresh vegetables, and seafood. Dishes like zeytinyağlı (olive oil dishes) and ege mezeleri (Aegean mezes) are popular.

Central Anatolia: Famous for hearty dishes like mantı (Turkish dumplings), etli ekmek (a type of flatbread with meat), and keşkek (a traditional dish made with wheat and meat).

Eastern Anatolia: Known for its robust and spicy cuisine, with dishes like kebabs, çiğ köfte (raw meatballs), and büryan (a type of roast lamb).

Southeastern Anatolia: Features rich and flavorful dishes, heavily influenced by Middle Eastern cuisine. Specialties include kebabs, baklava, and mezes like hummus and baba ghanoush.

Iconic Dishes

Turkish cuisine boasts an array of iconic dishes that have gained international acclaim. Some of the most notable include:

Kebabs: A variety of skewered and grilled meats, such as şiş kebab (marinated meat on skewers) and döner kebab (rotating roast meat).

Mezes: Small, flavorful dishes served as appetizers or snacks, including hummus, baba ghanoush, dolma (stuffed grape leaves), and muhammara (spicy red pepper and walnut dip).

Pide and Lahmacun: Turkish flatbreads topped with various ingredients. Pide is often referred to as Turkish pizza, while lahmacun is a thin, crispy flatbread topped with minced meat, vegetables, and herbs.

Pilav: Turkish rice dishes, often cooked with meat, vegetables, or dried fruits.

Börek: Savory pastries made with thin layers of dough, filled with ingredients like cheese, spinach, or minced meat.

Baklava: A rich, sweet pastry made of layers of filo dough filled with chopped nuts and sweetened with syrup or honey.

Beverages

Turkish cuisine also includes a variety of traditional beverages that complement the food:

Turkish Tea (Çay): A staple in Turkish culture, often served in small, tulip-shaped glasses.

Turkish Coffee: A strong, unfiltered coffee served in small cups, known for its distinctive preparation and rich flavor.

Ayran: A refreshing yogurt-based drink, often served with meals.

Rakı: An anise-flavored spirit, commonly enjoyed with mezes.

Dining Culture

Dining in Turkey is often a communal experience, emphasizing hospitality and generosity. Meals are typically shared, and it's common to see large gatherings of family and friends enjoying a wide array of dishes together. Turkish hospitality is renowned, and guests are often treated with great respect and generosity.

Must-Try Traditional Turkish Dishes

1. Kebabs

Kebabs are a staple of Turkish cuisine, encompassing a wide variety of grilled meat dishes. Some of the most popular types include Adana Kebab, made from spicy minced lamb, and Shish Kebab, consisting of marinated meat chunks skewered and grilled. Doner Kebab, often made from lamb, beef, or chicken, is another favorite, where the meat is cooked on a vertical rotisserie and shaved off for serving. Kebabs are typically served with rice, grilled vegetables, and various sauces, reflecting the rich flavors of Turkish culinary traditions.

2. Meze

Meze refers to a selection of small dishes served as appetizers or with drinks, often enjoyed in social settings. A typical meze spread might include dishes like hummus (chickpea dip), baba ghanoush (smoky eggplant dip), and dolma (grape leaves stuffed with rice, pine nuts, and currants). Other popular meze items include haydari (thick yogurt dip with herbs), ezme (spicy tomato and pepper salad), and cacık (yogurt with cucumbers and garlic). Meze showcases the diverse and vibrant flavors of Turkish cuisine, emphasizing fresh ingredients and bold seasonings.

3. Pide

Pide, often referred to as Turkish pizza, is a popular dish made with a flatbread base topped with various ingredients and baked until crispy. Common toppings include minced meat, cheese, eggs, and vegetables. One of the most popular varieties is the "Kıymalı Pide," which is topped with seasoned minced meat. Pide is typically served in boat-shaped pieces, making it easy to share. It's a beloved comfort food in Turkey, enjoyed by locals and visitors alike.

4. Lahmacun

Lahmacun, sometimes called Turkish flatbread, is a thin, crispy dough topped with a mixture of minced meat, vegetables, and herbs, then baked to perfection. It is often garnished with fresh parsley, lemon juice, and sometimes a sprinkle of sumac. Lahmacun is typically rolled up and eaten as a wrap, making it a convenient and delicious street food. It offers a delightful combination of savory, tangy, and slightly spicy flavors.

5. Manti

Manti is Turkish dumplings filled with spiced ground meat, typically lamb or beef, and served with a garlic yogurt sauce and a drizzle of melted butter infused with paprika or red pepper flakes. They are often topped with a sprinkling of dried mint or sumac. Manti are beloved for their delicate texture and rich, savory filling, offering a satisfying and comforting meal. The combination of creamy yogurt and spicy butter sauce enhances the dish's complexity and flavor.

6. Köfte

Köfte are Turkish meatballs made from ground meat (usually beef or lamb) mixed with onions, parsley, breadcrumbs, and various spices. They can be grilled, fried, or baked, and are often served with rice or bulgur, grilled vegetables, and a side of yogurt or tomato sauce. Variations of köfte include "İzmir Köfte," cooked in a tomato sauce with potatoes and green peppers, and "Çiğ Köfte," a raw version made with bulgur and finely ground meat, seasoned with spices and herbs.

7. Börek

Börek is a savory pastry made with thin layers of dough (yufka) filled with various ingredients such as cheese, spinach, minced meat, or potatoes. It can be baked or fried and is enjoyed as a snack, breakfast item, or appetizer. One popular version is "Su Böreği," which has a rich, buttery flavor and is often filled with cheese and parsley. Börek's flaky texture and delicious fillings make it a favorite in Turkish households and bakeries.

8. Dolma and Sarma

Dolma and sarma refer to stuffed vegetables and wrapped vine leaves, respectively. Dolma typically involves bell peppers, zucchinis, or eggplants filled with a mixture of rice, pine nuts, currants, and spices. Sarma involves grape leaves wrapped around a similar filling. Both versions are often served with a side of yogurt and are enjoyed either warm or cold. These dishes highlight the use of fresh ingredients and aromatic spices in Turkish cuisine, offering a delightful and healthy option.

9. Balık Ekmek

Balık Ekmek, or fish sandwich, is a popular street food in Istanbul, especially near the waterfront areas like the Galata Bridge. It consists of freshly grilled fish (usually mackerel) served inside a piece of Turkish bread, often accompanied by lettuce, onions, and a squeeze of lemon. The simplicity and freshness of the ingredients make this sandwich a beloved fast-food option, providing a taste of the sea with every bite.

10. Baklava

Baklava is a rich, sweet pastry made of layers of thin filo dough filled with chopped nuts, such as walnuts, pistachios, or almonds, and sweetened with syrup or honey. The layers are meticulously arranged and baked to golden perfection, then soaked in a sugary syrup that gives the dessert its signature sweetness and sticky texture. Baklava is a staple in Turkish cuisine, enjoyed during special occasions and festivals, and appreciated for its flaky texture and delectable filling.

Street Food and Snacks

1. Simit

Simit, often referred to as the Turkish bagel, is a popular street food found throughout Istanbul. This circular bread, encrusted with sesame seeds, is crispy on the outside and soft on the inside. Simit is typically enjoyed plain, but it can also be served with cheese, olives, or a spread of jam for added flavor. Vendors sell simit from red pushcarts on almost every corner, especially in busy areas like Taksim Square and near ferry terminals. Its simple yet delicious taste makes it a perfect snack for any time of the day.

2. Balık Ekmek

Balık ekmek, or fish sandwich, is a must-try street food for visitors to Istanbul, especially along waterfront areas like Eminönü. Freshly grilled fish, usually mackerel, is placed in a crusty bread roll and garnished with lettuce, onions, and a squeeze of lemon. The sandwich is typically prepared on boats anchored by the shore, adding to the unique dining experience. The combination of the smoky flavor of the grilled fish and the freshness of the vegetables makes it a delightful snack, capturing the essence of Istanbul's maritime culture.

3. Kokoreç

Kokoreç is a unique and flavorful street food that may not be for the faint-hearted. It consists of lamb intestines and sweetbreads seasoned with oregano, chili, and other spices, then wrapped around a skewer and grilled over charcoal. The cooked meat is finely chopped and typically served in a bread roll with tomatoes and green peppers.

Kokoreç is particularly popular late at night and can be found at various street vendors and small eateries across Istanbul, such as in the lively district of Beyoğlu.

4. Kumpir

Kumpir is a versatile and indulgent street food, perfect for those who love loaded baked potatoes. Originating from the Ortaköy neighborhood, kumpir starts with a large baked potato that is mashed and mixed with butter and cheese. It is then topped with a wide array of ingredients such as olives, sausages, pickles, corn, Russian salad, and more. The customization options are endless, making it a favorite snack for both locals and tourists. You can find kumpir stands throughout Istanbul, especially in busy districts like Ortaköy and Kadıköy.

5. Midye Dolma

Midye dolma, or stuffed mussels, is a beloved street snack in Istanbul, particularly enjoyed with a cold drink. These mussels are filled with a mixture of spiced rice, pine nuts, and currants, then steamed until tender. Vendors typically serve them fresh, often from trays carried on their heads or from small stalls. Midye dolma is eaten by squeezing a bit of lemon juice over the mussel and enjoying it in one bite. Popular spots to find this delicacy include the areas around the Galata Bridge and Istiklal Avenue.

6. Lahmacun

Lahmacun, sometimes called Turkish pizza, is a thin, crispy flatbread topped with a mixture of minced meat, tomatoes, onions, and spices. It's cooked quickly in a hot oven and often rolled up with fresh herbs, lettuce, and a squeeze of lemon juice before being eaten. Lahmacun is a quick and satisfying snack that can be found at street vendors, bakeries, and small restaurants throughout Istanbul. It's particularly popular in areas with high foot traffic, such as the bustling markets and shopping streets.

7. Dürüm

Dürüm is a delicious wrap made with lavash or yufka flatbread filled with various types of kebabs, such as chicken (tavuk), lamb (kuzu), or beef (dana). The meat is typically grilled on a skewer, then wrapped with fresh vegetables, herbs, and sometimes yogurt or a spicy sauce. Dürüm is a convenient and tasty street food that you can find at numerous kebab stands and street vendors across Istanbul. It's especially popular in areas like Taksim and Kadıköy, where it serves as a quick meal for people on the go.

8. Börek

Börek is a savory pastry that comes in many forms, made with layers of thin dough (yufka) filled with various ingredients such as cheese, spinach, potatoes, or minced meat. These pastries are baked to a golden perfection, resulting in a crispy and flaky texture. Börek can be found in bakeries and street stalls throughout Istanbul, often enjoyed as a breakfast item or a quick snack. Variants include su böreği (water börek), sigara böreği (cigar-shaped fried rolls), and kol böreği (spiral-shaped pastry).

9. Çiğ Köfte

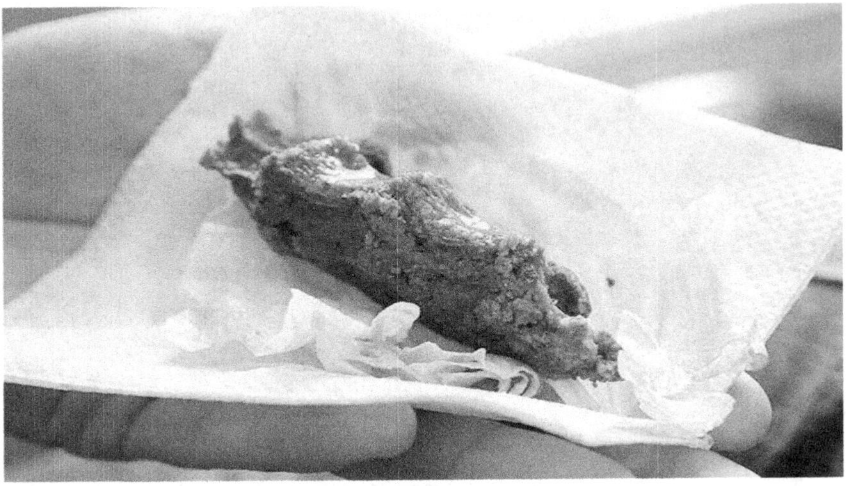

Çiğ köfte, which translates to "raw meatballs," is traditionally made with raw minced meat, bulgur, and a blend of spices. However, the street food version is typically meat-free, made with a mixture of bulgur, tomato paste, spices, and pomegranate molasses. The mixture is kneaded until soft and served in a lettuce wrap or flatbread, often accompanied by fresh herbs and a squeeze of lemon. Çiğ köfte vendors are common in Istanbul, especially in areas with a lot of pedestrian traffic.

10. Döner

Döner kebab is a quintessential Turkish street food that has gained popularity worldwide. In Istanbul, you'll find it at numerous street vendors and small eateries. The döner is made from seasoned meat (usually lamb, beef, or chicken) that is stacked in a cone shape and slowly roasted on a vertical rotisserie. The meat is thinly sliced and served in a bread roll, pita, or flatbread, often with vegetables, pickles, and a variety of sauces. Döner is a flavorful and filling snack, perfect for a quick bite.

Traditional Turkish Breakfast Spots

Van Kahvaltı Evi

Van Kahvaltı Evi is a beloved breakfast spot in Istanbul, famous for its traditional Van-style breakfast. This extensive spread includes a variety of cheeses, olives, honey, fresh bread, eggs, and a selection of regional specialties like "murtuğa" (scrambled eggs with flour and butter) and "sucuklu yumurta" (eggs with Turkish sausage). The atmosphere is cozy and welcoming, making it a perfect place to start your day with a hearty and authentic Turkish breakfast.

- **Location:** Defterdar Yokuşu No:52/A, Cihangir, Beyoğlu
- **Opening Hours:** 7:00 AM - 5:00 PM (Mon-Sun)
- **Phone Number:** +90 212 293 64 37

Namlı Gurme

Namlı Gurme is a gourmet delicatessen and restaurant located in Karaköy. Known for its lavish breakfast platters, Namlı Gurme offers a wide array of Turkish breakfast items including a variety of cheeses, cured meats, olives, jams, and freshly baked bread. You can also enjoy hot dishes like "menemen" (scrambled eggs with tomatoes and peppers) and "sucuk" (Turkish sausage). The vibrant and bustling atmosphere adds to the charm of this popular breakfast spot.

- **Location:** Rıhtım Cd. No:1/1, Karaköy, Beyoğlu
- **Opening Hours:** 8:00 AM - 10:00 PM (Mon-Sun)
- **Phone Number:** +90 212 293 68 80

Kale Café

Kale Café, located in the charming neighborhood of Rumelihisarı, offers stunning views of the Bosphorus along with its delightful breakfast. The breakfast menu includes a variety of cheeses, olives, fresh tomatoes and cucumbers, honey, jams, eggs, and traditional Turkish tea. The café's picturesque setting and delicious food make it a favorite among locals and tourists alike.

- **Location:** Yahya Kemal Cd. No:18, Rumelihisarı, Sarıyer
- **Opening Hours:** 7:00 AM - 10:00 PM (Mon-Sun)
- **Phone Number:** +90 212 263 19 01

Çakmak Kahvaltı Salonu

Çakmak Kahvaltı Salonu in Beşiktaş is a must-visit for breakfast enthusiasts. This local favorite serves a traditional Turkish breakfast with an array of cheeses, olives, honey, kaymak (clotted cream), fresh bread, and more. Their "menemen" are particularly popular. The casual and lively atmosphere makes it a great spot to experience an authentic Turkish breakfast.

- **Location:** Şehit Asım Cd. No:19, Beşiktaş
- **Opening Hours:** 6:00 AM - 5:00 PM (Mon-Sun)
- **Phone Number:** +90 212 261 19 76

Sütis Emirgan

Sütis Emirgan offers a picturesque breakfast experience by the Bosphorus. Their traditional Turkish breakfast spread includes a variety of fresh cheeses, olives, eggs, honey, and a selection of pastries. Guests can enjoy their meal in a beautiful garden setting, making it a relaxing and enjoyable breakfast spot. The café is known for its high-quality ingredients and attentive service.

- **Location:** Sakıp Sabancı Cd. No:14, Emirgan, Sarıyer
- **Opening Hours:** 7:00 AM - 12:00 AM (Mon-Sun)
- **Phone Number:** +90 212 323 50 30

Lokma

Located in Arnavutköy, Lokma offers an extensive breakfast menu with stunning views of the Bosphorus. Their breakfast includes a variety of Turkish cheeses, olives, fresh vegetables, eggs, and homemade jams. The ambiance is cozy and elegant, making it an ideal spot for a leisurely breakfast. Lokma is particularly known for its friendly staff and delicious "simit" (Turkish sesame bagel).

- **Location:** Arnavutköy Bebek Cd. No:15, Beşiktaş
- **Opening Hours:** 8:00 AM - 12:00 AM (Mon-Sun)
- **Phone Number:** +90 212 287 61 83

Van Kahvaltı Sofrası

Van Kahvaltı Sofrası in Beşiktaş is another excellent spot for a traditional Van-style breakfast. The menu features a wide selection of cheeses, honey, clotted cream, olives, fresh bread, and regional specialties like "kavut" (a type of roasted flour dish) and "mıhlama" (a cheesy cornmeal dish). The café's warm and inviting atmosphere makes it a perfect place to enjoy a traditional Turkish breakfast.

- **Location:** Süleyman Seba Cd. No:46/A, Beşiktaş
- **Opening Hours:** 7:00 AM - 6:00 PM (Mon-Sun)

- **Phone Number:** +90 212 258 51 95

Lades Menemen

Lades Menemen in Beyoğlu is renowned for its delicious "menemen," a classic Turkish breakfast dish made with eggs, tomatoes, peppers, and spices. In addition to menemen, the breakfast menu includes a variety of cheeses, olives, bread, and fresh vegetables. The casual and unpretentious setting makes it a great spot to enjoy a hearty and traditional Turkish breakfast.

- **Location:** Sadri Alışık Sk. No:11, Beyoğlu
- **Opening Hours:** 6:00 AM - 5:00 PM (Mon-Sun)
- **Phone Number:** +90 212 249 19 23

Privato Cafe

Privato Cafe in Galata offers a charming and rustic setting for a traditional Turkish breakfast. The menu features a variety of cheeses, olives, eggs, honey, and homemade jams, all served with freshly baked bread. The café's cozy and artistic ambiance, along with its delicious food, makes it a popular spot for breakfast. The outdoor seating area is particularly lovely, offering views of the historic Galata Tower.

- **Location:** Tımarcı Sk. No:3, Galata, Beyoğlu
- **Opening Hours:** 8:00 AM - 11:00 PM (Mon-Sun)
- **Phone Number:** +90 212 293 99 81

Cafe Privato

Cafe Privato, located in the picturesque neighborhood of Cihangir, is known for its extensive and delicious Turkish breakfast. The breakfast menu includes a variety of cheeses, olives, fresh tomatoes and cucumbers, eggs, honey, and homemade jams. The café's warm and cozy interior, along with its friendly service, makes it a great spot to enjoy a leisurely breakfast. The outdoor seating area offers beautiful views of the Bosphorus, adding to the charm of this popular breakfast spot.

- **Location:** Tımarcı Sk. No:3, Galata, Beyoğlu
- **Opening Hours:** 8:00 AM - 11:00 PM (Mon-Sun)
- **Phone Number:** +90 212 293 99 81

Fine Dining Restaurants and Modern Turkish Cuisine

1. Mikla

Mikla is a renowned restaurant located atop the Marmara Pera Hotel in Istanbul, offering breathtaking views of the city and the Bosphorus. Celebrated for its innovative approach to modern Turkish cuisine, Mikla blends traditional flavors with contemporary techniques, using locally sourced ingredients. The ambiance is chic and sophisticated, making it a perfect spot for a special occasion or a romantic dinner. The menu, crafted by Chef Mehmet Gürs, features a variety of seasonal dishes, and the extensive wine list highlights both local and international selections. Reservations are highly recommended due to its popularity.

- **Location:** The Marmara Pera, Meşrutiyet Cd. No:15, Beyoğlu
- Opening Hours: 6:00 PM - 12:00 AM (Mon-Sat)
- **Phone Number:** +90 212 293 56 56

Neolokal

Neolokal is a celebrated restaurant located in Istanbul's historic Karaköy district, known for its innovative approach to Turkish cuisine. Founded by Chef Maksut Aşkar, Neolokal focuses on farm-to-table dining, utilizing locally sourced ingredients to create contemporary dishes inspired by traditional recipes. The restaurant features a minimalist design with an open kitchen, allowing guests to witness the culinary process. Signature dishes highlight seasonal produce and regional flavors, offering a unique gastronomic experience. The ambiance is warm and inviting, making it a perfect spot for food enthusiasts seeking authentic yet modern Turkish cuisine.

- **Location:** Bankalar Cd. No:11, Karaköy, Beyoğlu
- **Opening Hours:** 12:00 PM - 2:30 PM, 6:00 PM - 11:00 PM (Tue-Sat)
- **Phone Number:** +90 212 244 00 16

Nicole

Located in the heart of Istanbul, Nicole Restaurant is renowned for its modern take on traditional Turkish cuisine. Nestled in a chic setting with panoramic views of the city, Nicole offers a unique dining experience that combines innovative culinary techniques with local flavors. The menu features a variety of dishes made from fresh, seasonal ingredients, often presented in artistic plating that reflects the restaurant's commitment to both taste and aesthetics. The ambiance is elegant yet inviting, making it perfect for special occasions or a romantic dinner. The knowledgeable staff provides exceptional service, guiding guests through the thoughtfully curated wine list that complements the meal beautifully. Nicole also hosts a seasonal tasting menu, allowing diners to explore a range of flavors in one sitting. Whether you're a local or a traveler, a visit to Nicole promises a memorable culinary journey in Istanbul.

- **Location:** Tomtom Suites, Boğazkesen Cd. No:18, Beyoğlu
- **Opening Hours:** 6:30 PM - 10:30 PM (Tue-Sat)
- **Phone Number:** +90 212 292 44 67

Spago

Spago, located in the luxurious St. Regis Hotel, offers a unique dining experience that blends Wolfgang Puck's innovative culinary vision with the rich flavors of Turkish cuisine. The restaurant boasts a stylish and contemporary atmosphere, featuring elegant decor and stunning views of the Bosphorus. Guests can indulge in a diverse menu that includes handmade pasta, fresh seafood, and artisanal pizzas, all crafted from locally sourced ingredients. With an extensive wine list and exceptional service, Spago provides an unforgettable setting for special occasions or intimate dinners, making it a top destination in Istanbul's vibrant culinary landscape.

- **Location:** St. Regis Istanbul, Mim Kemal Öke Cd. No:35, Nişantaşı
- **Opening Hours:** 12:00 PM - 11:00 PM (Mon-Sun)
- **Phone Number:** +90 212 368 08 08

Vogue

Vogue Restaurant offers a sophisticated dining experience with breathtaking views of the Bosphorus, making it a favorite among locals and tourists alike. The menu features a blend of Asian and Mediterranean cuisines, emphasizing fresh seafood, sushi, and inventive cocktails.

The elegant decor, combined with a vibrant atmosphere, creates the perfect setting for special occasions or romantic dinners. Vogue also boasts an extensive wine list, curated to complement its diverse offerings. With its stunning terrace and impeccable service, Vogue is a must-visit culinary destination in Istanbul.

Address: Akaretler, Süleyman Seba Caddesi No: 12, Beşiktaş

Opening Hours: Daily 12:00 PM - 12:00 AM

Phone: +90 212 227 4400

Sunset Grill & Bar

Sunset Grill & Bar is a renowned fine dining establishment offering a diverse menu that includes Turkish, Mediterranean, and Japanese cuisine. Situated on a hilltop in Ulus, the restaurant provides stunning views of the Bosphorus and Istanbul's skyline. The sushi bar is particularly popular, and the extensive wine list features selections from around the world. The elegant ambiance and impeccable service make Sunset Grill & Bar a top choice for fine dining in Istanbul.

- **Location:** Adnan Saygun Cd. Yol Sk. No:2, Ulus
- **Opening Hours:** 12:00 PM - 3:00 PM, 6:00 PM - 12:00 AM (Mon-Sun)
- **Phone Number:** +90 212 287 03 57

16 Roof

16 Roof, located in the Swissôtel The Bosphorus, offers an exquisite dining experience with breathtaking views of the Bosphorus. The restaurant's menu features a blend of international and Turkish dishes, with a focus on fresh and locally sourced ingredients. Signature dishes include grilled seafood, premium steaks, and a variety of creative appetizers. The chic and modern decor, combined with the stunning outdoor terrace, makes 16 Roof a perfect spot for a memorable dinner.

- **Location**: Swissôtel The Bosphorus, Visnezade Mh., Acisu Sok. No:19, Maçka
- **Opening Hours:** 6:00 PM - 2:00 AM (Mon-Sun)
- **Phone Number:** +90 212 326 11 00

Aqua

Aqua, located in the Four Seasons Hotel Istanbul at the Bosphorus, offers a luxurious dining experience with a focus on Italian and Turkish cuisine. The menu features a variety of fresh seafood, homemade pastas, and premium meats. Guests can dine indoors or on the stunning terrace overlooking the Bosphorus.

Aqua is known for its elegant ambiance, impeccable service, and exquisite dishes, making it a top choice for fine dining in Istanbul.

- **Location:** Four Seasons Hotel Istanbul at the Bosphorus, Çırağan Cd. No:28, Beşiktaş
- **Opening Hours:** 7:00 AM - 11:00 PM (Mon-Sun)
- **Phone Number:** +90 212 381 41 60

Ulus 29

Ulus 29 is a prestigious fine-dining restaurant that offers a unique blend of traditional Turkish and international cuisine. The menu includes dishes like lamb kebabs, sushi, and gourmet pizzas. The restaurant boasts a stylish and contemporary interior, with a large terrace offering panoramic views of the Bosphorus. Ulus 29 is also known for its extensive wine list and vibrant nightlife, making it a popular destination for both dining and entertainment.

- **Location:** Ahmet Adnan Saygun Cd. Ulus Parkı İçi, Ulus
- **Opening Hours:** 6:00 PM - 2:00 AM (Mon-Sun)
- **Phone Number:** +90 212 358 29 29

Zuma

Zuma, located in the chic Ortaköy neighborhood, offers a modern take on traditional Japanese izakaya dining. The menu features a variety of sushi, sashimi, and robata-grilled dishes, all prepared with the highest quality ingredients. The stylish and contemporary interior, combined with a stunning terrace overlooking the Bosphorus, creates a sophisticated dining atmosphere. Zuma is renowned for its exceptional food, service, and ambiance, making it a top choice for fine dining in Istanbul.

- **Location:** Salhane Sk. No:7, Ortaköy, Beşiktaş
- **Opening Hours:** 12:00 PM - 1:00 AM (Mon-Sun)
- **Phone Number:** +90 212 236 22 96

Oligark

Oligark offers a luxurious dining experience with a focus on modern Turkish and Mediterranean cuisine. The restaurant's menu features a variety of seafood, grilled meats, and creative appetizers, all made with fresh and locally sourced ingredients.

Oligark's stylish and contemporary interior, combined with a large outdoor terrace offering stunning views of the Bosphorus, makes it a perfect spot for a special dinner. The vibrant nightlife and live music add to the overall experience, making Oligark a popular destination for both dining and entertainment.

- **Location:** Muallim Naci Cd. No:65, Kuruçeşme, Beşiktaş
- **Opening Hours:** 12:00 PM - 2:00 AM (Mon-Sun)
- **Phone Number:** +90 212 265 00 77

Local Eateries and Casual Dining Spots

Dürümzade

Dürümzade is a casual eatery in the heart of Beyoğlu, renowned for its mouthwatering dürüms (wraps). The simple yet flavorful menu features a variety of grilled meats wrapped in freshly baked lavash bread, served with a side of tangy sumac onions and fresh herbs. The unpretentious setting and the quick service make it an ideal spot for a casual meal. It gained international fame after being featured on Anthony Bourdain's travel show, making it a must-visit for anyone looking to experience authentic Turkish street food.

- **Location:** Kamer Hatun Caddesi No:26/A, Beyoğlu

- **Opening Hours:** 11:00 AM - 4:00 AM (Mon-Sun)
- **Phone Number:** +90 212 249 01 47

Karaköy Lokantası

Karaköy Lokantası is a beloved dining spot in Karaköy, offering a modern twist on traditional Turkish cuisine. The menu changes daily, featuring a variety of mezes, fresh seafood, and hearty mains. The beautifully tiled interior and friendly service create a welcoming atmosphere. This restaurant is particularly known for its lunch specials and vibrant ambiance. It's an excellent place to enjoy a leisurely meal while exploring one of Istanbul's trendiest neighborhoods.

- **Location:** Kemankeş Karamustafa Paşa Mahallesi, Kemankeş Caddesi No:37/A, Karaköy
- **Opening Hours:** 12:00 PM - 10:30 PM (Mon-Sat), Closed on Sundays
- **Phone Number:** +90 212 292 44 55

Çiya Sofrası

Located in the bustling Kadıköy district, Çiya Sofrası offers an extensive menu of traditional Anatolian dishes. This restaurant is known for its diverse and authentic selection of mezes, kebabs, and stews, highlighting regional recipes from across Turkey. The vibrant and cozy setting, combined with the rich flavors of the food, makes for an unforgettable dining experience. Çiya Sofrası is perfect for those looking to explore the depth and variety of Turkish cuisine in a casual setting.

- **Location:** Güneşlibahçe Sokak No:43, Kadıköy
- **Opening Hours:** 11:30 AM - 10:00 PM (Mon-Sun)
- **Phone Number:** +90 216 336 30 13

Balıkçı Sabahattin

Balıkçı Sabahattin, situated in a historic wooden house in Sultanahmet, is a casual seafood restaurant known for its fresh and flavorful dishes. The menu features a variety of mezes, grilled fish, and seafood specialties, all prepared with high-quality ingredients. The charming ambiance and attentive service make it a favorite among locals and tourists alike. It's an ideal spot for a relaxed meal after exploring the nearby historical sites.

- **Location:** Cankurtaran Mahallesi, Seyit Hasan Kuyu Sokak No:1, Sultanahmet
- **Opening Hours:** 12:00 PM - 11:00 PM (Mon-Sun)
- **Phone Number:** +90 212 458 18 24

Antiochia

Antiochia is a cozy restaurant in Beyoğlu, specializing in dishes from the Antakya region of Turkey. The menu includes a variety of mezes, kebabs, and unique regional specialties such as "Antakya-style liver" and "stuffed grape leaves." The warm and inviting atmosphere, combined with the rich and aromatic flavors of the food, make it a popular spot for casual dining. The friendly staff and quick service add to the overall delightful experience.

- **Location:** Asmalı Mescit Mahallesi, Minare Sokak No:21, Beyoğlu
- **Opening Hours:** 12:00 PM - 11:00 PM (Mon-Sun)
- **Phone Number:** +90 212 292 11 42

Pandeli

Located inside the historic Spice Bazaar, Pandeli is a timeless Istanbul institution serving traditional Turkish cuisine. The restaurant's interior, adorned with blue Iznik tiles, offers a charming and nostalgic dining experience. The menu features classic dishes such as "hünkar beğendi" (sultan's delight), "karnıyarık" (stuffed eggplant), and a variety of flavorful mezes. The casual yet elegant ambiance makes it a perfect spot for enjoying a leisurely meal while soaking in the history of Istanbul.

- **Location:** Mısır Çarşısı, No:1, Eminönü
- **Opening Hours:** 11:30 AM - 6:30 PM (Mon-Sat), Closed on Sundays
- **Phone Number:** +90 212 527 39 09

Galata Kitchen

Galata Kitchen is a family-run restaurant offering a homey and casual dining experience in the Galata neighborhood. The menu features a variety of Turkish and Mediterranean dishes, with a focus on fresh and seasonal ingredients. Popular dishes include "grilled lamb chops," "stuffed zucchini flowers," and a range of delicious mezes. The cozy atmosphere and friendly service make it a great place to enjoy a relaxed meal with friends or family.

- **Location:** Tımarcı Sokak No:6, Galata, Beyoğlu
- **Opening Hours:** 12:00 PM - 11:00 PM (Mon-Sun)
- **Phone Number:** +90 212 244 42 63

Mangerie

Located in the upscale Bebek neighborhood, Mangerie offers a casual yet chic dining experience with stunning views of the Bosphorus. The menu includes a variety of international and Turkish dishes, from breakfast items to light bites and hearty mains. The rooftop terrace is particularly popular for its beautiful setting and relaxed ambiance. Mangerie is a perfect spot for a leisurely brunch or a casual dinner with a view.

- **Location:** Cevdet Paşa Caddesi No:69, Bebek
- **Opening Hours**: 9:00 AM - 12:00 AM (Mon-Sun)
- **Phone Number:** +90 212 263 51 99

Delicatessen

Delicatessen in Nişantaşı is a trendy eatery known for its diverse menu and stylish interior. The casual dining spot offers a variety of dishes, from breakfast options to salads, sandwiches, and hearty mains. The open kitchen and deli counter add to the vibrant atmosphere, making it a popular spot for locals and visitors alike. Whether you're stopping by for a quick bite or a leisurely meal, Delicatessen provides a delightful dining experience.

- **Location:** Abdi İpekçi Caddesi No: 56/A, Nişantaşı
- **Opening Hours:** 8:00 AM - 12:00 AM (Mon-Sun)
- **Phone Number:** +90 212 296 29 29

Tarihi Sultanahmet Köftecisi

Tarihi Sultanahmet Köftecisi is an iconic casual dining spot in Istanbul, famous for its delicious meatballs (köfte). Located near the historic Sultanahmet Square, the restaurant has been serving its signature dish since 1920. The menu is simple but flavorful, featuring perfectly grilled köfte, fresh salads, and homemade bread. The relaxed and friendly atmosphere makes it a great place to enjoy a traditional Turkish meal after visiting nearby landmarks like the Hagia Sophia and the Blue Mosque.

- **Location:** Divan Yolu Caddesi No:12, Sultanahmet

- **Opening Hours:** 11:00 AM - 10:00 PM (Mon-Sun)
- **Phone Number:** +90 212 520 05 66

Seafood Restaurants

Balıkçı Sabahattin

Balıkçı Sabahattin is a renowned seafood restaurant located in the historic Sultanahmet district. Known for its fresh and high-quality seafood, the restaurant offers a wide range of dishes, including grilled fish, calamari, and shrimp. The menu also features a variety of traditional Turkish mezes that perfectly complement the main courses. The ambiance is cozy and inviting, with a charming garden setting that's ideal for a leisurely meal. Balıkçı Sabahattin is a favorite among both locals and tourists, making it a must-visit for seafood lovers.

- **Location:** Seyit Hasan Kuyu Sk. No:1, Sultanahmet, Fatih
- **Opening Hours:** 12:00 PM - 11:30 PM (Mon-Sun)
- **Phone Number:** +90 212 458 18 24

Bebek Balıkçısı

Bebek Balıkçısı is a popular seafood restaurant located in the upscale neighborhood of Bebek, offering stunning views of the Bosphorus. The restaurant is famous for its extensive seafood menu, which includes fresh fish, lobster, and a variety of shellfish. Diners can enjoy dishes like grilled sea bass, shrimp casserole, and calamari, all prepared with the freshest ingredients. The elegant setting and scenic views make it a perfect spot for a romantic dinner or a special celebration.

- **Location:** Cevdet Paşa Cd. No:26, Bebek, Beşiktaş
- **Opening Hours:** 12:00 PM - 12:00 AM (Mon-Sun)
- **Phone Number:** +90 212 263 34 47

Arnavutköy Balıkçısı

Located in the charming Arnavutköy neighborhood, Arnavutköy Balıkçısı offers a delightful seafood dining experience. The restaurant specializes in fresh fish and seafood dishes, including grilled octopus, shrimp, and a variety of fish options. The menu also features traditional Turkish mezes and salads.

The ambiance is elegant and relaxing, with a beautiful Bosphorus view that enhances the dining experience. It's an excellent choice for those looking to enjoy a high-quality seafood meal in a picturesque setting.

- **Location:** Bebek Arnavutköy Cd. No:9, Arnavutköy, Beşiktaş
- **Opening Hours:** 12:00 PM - 12:00 AM (Mon-Sun)
- **Phone Number:** +90 212 265 50 63

Kiyi Restaurant

Kiyi Restaurant in Tarabya is a long-established seafood restaurant known for its exquisite dishes and breathtaking views of the Bosphorus. The menu features a wide selection of fresh fish, shellfish, and seafood mezes. Signature dishes include grilled sea bass, jumbo shrimp, and octopus salad. The elegant interior and terrace seating offer a sophisticated dining experience, making it a popular choice for special occasions and business dinners.

- **Location:** Kefeliköy Cd. No:126, Tarabya, Sarıyer
- **Opening Hours:** 12:00 PM - 12:00 AM (Mon-Sun)
- **Phone Number:** +90 212 262 00 02

Tarihi Karaköy Balıkçısı

Tarihi Karaköy Balıkçısı, located in the bustling Karaköy district, is a historic seafood restaurant that has been serving customers since 1923. The menu offers a variety of fresh seafood options, including grilled fish, fried calamari, and seafood salads. The restaurant's traditional Turkish decor and lively atmosphere make it a favorite among locals and tourists alike. It's an excellent spot to enjoy a delicious seafood meal while exploring the vibrant Karaköy area.

- **Location:** Tersane Cd. No:4, Karaköy, Beyoğlu
- **Opening Hours:** 12:00 PM - 11:00 PM (Mon-Sun)
- **Phone Number:** +90 212 251 13 51

Eftalya Balık Restaurant

Eftalya Balık Restaurant, located in the upscale neighborhood of Tarabya, offers a luxurious seafood dining experience. The restaurant's menu features a variety of fresh fish, shellfish, and seafood mezes, all prepared with the finest ingredients. Signature dishes include grilled seabream, shrimp casserole, and octopus salad. The elegant interior and stunning views of the Bosphorus make it a perfect choice for a romantic dinner or special celebration.

- **Location:** Haydar Aliyev Cd. No:2, Tarabya, Sarıyer
- **Opening Hours:** 12:00 PM - 12:00 AM (Mon-Sun)
- **Phone Number:** +90 212 299 88 88

Fishmekan Restaurant

Fishmekan Restaurant in the Kuruçeşme neighborhood is a modern seafood restaurant known for its innovative dishes and stunning Bosphorus views. The menu features a variety of fresh fish and seafood options, including grilled octopus, shrimp, and sea bass. The restaurant also offers a selection of Turkish mezes and salads. The chic interior, along with the beautiful terrace seating, creates a sophisticated dining atmosphere.

- **Location:** Muallim Naci Cd. No:64, Kuruçeşme, Beşiktaş
- **Opening Hours:** 12:00 PM - 12:00 AM (Mon-Sun)
- **Phone Number:** +90 212 287 31 31

Park Fora Restaurant

Park Fora Restaurant, located in the picturesque Kuruçeşme neighborhood, is a renowned seafood restaurant offering a luxurious dining experience. The menu features a variety of fresh fish, shellfish, and seafood dishes, including grilled sea bass, lobster, and calamari. The restaurant's elegant setting, with its beautiful garden and stunning Bosphorus views, makes it a popular choice for romantic dinners and special occasions.

- **Location:** Muallim Naci Cd. Cemil Topuzlu Parkı İçi No:54, Kuruçeşme, Beşiktaş
- **Opening Hours:** 12:00 PM - 12:00 AM (Mon-Sun)
- **Phone Number:** +90 212 265 50 63

Sur Balık Restaurant

Sur Balık Restaurant, located in the historic Kumkapı neighborhood, offers a traditional Turkish seafood dining experience. The menu features a variety of fresh fish, shellfish, and seafood mezes. Signature dishes include grilled seabream, shrimp casserole, and octopus salad. The restaurant's warm and inviting atmosphere, along with its attentive service, makes it a popular choice for both locals and tourists.

- **Location:** Kennedy Cd. No:28, Kumkapı, Fatih
- **Opening Hours:** 12:00 PM - 12:00 AM (Mon-Sun)
- **Phone Number:** +90 212 517 35 35

Eleos Restaurant

Eleos Restaurant, located in the lively Beyoğlu district, offers a delightful seafood dining experience with a Greek twist. The menu features a variety of fresh fish, shellfish, and seafood dishes, including grilled octopus, shrimp saganaki, and sea bass. The restaurant's charming and elegant interior, along with its rooftop terrace offering stunning views of the Bosphorus, makes it a perfect spot for a romantic dinner or special celebration.

- **Location:** İstiklal Cd. No:231, Beyoğlu
- **Opening Hours:** 12:00 PM - 12:00 AM (Mon-Sun)
- **Phone Number:** +90 212 244 90 85

Street Food Vendors

Şehzade Cağ Kebap

Şehzade Cağ Kebap is a must-visit for anyone wanting to try authentic Turkish kebap. This small but famous street food vendor specializes in "cağ kebap," a horizontally stacked kebap made from marinated lamb. The meat is slowly roasted over a wood fire and served with lavash bread, grilled tomatoes, and peppers. The succulent flavors and tender texture of the meat make this a top choice for street food lovers. The casual and bustling atmosphere adds to the charm of this spot.

- **Location:** Hocapaşa Sok. No:6, Sirkeci, Fatih
- **Opening Hours:** 11:00 AM - 10:00 PM (Mon-Sun)
- **Phone Number:** +90 212 522 13 38

Tarihi Sultanahmet Köftecisi

Tarihi Sultanahmet Köftecisi is an iconic street food spot known for its delicious "köfte" (Turkish meatballs). The köfte are made from a special blend of spices and grilled to perfection. They are served with fresh bread, grilled green peppers, and a tangy tomato sauce. This legendary vendor has been serving locals and tourists alike for decades, offering a taste of traditional Turkish flavors in a simple yet satisfying meal.

- **Location**: Divanyolu Cd. No:12, Sultanahmet, Fatih
- **Opening Hours:** 10:00 AM - 10:00 PM (Mon-Sun)
- **Phone Number:** +90 212 513 64 69

Balık Ekmek at Eminönü

Balık ekmek, or fish sandwich, is a quintessential Istanbul Street food experience. The vendors at Eminönü serve freshly grilled fish fillets stuffed into a loaf of Turkish bread, along with onions, lettuce, and a squeeze of lemon. The fish is usually mackerel, and the simple yet flavorful combination makes for a delightful and satisfying meal. Eating a balık ekmek while overlooking the Bosphorus is a memorable experience for any visitor.

- **Location:** Eminönü Square, Fatih
- **Opening Hours:** 11:00 AM - 10:00 PM (Mon-Sun)

Çiya Sofrası

Çiya Sofrası offers a unique street food experience with its array of traditional Turkish dishes. Located in the bustling Kadıköy market, this vendor specializes in regional Turkish cuisine, including various kebabs, stews, and vegetable dishes.

The diverse menu and authentic flavors make it a popular spot for those looking to explore the rich culinary heritage of Turkey. The casual setting and friendly atmosphere add to its appeal.

- **Location:** Güneşli Bahçe Sk. No:43, Kadıköy
- **Opening Hours:** 11:30 AM - 10:00 PM (Mon-Sun)
- **Phone Number:** +90 216 336 30 13

Kızılkayalar Hamburger

Kızılkayalar Hamburger is famous for its unique "wet burger" or "islak hamburger," a Turkish twist on the classic hamburger. The burgers are drenched in a tangy tomato and garlic sauce and kept warm in a steam box, resulting in a moist and flavorful bite. This late-night snack is especially popular among locals and tourists exploring Taksim Square. The bold flavors and distinctive preparation methods make it a must-try street food.

- **Location:** Sıraselviler Cd. No:6, Taksim, Beyoğlu
- **Opening Hours:** 24 hours (Mon-Sun)
- **Phone Number:** +90 212 244 15 90

Karadeniz Pide ve Döner

Karadeniz Pide ve Döner is a renowned vendor for its delicious döner kebap and "pide" (Turkish flatbread). The döner is made from high-quality meat, marinated and cooked on a vertical rotisserie, then served on bread with fresh vegetables and sauces. The pide, often referred to as Turkish pizza, is baked to perfection with various toppings. The combination of freshly made bread and flavorful fillings makes this vendor a favorite among street food enthusiasts.

- **Location:** Beşiktaş Çarşı, Sinanpaşa Mahallesi, Beşiktaş
- **Opening Hours:** 10:00 AM - 11:00 PM (Mon-Sun)
- **Phone Number:** +90 212 261 64 60

Midyeci Ahmet

Midyeci Ahmet is the go-to spot for stuffed mussels, a popular street food in Istanbul. The mussels are filled with a flavorful mixture of rice, spices, and herbs, and then served with a squeeze of lemon. This vendor has earned a reputation for serving some of the best-stuffed mussels in the city, attracting locals and tourists alike. The simple yet delicious snack is perfect for enjoying on the go.

- **Location:** Balık Pazarı Sk. No:20, Beyoğlu
- **Opening Hours:** 11:00 AM - 2:00 AM (Mon-Sun)
- **Phone Number:** +90 532 065 19 20

Dürümzade

Dürümzade is a popular street food vendor specializing in "dürüm," a type of Turkish wrap. The wraps are filled with a variety of grilled meats, such as lamb, chicken, or beef, along with fresh vegetables and flavorful spices. The meats are cooked over an open flame, giving them a smoky, delicious taste. The friendly service and casual setting make it a favorite among locals and visitors alike.

- **Location:** Kalyoncu Kulluğu Cd. No:26/A, Beyoğlu
- **Opening Hours:** 11:00 AM - 2:00 AM (Mon-Sun)
- **Phone Number:** +90 212 249 01 47

Tarihi Samatya Balıkçısı

Tarihi Samatya Balıkçısı is a well-known vendor in the historic Samatya district, specializing in grilled seafood. The menu includes a variety of fresh fish and seafood, grilled to perfection and served with bread and salad. The casual setting and authentic flavors make it a popular choice for seafood lovers. The vendor's location in a vibrant neighborhood adds to the overall experience.

- **Location:** Samatya Meydanı, Kocamustafapaşa, Fatih
- **Opening Hours:** 12:00 PM - 11:00 PM (Mon-Sun)
- **Phone Number:** +90 212 585 20 98

Bambi Café

Bambi Café is a legendary street food spot in Istanbul, known for its "kokoreç" (grilled lamb intestines) and "dürüm" (wraps). The kokoreç is seasoned with spices and grilled, then chopped and served in bread or as a wrap. The intense flavors and unique preparation make it a favorite among adventurous eaters. The bustling atmosphere and friendly service make Bambi Café a must-visit for street food enthusiasts.

- **Location:** Sıraselviler Cd. No:10, Taksim, Beyoğlu
- **Opening Hours:** 24 hours (Mon-Sun)
- **Phone Number:** +90 212 243 05 15

Vegetarian and Vegan Options

Bi Nevi Deli

Bi Nevi Deli is a popular vegetarian and vegan restaurant located in the upscale neighborhood of Nişantaşı. This eatery offers a wide range of plant-based dishes made with fresh, organic ingredients. Their menu includes innovative salads, hearty soups, delicious grain bowls, and raw vegan desserts. The restaurant's minimalist and cozy atmosphere, coupled with its focus on healthy eating, makes it a favorite among health-conscious diners. Bi Nevi Deli also offers gluten-free and sugar-free options, catering to various dietary needs.

- **Location:** Ahmet Fetgari Sk. No:19/A, Nişantaşı, Şişli
- **Opening Hours:** 8:00 AM - 8:00 PM (Mon-Sun)
- **Phone Number:** +90 212 234 18 34

Zencefil

Zencefil, located in the heart of Beyoğlu, is one of Istanbul's oldest and most beloved vegetarian restaurants. The menu features a diverse selection of vegetarian and vegan dishes, including hearty soups, creative salads, flavorful main courses, and delicious desserts.

The restaurant's rustic interior, with its wooden furniture and warm lighting, creates a welcoming and relaxed ambiance. Zencefil is committed to using fresh, locally sourced ingredients, ensuring that each dish is both nutritious and flavorful.

- **Location:** Kurabiye Sk. No:3, Beyoğlu
- **Opening Hours:** 11:00 AM - 10:00 PM (Mon-Sun)
- **Phone Number:** +90 212 244 40 52

Parsifal

Parsifal is a charming vegetarian restaurant located near Taksim Square. The menu features a variety of vegetarian and vegan dishes, including lentil balls, stuffed grape leaves, vegetable casseroles, and delicious homemade desserts. Parsifal's cozy and intimate setting, with its colorful decor and friendly service, makes it a popular choice for both locals and tourists. The restaurant is dedicated to offering healthy and tasty meals, using fresh and natural ingredients in all their dishes.

- **Location:** Kurabiye Sk. No:9, Beyoğlu
- **Opening Hours:** 11:00 AM - 10:00 PM (Mon-Sun)
- **Phone Number:** +90 212 245 25 88

Vegan Istanbul

Vegan Istanbul is a dedicated vegan restaurant that offers a wide range of delicious plant-based dishes. Located in the lively district of Kadıköy, the restaurant's menu includes vegan burgers, wraps, salads, and desserts. They also offer a selection of vegan Turkish dishes, providing a unique twist on traditional cuisine. The modern and vibrant interior, along with the friendly staff, creates a welcoming atmosphere for diners. Vegan Istanbul is committed to promoting a cruelty-free lifestyle and sustainability.

- **Location:** Caferağa Mahallesi, Sakız Sk. No:13, Kadıköy
- **Opening Hours:** 11:00 AM - 10:00 PM (Mon-Sun)
- **Phone Number:** +90 216 418 17 17

Mahatma Cafe

Mahatma Cafe, located in the historic district of Sultanahmet, is a vegetarian and vegan-friendly restaurant known for its cozy atmosphere and delicious food. The menu features a variety of vegetarian and vegan dishes, including fresh salads, hearty soups, vegetable stews, and homemade desserts. The cafe's warm and inviting interior, with its eclectic decor and comfortable seating, makes it a perfect spot to relax and enjoy a healthy meal.

Mahatma Cafe is dedicated to using fresh and natural ingredients, ensuring each dish is both nutritious and flavorful.

- **Location:** Akbıyık Caddesi No:26, Sultanahmet, Fatih
- **Opening Hours:** 8:00 AM - 10:00 PM (Mon-Sun)
- **Phone Number:** +90 212 517 65 13

Helvetia

Helvetia is a cozy vegetarian restaurant located in Beyoğlu, known for its affordable and delicious vegetarian dishes. The menu includes a variety of Turkish and international vegetarian dishes, such as stuffed peppers, vegetable stews, salads, and hearty soups. The restaurant's simple and homey decor, combined with its friendly service, creates a welcoming atmosphere for diners. Helvetia is dedicated to using fresh and locally sourced ingredients, ensuring that each dish is both healthy and flavorful.

- **Location:** Asmalı Mescit Mahallesi, General Yazgan Sk. No:8, Beyoğlu
- **Opening Hours:** 12:00 PM - 10:00 PM (Mon-Sun)
- **Phone Number:** +90 212 292 80 74

Community Kitchen

Community Kitchen is a unique vegan restaurant located in the vibrant neighborhood of Kadıköy. The restaurant offers a diverse menu of plant-based dishes, including vegan kebabs, burgers, wraps, and salads. They also offer a selection of vegan desserts and smoothies. The casual and colorful interior, along with the communal seating, creates a friendly and relaxed dining atmosphere. Community Kitchen is committed to promoting veganism and sustainability, using organic and locally sourced ingredients whenever possible.

- **Location:** Caferağa Mahallesi, Kadife Sk. No:16, Kadıköy
- **Opening Hours:** 11:00 AM - 10:00 PM (Mon-Sun)
- **Phone Number:** +90 216 345 67 89

Rulo Lezzetler

Rulo Lezzetler is a popular vegetarian and vegan restaurant located in Beşiktaş. The restaurant is known for its delicious wraps and sandwiches, filled with a variety of fresh vegetables, legumes, and flavorful sauces. They also offer a selection of salads, soups, and smoothies. The modern and stylish interior, along with the friendly service, makes it a great spot for a quick and healthy meal. Rulo Lezzetler is dedicated to using high-quality, natural ingredients, ensuring each dish is both tasty and nutritious.

- **Location:** Ihlamurdere Cd. No:84, Beşiktaş
- **Opening Hours:** 11:00 AM - 9:00 PM (Mon-Sun)
- **Phone Number:** +90 212 259 00 10

Veganzade

Veganzade is a vegan restaurant located in the historic district of Sultanahmet. The restaurant offers a wide range of vegan dishes, including vegan versions of traditional Turkish cuisine. The menu features dishes such as vegan kebabs, stuffed grape leaves, vegetable stews, and a variety of desserts. The cozy and intimate interior, along with the friendly staff, creates a welcoming atmosphere for diners. Veganzade is committed to promoting a vegan lifestyle and sustainability, using organic and locally sourced ingredients.

- **Location:** Akbıyık Caddesi No:31, Sultanahmet, Fatih
- **Opening Hours:** 10:00 AM - 10:00 PM (Mon-Sun)
- **Phone Number:** +90 212 517 65 22

Zencefil Vegan & Vegetarian Cafe

Zencefil Vegan & Vegetarian Cafe, located in the heart of Kadıköy, offers a diverse menu of vegan and vegetarian dishes. The menu includes a variety of salads, soups, sandwiches, and main courses, all made with fresh and natural ingredients. The cafe's cozy and relaxed atmosphere, with its colorful decor and comfortable seating, makes it a perfect spot to enjoy a healthy meal. Zencefil is dedicated to providing delicious and nutritious food, catering to various dietary preferences.

- **Location:** Caferağa Mahallesi, Sakız Sk. No:11, Kadıköy
- **Opening Hours:** 10:00 AM - 10:00 PM (Mon-Sun)
- **Phone Number:** +90 216 345 67 88

Food Markets and Culinary Tours

Spice Bazaar (Mısır Çarşısı)

The Spice Bazaar, also known as Mısır Çarşısı, is one of Istanbul's most famous food markets. Dating back to the 17th century, it is a vibrant and bustling marketplace where visitors can find a wide variety of spices, dried fruits, nuts, sweets, and traditional Turkish delicacies. The aromatic scents of spices and herbs fill the air, creating an enticing atmosphere. The market is also home to numerous shops selling teas, Turkish delights, and other local products. It is a must-visit for anyone interested in Turkish cuisine and culture.

- **Location:** Rüstem Paşa, Erzak Ambarı Sok. No:92, Fatih
- **Opening Hours:** 8:00 AM - 7:30 PM (Mon-Sun)

Kadıköy Market

Kadıköy Market is a bustling food market located on the Asian side of Istanbul. It offers a wide range of fresh produce, seafood, meats, and dairy products. The market is known for its high-quality ingredients and vibrant atmosphere. In addition to the food stalls, there are numerous cafes and eateries where visitors can sample traditional Turkish dishes and street food. Kadıköy Market is a great place to experience the local culinary culture and shop for fresh ingredients.

- **Location:** Caferağa, Güneşli Bahçe Sokak No:10, Kadıköy
- **Opening Hours**: 8:00 AM - 8:00 PM (Mon-Sun)

Beşiktaş Fish Market

Beşiktaş Fish Market is a lively and bustling market located in the heart of Beşiktaş. It is renowned for its fresh seafood, including fish, shrimp, calamari, and mussels. The market also offers a variety of fresh fruits, vegetables, and other food products. The energetic atmosphere and the wide selection of seafood make it a popular spot for both locals and tourists. Visitors can also find several seafood restaurants nearby that serve freshly prepared dishes.

- **Location:** Sinanpaşa Mah, Beşiktaş Caddesi, Beşiktaş
- **Opening Hours:** 7:00 AM - 7:00 PM (Mon-Sun)

Balık Pazarı (Fish Market)

Balık Pazarı, located in the bustling Beyoğlu district, is another popular food market specializing in fresh seafood. It is part of the larger Nevizade Street, known for its lively nightlife and dining scene. The market offers a wide selection of fish and seafood, as well as fresh fruits, vegetables, and other food products. The vibrant atmosphere and the variety of stalls make it a great place to explore and sample local flavors. Visitors can also enjoy freshly prepared seafood dishes at the nearby restaurants.

- **Location:** Hüseyinağa, Sahne Sk. No:12, Beyoğlu
- **Opening Hours:** 9:00 AM - 9:00 PM (Mon-Sun)

Feriköy Organic Market

Feriköy Organic Market is a weekly market held every Saturday in the Şişli district. It is the first and largest organic market in Istanbul, offering a wide range of organic and natural products. Visitors can find fresh fruits and vegetables, dairy products, meats, honey, olives, and more. The market also features stalls selling organic beauty products and household items. The emphasis on organic and sustainable products makes it a popular choice for health-conscious shoppers.

- **Location:** Cumhuriyet Mahallesi, 34380 Şişli
- **Opening Hours:** 8:00 AM - 5:00 PM (Saturday only)

Balat Market

Balat Market is a historic market located in the Balat neighborhood, known for its vibrant and colorful atmosphere. The market offers a wide variety of fresh produce, meats, seafood, spices, and other food products. It is a great place to explore local flavors and shop for ingredients. The market is also surrounded by charming streets and historic buildings, making it a popular destination for tourists and locals alike. Balat Market is an excellent spot to experience the rich culinary heritage of Istanbul.

- **Location:** Balat, Hızır Çavuş Köprübaşı Cd. No:1, Fatih
- **Opening Hours:** 8:00 AM - 7:00 PM (Mon-Sun)

Şişli Market (Şişli Pazarı)

Şişli Market, also known as Şişli Pazarı, is a large and bustling market located in the Şişli district. It offers a wide range of fresh fruits, vegetables, meats, seafood, and other food products. The market is known for its vibrant atmosphere and affordable prices. In addition to food stalls, there are also vendors selling clothing, household items, and other goods. Şişli Market is a great place to experience the local market culture and shop for fresh ingredients.

- **Location:** Halaskargazi Cd. No:178, Şişli
- **Opening Hours:** 8:00 AM - 7:00 PM (Mon-Sun)

Bomonti Flea Market

Bomonti Flea Market is not only a treasure trove for vintage and antique lovers but also a great place to find unique food items and culinary delights. Held every Sunday, the market features a variety of stalls selling everything from fresh produce and spices to homemade jams and traditional Turkish sweets. The market's eclectic and vibrant atmosphere makes it a popular destination for both locals and tourists. Visitors can also enjoy street food and snacks while exploring the market.

- **Location:** Cumhuriyet Mahallesi, 34380 Şişli
- **Opening Hours:** 9:00 AM - 6:00 PM (Sunday only)

Eminönü Square Market

Eminönü Square Market is a bustling market located near the historic Eminönü district. It offers a wide range of fresh produce, seafood, meats, and spices. The market is also known for its variety of street food vendors, offering delicious snacks and traditional Turkish dishes. The lively and energetic atmosphere, combined with the market's proximity to the iconic Spice Bazaar and other historic sites, makes it a popular destination for food enthusiasts and tourists.

- **Location:** Eminönü Meydanı, Fatih
- **Opening Hours:** 8:00 AM - 7:00 PM (Mon-Sun)

Karaköy Fish Market

Karaköy Fish Market, located along the Bosphorus, is a popular spot for fresh seafood lovers. The market offers a wide selection of fish and seafood, including seasonal catches.

Visitors can also find fresh fruits, vegetables, and other food products. The market's waterfront location provides a picturesque setting, and there are several seafood restaurants nearby where visitors can enjoy freshly prepared dishes. The market's vibrant atmosphere and variety of offerings make it a must-visit for seafood enthusiasts.

- **Location:** Rıhtım Cd. No:3, Karaköy, Beyoğlu
- **Opening Hours:** 7:00 AM - 7:00 PM (Mon-Sun)

Food Tour and Culinary Experience

1. Istanbul Street Food Tour

This tour takes you on a delicious journey through Istanbul's bustling streets, where you'll sample a variety of street foods that define the city's culinary culture. From savory kebabs and mezes to sweet baklava and traditional Turkish tea, the tour covers a range of local specialties. The guide provides insights into the history and preparation of each dish, offering a comprehensive understanding of Istanbul's street food culture.

- **Meeting Point:** Galata Tower, Bereketzade Mahallesi, Galata Kulesi, 34421 Istanbul
- **Highlights:** Kebabs, mezes, baklava, Turkish tea, street food culture
- **Tour Provider:** Culinary Istanbul Tours
- **Duration:** 3 hours
- **Contact:** +90 212 345 67 89

2. Traditional Turkish Cooking Class

This hands-on cooking class allows you to learn how to prepare traditional Turkish dishes from scratch. You'll start with a market visit to pick fresh ingredients, followed by a cooking session where you'll make classic dishes such as kebabs, mezes, and desserts. The class concludes with a tasting of the dishes you've prepared, providing a thorough culinary experience and a chance to enjoy your creations.

- **Meeting Point:** Tour provider's kitchen, Nişantaşı, Istanbul
- **Highlights:** Market visit, hands-on cooking, traditional Turkish recipes, meal tasting
- **Tour Provider:** Istanbul Culinary Academy
- **Duration:** 4 hours

- **Contact:** +90 212 678 90 12

3. Bosphorus Food and Boat Tour

Combine scenic views with culinary delights on this tour, which includes a boat cruise along the Bosphorus Strait. You'll sample a variety of Turkish appetizers and local specialties while enjoying panoramic views of Istanbul's landmarks from the water. The guide provides commentary on the city's history and culture, enhancing the overall experience with both visual and culinary pleasures.

- **Meeting Point:** Kabataş Pier, Istanbul
- **Highlights:** Bosphorus cruise, Turkish appetizers, scenic views, historical commentary
- **Tour Provider:** Bosphorus Cruise and Food Tours
- **Duration:** 3 hours
- **Contact:** +90 212 456 78 90

4. Istanbul Food and Cultural Walking Tour

This comprehensive tour combines food tasting with cultural exploration. You'll visit local markets, traditional eateries, and historic sites while sampling a variety of Turkish foods. The tour includes dishes such as döner kebabs, simit (Turkish bagels), and various mezes. The guide provides insights into the cultural significance of each dish and the history of the neighborhoods you visit.

- **Meeting Point:** Sultanahmet Square, Istanbul
- **Highlights:** Local markets, traditional eateries, döner kebabs, simit, mezes
- **Tour Provider:** Foodie Istanbul Tours
- **Duration:** 4 hours
- **Contact:** +90 212 789 01 23

5. Private Gourmet Tour of Istanbul

For a more personalized experience, this private gourmet tour takes you to some of Istanbul's finest restaurants and hidden gems. The tour is customized based on your culinary preferences and interests, offering a mix of high-end dining and unique local spots. You'll enjoy a variety of dishes, from fine dining experiences to artisanal street food, with a knowledgeable guide providing insights and recommendations.

- **Meeting Point:** Flexible, based on tour preferences

- **Highlights:** Customized dining experience, high-end restaurants, unique local spots, personalized recommendations
- **Tour Provider:** Gourmet Istanbul Experiences
- **Duration:** 5 hours
- **Contact:** +90 212 345 67 88

6. Fish Market Tour and Cooking Class

Explore Istanbul's vibrant fish markets and learn how to prepare fresh seafood in this hands-on cooking class. The tour begins with a visit to the Karaköy Fish Market, where you'll select the catch of the day with the guidance of a local chef. Afterward, you'll head to a nearby cooking studio where you'll learn to prepare dishes such as grilled fish, seafood meze, and calamari. The class concludes with a meal, allowing you to savor the fruits of your labor.

- **Meeting Point:** Karaköy Fish Market, Istanbul
- **Highlights:** Fish market visit, seafood cooking, hands-on experience, chef guidance
- **Tour Provider:** Istanbul Cooking Studio
- **Duration:** 4 hours
- **Contact:** +90 212 567 89 01

7. Taste of Two Continents Food Tour

This unique tour takes you on a culinary journey across both the European and Asian sides of Istanbul. Starting in the historic Sultanahmet area, you'll sample Turkish delights, baklava, and fresh simit. After a short ferry ride to Kadıköy on the Asian side, the tour continues with traditional mezes, kebabs, and fish dishes at local eateries. The guide provides insights into the cultural significance of the dishes and the history of Istanbul's culinary evolution.

- **Meeting Point:** Sultanahmet Square, Istanbul
- **Highlights:** Turkish delight, baklava, simit, mezes, kebabs, local markets, ferry ride
- **Tour Provider:** Istanbul on Food
- **Duration:** 6 hours
- **Contact:** +90 212 987 67 89

8. Turkish Coffee and Baklava Experience

This tour is perfect for those with a sweet tooth and a love for coffee. You'll start with a visit to a historic coffee house where you'll learn about the preparation and cultural significance of Turkish coffee. After savoring your coffee, the tour continues to a traditional baklava shop, where you can watch the baklava being made and sample different varieties. The guide will explain the history of both Turkish coffee and baklava, providing a deeper understanding of these beloved Turkish treats.

- **Meeting Point:** Historic Coffee House, Sultanahmet, Istanbul
- **Highlights:** Turkish coffee making, baklava tasting, sweet treats, cultural history
- **Tour Provider:** Sweet Istanbul Experiences
- **Duration:** 2.5 hours
- **Contact:** +90 212 987 65 43

Chapter 10: Shopping in Istanbul

Shopping Districts and Streets

Grand Bazaar (Kapalı Çarşı)

The Grand Bazaar in Istanbul is one of the largest and oldest covered markets in the world, dating back to the 15th century. This labyrinthine market features over 4,000 shops sprawled across 61 covered streets. Visitors can find a wide variety of goods including jewelry, ceramics, spices, carpets, antiques, and textiles. Each area of the bazaar specializes in different products, providing a unique shopping experience that reflects the rich cultural heritage of Istanbul. The bazaar's vibrant atmosphere, bustling with locals and tourists alike, offers an authentic glimpse into traditional Turkish commerce and craftsmanship.

- **Location:** Beyazıt, Kalpakçılar Cd. No:22, 34126 Fatih/Istanbul, Turkey
- **Opening Hours:** Monday to Saturday: 9:00 AM - 7:00 PM; Closed on Sundays and public holidays
- **Phone Number:** +90 212 519 12 48

Spice Bazaar (Mısır Çarşısı)

The Spice Bazaar, also known as the Egyptian Bazaar, is a historical market that dates back to the 17th century. Renowned for its exotic spices, dried fruits, nuts, and sweets, the bazaar is a sensory delight. Aromas of saffron, cinnamon, and countless other spices fill the air, inviting visitors to explore the colorful stalls. In addition to spices, you can find a variety of other products such as Turkish delight, tea, oils, and traditional Turkish textiles. The bazaar's vibrant ambiance and rich array of goods make it a must-visit destination for those looking to experience the flavors and scents of Turkey.

- **Location:** Rüstem Paşa, Erzak Ambarı Sok. No:92, 34116 Fatih/Istanbul, Turkey
- **Opening Hours:** Monday to Saturday: 9:00 AM - 7:00 PM; Sunday: 10:00 AM - 6:00 PM
- **Phone Number:** +90 212 513 65 97

Istiklal Street (Istiklal Caddesi)

Istiklal Street is a lively pedestrian avenue stretching from Taksim Square to Galata Tower. Lined with 19th-century buildings, it houses a mix of international brands, Turkish boutiques, cafes, restaurants, and historic sites.

Street performers add to the vibrant atmosphere, and the historic red tram offers a nostalgic ride through the district. This area is also known for its nightlife, with numerous bars and clubs that come alive after dark.

- **Location:** Beyoğlu, Istanbul
- **Opening Hours:** Stores generally open daily from 10:00 AM to 10:00 PM

Nişantaşı

Nişantaşı is an upscale district renowned for its luxury shopping, elegant cafes, and high-end boutiques. Abdi İpekçi Street, the heart of Nişantaşı, is lined with flagship stores of international designer brands like Louis Vuitton, Chanel, and Prada, as well as top Turkish designers. The area is also known for its vibrant street life, art galleries, and stylish residents. It's a favorite among Istanbul's elite and fashion enthusiasts.

- **Location:** Şişli, Istanbul
- **Opening Hours:** Stores generally open daily from 10:00 AM to 10:00 PM

Bağdat Avenue (Bağdat Caddesi)

Bagdat Street is a bustling, 14-kilometer-long avenue on Istanbul's Asian side. It is famous for its wide sidewalks, tree-lined streets, and an array of shops ranging from high-street brands to luxury boutiques. This area also features numerous cafes, restaurants, and entertainment options, making it a popular destination for both shopping and socializing. The street is particularly vibrant on weekends, with locals and tourists alike enjoying the lively atmosphere.

- **Location:** Kadıköy, Istanbul (Asian Side)
- **Opening Hours:** Stores generally open daily from 10:00 AM to 10:00 PM

Karaköy

Karaköy has transformed from an industrial port area into one of Istanbul's trendiest neighborhoods. It is known for its eclectic mix of boutiques, art galleries, cafes, and restaurants. The area is particularly popular among young locals and tourists looking for unique fashion pieces, vintage items, and contemporary art. Its cobblestone streets and historic buildings add to the charm, making it a delightful area to explore.

- **Location:** Beyoğlu, Istanbul

- **Opening Hours:** Stores generally open daily from 10:00 AM to 10:00 PM

Çukurcuma

Çukurcuma is a charming neighborhood in Beyoğlu, Istanbul, renowned for its antique shops, art galleries, and vintage boutiques. Walking through its narrow, cobblestone streets feels like stepping back in time, with each shop offering unique treasures from different eras. The area is a haven for collectors and those interested in history and art, featuring a mix of Ottoman and European influences.

- **Location:** Beyoğlu, Istanbul
- **Opening Hours:** Stores generally open daily from 10:00 AM to 7:00 PM

Galata

Galata is a historic district known for the iconic Galata Tower and its artistic vibe. The area is filled with boutiques selling designer clothing, handmade jewelry, and unique home decor. Galata's narrow streets and historic architecture create a bohemian atmosphere, attracting creative minds and shoppers looking for one-of-a-kind items. The numerous cafes and rooftop bars also offer stunning views of the Bosphorus and the Golden Horn.

- **Location:** Beyoğlu, Istanbul
- **Opening Hours:** Stores generally open daily from 10:00 AM to 10:00 PM

Modern Malls and Shopping Centers

Istinye Park

Istinye Park is one of Istanbul's premier shopping destinations, known for its upscale stores and luxurious ambiance. Located in the affluent Sariyer district, this mall offers a mix of international and Turkish brands, from fashion and accessories to electronics and home decor. Its architecture blends modern design with elements inspired by traditional Ottoman motifs, creating a unique shopping experience. Istinye Park also features a variety of dining options and a cinema complex, making it a popular spot for both locals and tourists.

- **Location:** Pinar Mahallesi, Istinye Bayiri Cd. No:73, 34460 Sariyer/Istanbul, Turkey
- **Opening Hours:** Monday to Saturday, 10:00 AM to 10:00 PM; Sunday, 10:00 AM to 8:00 PM

- **Phone Number:** +90 212 345 55 55

Kanyon

Kanyon is a contemporary shopping and lifestyle center located in the Levent business district of Istanbul. Designed by renowned architects, it features a distinctive canyon-like structure with open-air spaces and glass roofs that allow natural light to flood the interior. Kanyon offers a wide range of shops, including fashion boutiques, electronics stores, and gourmet markets. It's also home to cafes, restaurants, and a cinema complex, providing a complete leisure experience amidst modern architecture.

- **Location:** Buyukdere Cad. No:185, Levent, 34394 Istanbul, Turkey
- **Opening Hours:** Monday to Saturday, 10:00 AM to 10:00 PM; Sunday, 10:00 AM to 8:00 PM
- **Phone Number:** +90 212 317 53 00

Zorlu Center

Zorlu Center is a luxury mixed-use complex in Istanbul's Zincirlikuyu district, combining shopping, entertainment, and residential spaces. It houses a high-end shopping mall with designer boutiques, upscale department stores, and exclusive brands. The architecture is modern and sleek, complemented by landscaped outdoor areas and art installations. Zorlu Center also features a performing arts center, luxury residences, a hotel, and a wide selection of restaurants and cafes, catering to a sophisticated clientele.

- **Location:** Koru Sk. No:2, Zincirlikuyu, 34340 Istanbul, Turkey
- **Opening Hours:** Daily, 10:00 AM to 10:00 PM
- **Phone Number:** +90 212 924 01 00

Cevahir Istanbul

Cevahir Istanbul, officially known as Istanbul Cevahir Shopping and Entertainment Centre, is one of the largest malls in Europe and a landmark in the Sisli district. It boasts a vast array of shops offering fashion, electronics, home goods, and more across its multiple floors. The mall features an indoor roller coaster, a cinema complex, and a food court with international and Turkish cuisine options. Its sheer size and comprehensive offerings make it a popular destination for shoppers of all ages.

- **Location:** Buyukdere Cad. No:22, Sisli, 34360 Istanbul, Turkey
- **Opening Hours:** Monday to Saturday, 10:00 AM to 10:00 PM; Sunday, 10:00 AM to 9:00 PM
- **Phone Number**: +90 212 368 69 00

Akasya Acibadem

Akasya Acibadem is a modern shopping and lifestyle center situated on Istanbul's Asian side in the Uskudar district. Designed with sustainability in mind, it features green spaces and natural light-filled interiors. The mall offers a diverse range of shops, from fashion and beauty to electronics and home decor. Akasya Acibadem also includes entertainment options like a cinema, fitness center, and family-friendly activities, along with a variety of dining choices, making it a popular spot for both shopping and leisure.

- **Location:** Acıbadem Mahallesi, Cendere Cd. No:40, 34660 Uskudar/Istanbul, Turkey
- **Opening Hours:** Monday to Saturday, 10:00 AM to 10:00 PM; Sunday, 10:00 AM to 8:00 PM
- **Phone Number:** +90 216 622 00 66

Mall of Istanbul

The Mall of Istanbul, located in the Basaksehir district, is a vast shopping and entertainment complex catering to diverse tastes and preferences. It features a wide range of shops offering fashion, electronics, and home furnishings. The mall is designed with modern architecture and includes indoor and outdoor spaces, a cinema complex, and a variety of restaurants and cafes. The Mall of Istanbul is a popular destination for families and shoppers looking for a comprehensive retail and leisure experience.

- **Location:** Mahmutbey Mahallesi, Tasocagi Cd. No:5, 34217 Basaksehir/Istanbul, Turkey
- **Opening Hours:** Daily, 10:00 AM to 10:00 PM
- **Phone Number:** +90 212 444 44 99

Istanbul Cevahir

Istanbul Cevahir is one of the largest and most popular shopping malls in Istanbul, located in the Sisli district. It offers a vast selection of shops, including international brands, fashion boutiques, electronics stores, and more.

The mall also features entertainment options like a cinema complex and a food court with diverse dining choices. Istanbul Cevahir's central location and extensive offerings make it a convenient and enjoyable destination for shopping and leisure activities.

- **Location:** Buyukdere Cad. No:22, Sisli, 34360 Istanbul, Turkey
- **Opening Hours:** Monday to Saturday, 10:00 AM to 10:00 PM; Sunday, 10:00 AM to 9:00 PM
- **Phone Number:** +90 212 368 69 00

Capacity Istanbul

Capacity Istanbul is a large shopping mall located in the Bakirkoy district, known for its comprehensive shopping and entertainment options. It houses a variety of shops ranging from fashion and accessories to electronics and home decor. The mall also features a cinema complex, fitness center, and diverse dining choices in its food court. Capacity Istanbul's convenient location and extensive facilities make it a popular choice for both locals and visitors looking for a complete retail and leisure experience.

- **Location:** Bakirkoy, Istanbul, Turkey
- **Opening Hours:** Monday to Saturday, 10:00 AM to 10:00 PM; Sunday, 10:00 AM to 8:00 PM
- **Phone Number:** +90 212 560 00 60

Palladium Istanbul

Palladium Istanbul is a modern shopping mall situated in the Atasehir district on Istanbul's Asian side. It offers a variety of shops featuring international and Turkish brands, along with electronics, home goods, and more. The mall's design includes open spaces and natural light, creating a pleasant shopping environment. Palladium Istanbul also includes a cinema complex, fitness center, and a range of dining options from casual eateries to upscale restaurants, catering to different tastes and preferences.

- **Location:** Barbaros Mahallesi, Halk Cad. No:8, 34746 Atasehir/Istanbul, Turkey
- **Opening Hours:** Monday to Saturday, 10:00 AM to 10:00 PM; Sunday, 10:00 AM to 8:00 PM
- **Phone Number:** +90 216 663 56 00

Forum Istanbul

Forum Istanbul is a large shopping and entertainment complex located in the Bayrampasa district, known for its diverse retail offerings and leisure facilities. The mall features a wide range of shops, including fashion, electronics, and home decor stores. It also includes entertainment options such as a cinema complex, bowling alley, and children's play areas. Forum Istanbul's convenient location and comprehensive amenities make it a popular destination for shopping, dining, and family-friendly activities.

- **Location:** Kocatepe Mahallesi, Paşa Cd. No:5/5, 34045 Bayrampasa/Istanbul, Turkey
- **Opening Hours:** Daily, 10:00 AM to 10:00 PM
- **Phone Number:** +90 212 443 13 00

Local Markets and Boutiques

Arasta Bazaar

Nestled near the Blue Mosque, Arasta Bazaar offers a quieter alternative to the Grand Bazaar. This historic market features small shops selling Turkish carpets, ceramics, textiles, and handicrafts. It's known for its authentic atmosphere and is a great place to find unique souvenirs away from the crowds.

- **Location:** Sultan Ahmet Mahallesi, 34122 Fatih/Istanbul, Turkey
- **Opening Hours:** Daily, 9:00 AM to 7:00 PM
- **Phone Number:** +90 212 518 13 19

Cukurcuma Antiques Market

Cukurcuma is famous for its antique shops and vintage boutiques, making it a paradise for collectors and enthusiasts. Located in Beyoglu, this charming neighborhood boasts cobblestone streets lined with shops selling antique furniture, retro clothing, and unique decor items.

- **Location:** Cukurcuma, 34425 Beyoglu/Istanbul, Turkey
- **Opening Hours:** Varies by shop; generally open daily

Kadikoy Market

Located on the Asian side of Istanbul, Kadikoy Market is a vibrant hub of activity offering fresh produce, spices, seafood, and more.

The market also features stalls selling clothing, accessories, and household goods. It's a favorite among locals and visitors alike for its bustling atmosphere and diverse offerings.

- **Location:** Kadikoy, Istanbul, Turkey
- **Opening Hours:** Daily, 8:00 AM to 7:00 PM

Istiklal Avenue Boutiques

Istiklal Avenue, in the heart of Beyoglu, is lined with trendy boutiques offering fashion, accessories, and unique finds. It's a popular shopping destination known for its European flair and diverse range of stores, from high-end brands to independent designers.

- **Location:** Istiklal Avenue, Beyoglu, Istanbul, Turkey
- **Opening Hours:** Varies by store; generally open daily

Galata Tower Shops

Surrounding the iconic Galata Tower, this area is dotted with small shops and boutiques selling jewelry, art, and traditional Turkish crafts. It's a picturesque spot to shop while enjoying views of Istanbul's skyline.

- **Location:** Bereketzade, Galata Kulesi, 34421 Beyoglu/Istanbul, Turkey
- **Opening Hours:** Varies by shop; generally open daily

Ortakoy Market

Situated along the Bosphorus on the European side, Ortakoy Market is known for its lively atmosphere and scenic views. It features a mix of stalls selling handmade jewelry, crafts, clothing, and artwork. The market also offers a variety of street food, making it a popular destination for both shopping and dining.

- **Location:** Ortakoy, Istanbul, Turkey
- **Opening Hours:** Weekends are busiest; open from morning until late evening

Nisantasi Boutiques

Nisantasi is Istanbul's upscale shopping district, known for its designer boutiques, luxury brands, and chic cafes. It's a hub for fashion enthusiasts and those seeking high-end shopping experiences in a stylish setting.

- **Location:** Nisantasi, Sisli, Istanbul, Turkey

- **Opening Hours:** Varies by store; generally open daily

Spice Shops in Eminonu

Along the streets near the Spice Bazaar in Eminonu, you'll find numerous spice shops offering a variety of aromatic spices, herbs, teas, and Turkish delights. These shops are a feast for the senses, with colorful displays and enticing aromas.

- **Location:** Eminonu, 34116 Fatih/Istanbul, Turkey
- **Opening Hours:** Daily, typically from early morning to evening

Sahaflar Carsisi (Secondhand Book Market)

Located near the Grand Bazaar, Sahaflar Carsisi is a haven for book lovers and collectors. It features stalls selling rare books, manuscripts, and antique prints, making it a unique destination for literary enthusiasts.

- **Location:** Beyazit, Istanbul, Turkey
- **Opening Hours:** Daily, generally from morning until early evening

Beyoglu Street Markets

Beyoglu's diverse street markets offer a mix of goods, from fresh produce and clothing to household items and souvenirs. These local markets are a great way to experience everyday life in Istanbul and discover hidden gems.

- **Location:** Beyoglu, Istanbul, Turkey
- **Opening Hours:** Varies by market and day of the week

Souvenirs and Handicrafts

When visiting Istanbul, shopping for souvenirs and handicrafts offers a glimpse into Turkey's rich cultural heritage and craftsmanship. Here are some popular items you can find:

1. Ceramics:

Turkish ceramics are renowned for their intricate patterns and vibrant colors. You can find everything from decorative plates and bowls to tiles and traditional Turkish coffee sets. The designs often draw inspiration from Ottoman and Anatolian motifs, making them unique and highly sought after by visitors.

2. Carpets and Kilims:

Handwoven carpets and kilims (flat-woven rugs) are a staple of Turkish craftsmanship. Each region in Turkey produces carpets with distinct patterns and colors, such as the famous Anatolian motifs or the geometric designs of Kilims. These carpets are not only beautiful but also reflect a centuries-old tradition of weaving passed down through generations.

3. Spices and Turkish Delights:

Istanbul's Spice Bazaar is a treasure trove of aromatic spices, including saffron, sumac, and Turkish red pepper. Alongside spices, Turkish delights (lokum) come in various flavors like rose, pistachio, and pomegranate. They make for delicious and colorful gifts packed in ornate boxes.

4. Calligraphy and Illumination Art:

Ottoman calligraphy, known as Hat, and illumination art (Tezhip) are intricate forms of Islamic art. You can find beautifully handcrafted calligraphy works on paper or ceramics, often featuring verses from the Quran or poetic texts. Illumination art adorns manuscripts and decorative items with gold leaf and colorful designs.

5. Turkish Tea and Coffee Sets:

Tea (çay) and coffee (kahve) hold significant cultural importance in Turkey. Authentic Turkish tea sets usually include small glasses and ornate tea trays, while coffee sets often feature delicate cups and coffee pots (cezve). These sets are not only functional but also serve as decorative pieces in homes.

6. Jewelry:

Turkish jewelry combines traditional craftsmanship with unique designs. Look for pieces adorned with turquoise (a stone believed to bring luck), filigree work, and Ottoman motifs. Items range from earrings and bracelets to ornate necklaces and rings, each telling a story of Turkish artistry and history.

7. Leather Goods:

Turkey is known for its high-quality leather products, including bags, wallets, and jackets. Istanbul's markets and boutiques offer a wide selection of leather goods, often handcrafted using traditional methods. Look for items made from genuine Turkish leather for durability and style.

8. Evil Eye Talismans:

The Nazar Boncuk, or evil eye bead, is a popular protective amulet in Turkey. It's believed to ward off the evil eye and bring good luck to its wearer. You can find Nazar beads in various forms, from small glass charms to larger decorative items like wall hangings and jewelry. They are a ubiquitous symbol in Turkish culture and make for meaningful and symbolic souvenirs.

9. Musical Instruments:

Turkey has a rich musical heritage, and traditional musical instruments like the saz (a long-necked lute), darbuka (goblet drum), and ney (reed flute) are crafted with care and precision. These instruments not only serve as souvenirs but also allow you to delve into Turkey's musical traditions, whether through performances or personal practice.

10. Antiques and Vintage Items:

Istanbul's antique shops and markets offer a treasure trove of vintage items, including old coins, Ottoman-era furniture, vintage textiles, and decorative pieces. Collectors and history enthusiasts will find unique pieces that reflect Turkey's historical legacy and cultural evolution over the centuries.

Antique Shops and Vintage Finds

Exploring Istanbul's antique shops and vintage finds is a journey through history, art, and culture. Here are some of the best spots where you can discover unique treasures:

Çukurcuma Antikacılar Sokağı (Çukurcuma Antique Shops Street)

The Çukurcuma Antique District is a haven for antique lovers. Located in the Beyoğlu district, this area is filled with narrow streets lined with antique shops and boutiques. You can find everything from Ottoman-era furniture, vintage jewelry, and old books to unique collectibles and art pieces. The charming ambiance of the district, with its historical buildings and cobblestone streets, makes for a delightful shopping experience.

- **Location:** Çukurcuma, Beyoğlu, Istanbul

- **Opening Hours:** Varies by shop; typically, open daily from 10 AM to 7 PM

Antika Pazari

Located near the Grand Bazaar, Antika Pazari is renowned for its extensive collection of antiques and vintage goods. From ornate ceramics to exquisite carpets and ancient manuscripts, this market appeals to both collectors and casual shoppers seeking authentic Turkish treasures.

- **Location:** Beyazıt Mh., Beyazıt, Fatih, Istanbul
- **Opening Hours:** Open daily from 9 AM to 7 PM
- **Phone Number**: +90 212 518 18 68

Feriköy Antikacılar Sokağı (Feriköy Antique Shops Street)

Known for its charming ambiance and diverse offerings, Feriköy Antikacılar Sokağı is a hidden gem in Istanbul's antique scene. Visitors can explore a variety of shops selling vintage furniture, retro clothing, and unique curiosities, making it a favorite haunt for collectors and interior decorators alike.

- **Location:** Feriköy, Şişli, Istanbul
- **Opening Hours:** Typically open daily; hours vary by shop

Cihangir Antikacılar Sokağı (Cihangir Antique Shops Street)

Situated in the trendy Cihangir neighborhood, this street is home to several boutique antique shops offering a mix of European and Ottoman antiques. Visitors can browse through items such as vintage posters, old maps, and intricate silverware, all reflecting Istanbul's cultural diversity.

- **Location:** Cihangir, Beyoğlu, Istanbul
- **Opening Hours:** Varies by shop; generally open from 11 AM to 6 PM

Kadıköy Antikacılar Çarşısı (Kadıköy Antique Market)

Located on Istanbul's Asian side, Kadıköy Antique Market is a bustling hub for antique enthusiasts. Here, you can find a wide range of goods including vintage cameras, retro furnishings, and traditional Turkish artifacts, all set amidst the vibrant atmosphere of Kadıköy.

- **Location:** Kadıköy, Istanbul
- **Opening Hours:** Open daily from 10 AM to 8 PM

Galata Antik

Galata Antik offers a curated selection of antique furniture, artwork, and decorative items. Located in the historic Galata neighborhood, this shop is known for its knowledgeable staff and quality pieces that cater to both seasoned collectors and first-time buyers.

- **Location:** Galata, Beyoğlu, Istanbul
- **Opening Hours:** Open daily from 10 AM to 7 PM
- **Phone Number:** +90 212 244 66 85

Pandora Antique

Pandora Antique specializes in Ottoman-era artifacts, including ceramics, textiles, and jewelry. Situated in the heart of Sultanahmet, near major historic sites, it offers a glimpse into Istanbul's imperial past through its meticulously curated collection.

- **Location:** Sultanahmet, Fatih, Istanbul
- **Opening Hours:** Open daily from 9 AM to 6 PM
- **Phone Number:** +90 212 517 33 44

Feriköy Antik

Feriköy Antik is renowned for its selection of vintage Turkish carpets, kilims, and tribal textiles. Located in the Feriköy neighborhood, it attracts collectors and interior designers seeking unique pieces that blend history with contemporary design sensibilities.

- **Location:** Feriköy, Şişli, Istanbul
- **Opening Hours:** Open daily from 10 AM to 7 PM
- **Phone Number:** +90 212 231 21 12

Beyoğlu Antikacılar Çarşısı (Beyoğlu Antique Market)

Beyoğlu Antique Market offers a mix of shops selling everything from vintage toys to retro clothing and nostalgic memorabilia. Located near İstiklal Avenue, it's a vibrant spot where visitors can uncover hidden gems from Turkey's past.

- **Location:** Beyoğlu, Istanbul
- **Opening Hours:** Open daily from 11 AM to 8 PM

Karaköy Antikacılar Çarşısı (Karaköy Antique Market)

Nestled in the bustling Karaköy district, this market is known for its eclectic mix of antique shops offering a diverse range of items, from retro furniture to ancient coins and vintage books. It's a must-visit for those looking to explore Istanbul's antique scene off the beaten path.

- **Location:** Karaköy, Beyoğlu, Istanbul
- **Opening Hours:** Open daily from 10 AM to 7 PM

Chapter 11: Nightlife and Entertainment

Bars and Pubs

Istanbul offers a vibrant nightlife scene with an array of bars and pubs that cater to different tastes and preferences. Here are some of the best bars and pubs in the city:

360 Istanbul

Located on the rooftop of a historic building in the heart of Beyoğlu, 360 Istanbul offers a unique 360-degree view of the city. The venue combines a chic restaurant, bar, and nightclub, making it a popular choice for both dining and nightlife. The bar serves creative cocktails, premium spirits, and an extensive wine list. The lively atmosphere, combined with the stunning views, makes it a favorite among locals and tourists alike.

- **Location:** Istiklal Ave Misir Apt. K8, Beyoglu, Istanbul
- **Opening Hours:** Daily, 5:00 PM - 2:00 AM
- **Phone Number:** +90 212 251 1042

Babylon Bomonti

Located in an old beer factory, Babylon Bomonti is a beloved venue for live music enthusiasts. It hosts a range of performances from local bands to international acts, spanning various genres including jazz, rock, and electronic. The industrial-chic setting adds to its appeal, making it a cultural hub in Istanbul's nightlife scene.

- **Location:** Bomontiada, Silahsor Cad. No: 1, Bomonti, Sisli, Istanbul
- **Opening Hours:** Varies based on events, typically evenings
- **Phone Number:** +90 212 334 01 00

Mikla Bar

Mikla Rooftop Bar is situated on the top floor of the Marmara Pera Hotel, offering stunning panoramic views of Istanbul's skyline, including the Golden Horn and the Bosphorus. The bar features a stylish and modern ambiance, perfect for enjoying signature cocktails, fine wines, and a variety of spirits. The combination of breathtaking views, sophisticated atmosphere, and excellent service makes Mikla a must-visit spot for an unforgettable night out.

- **Location:** The Marmara Pera, Mesrutiyet Cad. Tepebasi, Beyoglu, Istanbul
- **Opening Hours:** Daily, 6:00 PM - 2:00 AM
- **Phone Number:** +90 212 293 5656

Alexandra Cocktail Bar

Known for its cozy and intimate ambiance, Alexandra Cocktail Bar is tucked away in the lively Beyoglu district. It specializes in craft cocktails prepared with precision and flair. The bar's vintage decor and attentive service create an inviting atmosphere perfect for unwinding after a day of exploring the city.

- **Location:** Kucukparmakkapi Sokak No: 5/A, Beyoglu, Istanbul
- **Opening Hours:** Daily, 6:00 PM - 2:00 AM
- **Phone Number:** +90 212 249 0915

Arka Oda

Translating to the "back room," Arka Oda offers a laid-back and artistic vibe in Istanbul's Kadikoy district. It's a favorite among locals for its eclectic decor, featuring vintage furniture and an extensive collection of vinyl records. The bar serves a variety of Turkish and international beers, making it a perfect spot for casual gatherings.

- **Location:** Caferaga Mahallesi, Bademalti Sokak No: 21/A, Kadikoy, Istanbul
- **Opening Hours:** Daily, 6:00 PM - 2:00 AM
- **Phone Number:** +90 216 336 3796

Karakoy Lokantasi Meyhanesi

Located in the trendy Karakoy neighborhood, this meyhane (traditional Turkish tavern) offers a warm and inviting atmosphere. It's known for its selection of mezes (appetizers) and rakı (aniseed-flavored spirit), creating an authentic Turkish dining experience. Live music performances often enhance the lively ambiance.

- **Location:** Kemankes Karamustafa Pasa Mescidi Sk. No: 10/A, Karakoy, Istanbul
- **Opening Hours:** Daily, 12:00 PM - 2:00 AM
- **Phone Number:** +90 212 292 4455

Lucca

A staple in Istanbul's nightlife, Lucca offers a sophisticated setting with a sleek interior and stylish crowd. It's popular for its DJ performances that keep the atmosphere lively until late. The bar serves a wide range of cocktails and premium spirits, making it a go-to spot for those seeking a chic night out.

- **Location:** Istiklal Caddesi, No: 185, Beyoglu, Istanbul
- **Opening Hours:** Daily, 6:00 PM - 4:00 AM
- **Phone Number:** +90 212 293 9602

Beyoglu Hayal Kahvesi

Known for its live music and cozy atmosphere, Beyoglu Hayal Kahvesi is a popular venue for both Turkish and international artists. It offers a diverse program including jazz, rock, and folk performances, catering to a wide range of musical tastes. The venue's intimate setting enhances the overall experience.

- **Location:** Istiklal Cad. Misir Apt. No: 163 K: 6, Beyoglu, Istanbul
- **Opening Hours:** Daily, 9:00 PM - 4:00 AM
- **Phone Number:** +90 212 244 2556

Chanta Club

Located in Ortakoy, Chanta Club is famous for its lively nightlife scene and stunning Bosphorus views. It offers both indoor and outdoor seating, with a spacious dance floor where DJs spin a mix of Turkish and international beats. The club's energetic atmosphere attracts party-goers looking to dance the night away.

- **Location:** Muallim Naci Cad. No: 65, Ortakoy, Istanbul
- **Opening Hours:** Daily, 10:00 PM - 4:00 AM
- **Phone Number:** +90 212 261 4050

Kasette

A unique blend of a bar and a record shop, Kasette in Cihangir appeals to music lovers and cocktail enthusiasts alike. It offers a curated selection of vinyl records spanning various genres, which guests can browse while enjoying their drinks. The cozy space and friendly vibe make it a favorite among locals and visitors.

- **Location:** Cihangir Mah. Soganci Sok. No: 6/B, Beyoglu, Istanbul
- **Opening Hours:** Daily, 6:00 PM - 2:00 AM

- **Phone Number:** +90 532 245 8920

Nightclubs and Lounges

Istanbul's nightlife scene is vibrant and diverse, offering a range of nightclubs and lounges that cater to various tastes and preferences. Here are some of the top spots for an unforgettable night out in the city:

360 Istanbul:

Perched on a rooftop offering breathtaking views of the city, 360 Istanbul is renowned for its vibrant atmosphere and eclectic music. It's a hotspot for both locals and tourists looking to dance the night away amidst a sophisticated setting. The venue often hosts live music performances and DJs spinning a mix of international beats. Located in Beyoglu, it's open from evening till late night, making it ideal for a memorable night out.

- **Location:** Istiklal Caddesi Mısır Apt. Kat 8, Beyoğlu, Istanbul
- **Opening Hours:** Daily from 6:00 PM to 4:00 AM
- **Phone Number:** +90 212 251 1042

Sortie Club:

Situated on the Bosphorus waterfront, Sortie Club offers an elegant ambiance with multiple outdoor terraces and stylish interiors. It features a variety of music genres across its several themed areas, ensuring there's something for every taste. The club attracts a fashionable crowd and is known for its upscale dining options and lively nightlife scene.

- **Location:** Muallim Naci Cad. No: 141, Kuruçeşme, Istanbul
- **Opening Hours:** Daily from 7:00 PM to 4:00 AM
- **Phone Number:** +90 212 327 8585

Anjelique:

Another Bosphorus-side gem, Anjelique is celebrated for its chic design and spectacular views. The venue combines a restaurant, bar, and nightclub, offering a seamless transition from dining to dancing. Its sophisticated ambiance, international music, and trendy crowd make it a must-visit for those seeking a luxurious nightlife experience.

- **Location:** Muallim Naci Cad. Salhane Sok. No: 5, Ortaköy, Istanbul

- **Opening Hours:** Daily from 6:00 PM to 4:00 AM
- **Phone Number:** +90 212 327 2844

Indigo:

Situated in the heart of Beyoglu, Indigo is a longstanding favorite among Istanbul's club-goers. Known for its alternative music scene, live performances, and laid-back atmosphere, Indigo attracts a diverse crowd of music enthusiasts. The club often hosts local and international bands, DJs, and themed nights, creating a dynamic nightlife experience.

- **Location:** Istiklal Caddesi No: 136, Beyoğlu, Istanbul
- **Opening Hours:** Daily from 9:00 PM to 4:00 AM
- **Phone Number:** +90 212 244 8567

Klein:

Tucked away in the lively nightlife district of Taksim, Klein is a compact yet vibrant nightclub known for its underground electronic music scene. The intimate setting, pulsating beats, and energetic crowd create an electrifying atmosphere perfect for dancing until dawn. It's a favorite among locals and visitors seeking a more underground clubbing experience.

- **Location:** Şehbender Sokak No: 3, Taksim, Istanbul
- **Opening Hours:** Daily from 10:00 PM to 5:00 AM
- **Phone Number**: +90 533 387 6101

Ruby Istanbul:

Located in the historic district of Karaköy, Ruby Istanbul combines a bar and nightclub in a stylish industrial setting. Known for its craft cocktails, live DJ performances, and retro-futuristic decor, Ruby attracts a trendy crowd looking for a unique nightlife experience. The venue's intimate yet lively vibe makes it a popular choice for late-night revelers.

- **Location:** Kemankes Mah. Necatibey Cad. No: 57/A, Karaköy, Istanbul
- **Opening Hours:** Daily from 6:00 PM to 4:00 AM
- **Phone Number:** +90 212 244 8567

Lucca:

Situated in Istanbul's chic Beşiktaş district, Lucca is a sophisticated lounge and nightclub known for its stylish design and upscale ambiance. The venue features a restaurant serving Mediterranean cuisine, a sleek bar area, and a dance floor where DJs spin international hits. Lucca is popular among affluent locals and visitors seeking a classy night out.

- **Location:** Vişnezade Mah. Süleyman Seba Cad. No: 57, Beşiktaş, Istanbul
- **Opening Hours:** Daily from 6:00 PM to 4:00 AM
- **Phone Number:** +90 212 327 9947

Babylon:

A pioneer in Istanbul's live music scene, Babylon offers a laid-back yet vibrant atmosphere with regular performances by local and international bands. Located in Beyoğlu, the venue has a relaxed setting with a diverse program of jazz, rock, electronic, and world music concerts, making it a favorite among music aficionados.

- **Location:** Şehbender Sokak No: 3, Taksim, Istanbul
- **Opening Hours:** Varies based on event schedule
- **Phone Number:** +90 212 292 7368

Wan-na:

Situated in the lively neighborhood of Beşiktaş, Wan-na is a popular nightclub known for its energetic DJ sets and vibrant dance floors. The venue offers a mix of electronic, pop, and Turkish music, catering to a young and energetic crowd. Wan-na's lively atmosphere and central location make it a go-to spot for late-night partygoers.

- **Location:** Vişnezade Mah. Süleyman Seba Cad. No: 57, Beşiktaş, Istanbul
- **Opening Hours:** Daily from 10:00 PM to 5:00 AM
- **Phone Number:** +90 212 227 8000

Live Music Venues

Babylon Bomonti

Babylon Bomonti is a renowned venue known for hosting a diverse range of musical genres including jazz, rock, electronic, and world music.

Located in the historic Bomonti Beer Factory, this spacious venue offers both indoor and outdoor stages, creating an immersive concert experience. With its trendy ambiance and top-notch sound system, Babylon Bomonti attracts both local and international artists.

- **Location:** Merkez Mahallesi, Silahsor Cd. No:1, Bomonti, Şişli, Istanbul
- **Opening Hours:** Varies based on event schedule
- **Phone Number:** +90 212 334 01 00

Nardis Jazz Club

Situated in the heart of Istanbul's vibrant Beyoğlu district, Nardis Jazz Club is a cozy and intimate venue dedicated to jazz enthusiasts. Featuring performances by talented local and international jazz artists, Nardis offers an authentic jazz club atmosphere with a well-curated selection of drinks. The club's small size ensures an up-close experience with the musicians, making it a favorite among jazz lovers.

- **Location:** Kuledibi Sokak No:14, Galata, Beyoğlu, Istanbul
- **Opening Hours:** Daily from 20:00 onwards
- **Phone Number:** +90 212 244 63 27

Babylon Çeşme

Babylon Çeşme, located in the popular coastal town of Çeşme, offers a unique summer concert experience. Set in a beautiful garden setting, this venue hosts a variety of live music events ranging from rock and pop to electronic music. Babylon Çeşme is known for its relaxed vibe and stunning outdoor stage, making it a perfect spot to enjoy live music under the stars.

- **Location:** Dalyan Mah. 3436 Sokak No:3, Çeşme, İzmir
- **Opening Hours:** Varies based on event schedule
- **Phone Number:** +90 232 712 00 36

IF Performance Hall

IF Performance Hall in Beşiktaş is a popular choice for live music enthusiasts seeking a dynamic atmosphere. Known for its diverse lineup of concerts featuring Turkish and international artists, IF Performance Hall offers an energetic setting with impressive acoustics. The venue's central location and modern facilities make it a go-to spot for both music lovers and performers.

- **Location:** Yıldız Posta Cad. No: 50/1, Beşiktaş, Istanbul
- **Opening Hours:** Varies based on event schedule
- **Phone Number:** +90 212 327 70 70

Jolly Joker Istanbul

Jolly Joker Istanbul, located in the heart of Beyoğlu, is a prominent venue known for its lively atmosphere and diverse music lineup. From rock and pop to blues and electronic, Jolly Joker hosts both renowned international acts and emerging local bands. The venue's spacious layout and state-of-the-art sound system ensure an unforgettable concert experience.

- **Location:** Balo Sokak No: 22, Beyoğlu, Istanbul
- **Opening Hours:** Varies based on event schedule
- **Phone Number:** +90 212 249 73 93

Salon İKSV

Salon İKSV, part of the Istanbul Foundation for Culture and Arts (İKSV), is a cultural hub located near Taksim Square. Known for its eclectic programming, Salon İKSV hosts a wide range of live music performances including indie, alternative, and experimental music. The venue's intimate setting and commitment to artistic diversity attract music aficionados seeking unique and innovative sounds.

- **Location:** Nejat Eczacıbaşı Binası, Sadi Konuralp Caddesi No:5, Şişhane, Istanbul
- **Opening Hours:** Varies based on event schedule
- **Phone Number:** +90 212 334 07 00

Kadıköy Sahne

Kadıköy Sahne, located in Istanbul's Kadıköy district, offers a cozy and welcoming space for live music enthusiasts. Known for its laid-back ambiance and community-oriented approach, Kadıköy Sahne hosts a variety of musical genres including folk, jazz, and Turkish rock. The venue's commitment to showcasing local talent makes it a beloved spot among Istanbul's music scene.

- **Location:** Osmanağa Mahallesi, Halitağa Cad. No: 25, Kadıköy, Istanbul
- **Opening Hours:** Varies based on event schedule
- **Phone Number:** +90 216 450 00 00

Zorlu PSM

Zorlu PSM (Performing Arts Center), located in the upscale Zorlu Center, is a multifaceted cultural complex that hosts a wide range of live music performances. From classical concerts and opera to contemporary music and jazz, Zorlu PSM offers diverse programming in a modern and sophisticated setting. The venue's state-of-the-art facilities and central location make it a premier destination for cultural events.

- **Location:** Koru Sokak No:2, Zincirlikuyu, Istanbul
- **Opening Hours:** Varies based on event schedule
- **Phone Number:** +90 212 924 01 28

Tamirane

Tamirane, located in Beşiktaş, is a stylish venue known for its vibrant nightlife and live music performances. Featuring a spacious indoor area and a cozy outdoor terrace, Tamirane hosts a variety of music events including live bands, DJs, and themed parties. The venue's trendy ambiance and eclectic music selection appeal to Istanbul's young and cosmopolitan crowd.

- **Location:** Akaretler Spor Cad. No: 43, Beşiktaş, Istanbul
- **Opening Hours:** Varies based on event schedule
- **Phone Number:** +90 533 478 53 13

Babylon Aya Yorgi

Babylon Aya Yorgi, situated in the seaside village of Aya Yorgi near Çeşme, offers a picturesque setting for live music performances during the summer months. With its stunning views of the Aegean Sea and vibrant music scene, Babylon Aya Yorgi hosts an array of concerts featuring Turkish and international artists across various genres. The venue's relaxed atmosphere and seaside location make it a favorite among music lovers.

- **Location:** Aya Yorgi Mahallesi, 3133. Sokak, No:3, Çeşme, İzmir
- **Opening Hours:** Varies based on event schedule
- **Phone Number:** +90 232 712 00 36

Rooftop Bars and Scenic Views

Istanbul's skyline is breathtaking, and the city offers a variety of rooftop bars where you can enjoy stunning views along with delicious drinks.

360 Istanbul

Located in Beyoglu, 360 Istanbul offers panoramic views of the city skyline, including iconic landmarks like the Galata Tower and Bosphorus Bridge. The chic ambiance is complemented by a diverse menu of international cuisine and creative cocktails. It's perfect for both sunset and late-night outings, providing a lively atmosphere with DJs spinning tunes into the night.

- **Location:** Istiklal Avenue, Misir Apartment, No: 163, Beyoglu
- **Opening Hours:** Daily from 5:00 PM to 2:00 AM
- **Phone Number:** +90 212 251 1042

Leb-i Derya

Perched atop the Richmond Hotel in Beyoglu, Leb-i Derya offers breathtaking views of the Golden Horn and historical peninsula. The menu features Mediterranean-inspired dishes, while the bar serves an array of wines and signature cocktails. The ambiance is sophisticated yet relaxed, making it ideal for romantic evenings or casual gatherings with friends.

- **Location:** Istiklal Avenue, Misir Apartment, No: 163, Beyoglu
- **Opening Hours:** Daily from 12:00 PM to 2:00 AM
- **Phone Number:** +90 212 293 4989

Mikla

Situated on the rooftop of the Marmara Pera Hotel, Mikla offers stunning views of Istanbul's skyline and the Bosphorus. Renowned chef Mehmet Gürs combines Turkish and Scandinavian influences in the menu, complemented by an extensive wine list. The ambiance is sophisticated with a minimalist design, perfect for a memorable dining experience.

- **Location:** Meşrutiyet Caddesi, Beyoğlu
- **Opening Hours:** Daily from 6:00 PM to 2:00 AM
- **Phone Number:** +90 212 293 5656

Nu Teras

Located in Galata, Nu Teras offers panoramic views of the Golden Horn and the Galata Tower.

The terrace is adorned with cozy seating areas surrounded by greenery, creating a tranquil atmosphere. The menu features Mediterranean cuisine with a Turkish twist, alongside a variety of refreshing cocktails and wines.

- **Location:** Sofyalı Sokak No: 1/1, Beyoğlu
- **Opening Hours:** Daily from 12:00 PM to 2:00 AM
- **Phone Number**: +90 212 252 4747

Anjelique

Situated in Ortakoy, Anjelique boasts breathtaking views of the Bosphorus Bridge and the Old City. The venue offers a blend of restaurant, bar, and nightclub experiences with a focus on seafood and international cuisine. The modern design and lively atmosphere make it a popular spot for both dining and nightlife.

- **Location:** Muallim Naci Caddesi Salhane Sokak No: 5, Ortakoy
- **Opening Hours:** Daily from 6:00 PM to 4:00 AM
- **Phone Number:** +90 212 327 2844

Babylon Bomonti

Located in Bomonti, Babylon offers panoramic views of Istanbul's skyline, with a terrace that hosts live music performances and DJ sets. The menu features a fusion of Mediterranean and international flavors, accompanied by a diverse selection of cocktails and craft beers. The vibrant atmosphere makes it a popular spot among locals and tourists alike.

- **Location:** Bomontiada, Birahane Sokak No: 1, Bomonti
- **Opening Hours:** Daily from 6:00 PM to 2:00 AM
- **Phone Number:** +90 212 334 0100

Lavazza Espression

Situated on Istiklal Avenue, Lavazza Espression offers stunning views of the historic peninsula and Galata Tower. The rooftop cafe specializes in gourmet coffee and Italian cuisine, with a relaxed ambiance ideal for enjoying both day and night views of the city.

- **Location:** Istiklal Avenue, Misir Apartment, No: 163, Beyoglu
- **Opening Hours:** Daily from 8:00 AM to 10:00 PM
- **Phone Number:** +90 212 252 0956

Maiden's Tower

Floating in the Bosphorus, Maiden's Tower provides a unique perspective of Istanbul's skyline and the waterside. The venue serves as both a restaurant and a bar, offering seafood specialties and a variety of drinks. Accessible by boat, it's an excellent choice for a romantic dinner or a casual drink with spectacular views.

- **Location:** Salacak Mevkii, Üsküdar
- **Opening Hours:** Daily from 12:00 PM to 2:00 AM
- **Phone Number:** +90 216 342 4747

Flamingo Lounge

Located in Kurucesme, Flamingo Lounge offers panoramic views of the Bosphorus Bridge and the Asian side of Istanbul. The lounge features a modern design with comfortable seating, serving a menu of international cuisine and creative cocktails. Live DJ performances create a vibrant atmosphere, perfect for evening gatherings.

- **Location:** Muallim Naci Caddesi No: 16, Kurucesme
- **Opening Hours:** Daily from 6:00 PM to 4:00 AM
- **Phone Number:** +90 212 263 5606

The Marmara Pera

The rooftop terrace of The Marmara Pera offers stunning views of the Golden Horn and the historic peninsula. It features a stylish bar serving a variety of cocktails and beverages, making it an ideal spot for enjoying sunset views or evening drinks with friends.

- **Location:** Mesrutiyet Caddesi Tepebasi, Beyoglu
- **Opening Hours:** Daily from 5:00 PM to 1:00 AM
- **Phone Number:** +90 212 251 4646

Chapter 12: Outdoor Activities and Recreation

Parks and Gardens

Istanbul is home to numerous parks and gardens that offer lush green spaces, beautiful landscapes, and a serene escape from the bustling city. Here are some of the best parks and gardens to explore:

1. Emirgan Park

Emirgan Park is renowned for its stunning collection of tulips, making it a must-visit during the Istanbul Tulip Festival in April. Nestled along the Bosphorus, this historic park dates back to the Ottoman era and offers tranquil pathways, vibrant flower beds, and scenic views of the water. Its expansive green spaces and numerous picnic areas make it ideal for a relaxing day out.

- **Location:** Sarıyer, Istanbul
- **Best Time to Visit:** April during the Istanbul Tulip Festival
- **Opening Hours:** 24 hours; generally, the tulip gardens are accessible during daylight hours.

2. Gülhane Park

Gülhane Park is one of Istanbul's oldest and most picturesque parks, located adjacent to the Topkapi Palace. It offers a serene escape from the bustling city, featuring lush greenery, colorful flower beds, and historical landmarks like the Archaeology Museum. Visitors can relax by the fountain or stroll through its pathways lined with century-old trees.

- **Location:** Eminönü, Istanbul
- **Best Time to Visit:** Spring and early summer for blooming flowers
- **Opening Hours:** 9 AM to 7 PM (Varies slightly by season)

3. Yıldız Park

Yıldız Park is a tranquil oasis in the heart of Istanbul, known for its expansive woodlands, landscaped gardens, and picturesque views of the Bosphorus. Once part of the Ottoman imperial gardens, it offers shaded pathways, ornamental ponds, and secluded picnic spots. The park also houses historical pavilions and a charming café, making it a favorite among locals and tourists alike.

- **Location:** Beşiktaş, Istanbul
- **Best Time to Visit:** Spring and autumn for mild weather
- **Opening Hours:** 24 hours; main entrances are generally open from dawn to dusk.

4. Macka Park

Macka Park, centrally located near Nişantaşı, offers a peaceful retreat with its lush green lawns, jogging tracks, and children's playgrounds. The park is surrounded by upscale neighborhoods and is popular for its relaxing atmosphere and scenic views of the city skyline. Visitors can unwind amidst nature or enjoy a cup of Turkish tea at one of the park's charming cafés.

- **Location:** Şişli, Istanbul
- **Best Time to Visit:** Late spring and early autumn
- **Opening Hours:** 7 AM to 10 PM

5. Fenerbahçe Park

Fenerbahçe Park is a coastal park overlooking the Sea of Marmara, offering panoramic views of the Istanbul skyline and Princes' Islands. Known for its expansive green spaces, jogging paths, and seaside promenades, it's a favorite spot for both recreation and relaxation. The park also features sports facilities, playgrounds, and several cafés serving traditional Turkish cuisine.

- **Location:** Kadıköy, Istanbul
- **Best Time to Visit:** Summer evenings for cool sea breezes
- **Opening Hours:** 24 hours; facilities may have varying hours.

6. Belgrad Forest

Belgrad Forest is a vast natural reserve on Istanbul's European side, offering dense woodlands, scenic hiking trails, and tranquil picnic areas. Spanning over 5,000 hectares, it's a haven for nature lovers and outdoor enthusiasts seeking to escape the urban hustle. The forest also houses historical aqueducts and reservoirs, adding to its cultural significance.

- **Location:** Sarıyer, Istanbul
- **Best Time to Visit:** Spring and autumn for comfortable temperatures
- **Opening Hours:** 24 hours; trails and picnic areas accessible during daylight hours.

7. Miniaturk Park

Miniaturk Park is a unique attraction featuring miniature replicas of famous Turkish landmarks and historical sites from around the country. Located near the Golden Horn, it offers an educational and visually captivating experience, allowing visitors to explore Turkey's rich cultural heritage in a single park. The meticulously crafted models include iconic mosques, palaces, and ancient ruins.

- **Location:** Sütlüce, Istanbul
- **Best Time to Visit:** Year-round; weekdays for fewer crowds
- **Opening Hours:** 9 AM to 7 PM (Varies by season)

8. Ihlamur Pavilion and Gardens

Ihlamur Pavilion and its surrounding gardens are a serene retreat in the heart of Istanbul, known for their historical significance and lush greenery. The pavilions were once favored by Ottoman sultans for strolls and tea ceremonies, offering visitors a glimpse into Istanbul's imperial past. The gardens are meticulously landscaped, featuring blooming flowers and tranquil fountains.

- **Location:** Beşiktaş, Istanbul
- **Best Time to Visit:** Spring and early summer for blooming gardens
- **Opening Hours:** 9 AM to 6 PM (Closed Mondays)

9. Mihrabat Grove

Mihrabat Grove is a lesser-known gem located on the Asian side of Istanbul, offering panoramic views of the Bosphorus and the historic peninsula. This seaside park is ideal for picnics, jogging, and birdwatching, with its quiet pathways and shaded areas. Visitors can enjoy stunning sunset views over the water and explore nearby cafes and seafood restaurants.

- **Location:** Üsküdar, Istanbul
- **Best Time to Visit:** Late afternoon for sunset views
- **Opening Hours:** 24 hours; recommended during daylight hours.

10. Abdi Ipekci Park

Abdi Ipekci Park, named after a renowned Turkish athlete, is a vibrant urban park in the heart of Istanbul's bustling Nişantaşı district. It features landscaped gardens, modern sculptures, and a popular children's playground. The park hosts cultural events, outdoor concerts, and art exhibitions throughout the year, making it a lively hub for both locals and visitors.

- **Location:** Nişantaşı, Istanbul
- **Best Time to Visit:** Spring and summer for outdoor events
- **Opening Hours:** 7 AM to 10 PM

Bosphorus Cruise

A Bosphorus cruise is a must-do experience when visiting Istanbul, offering stunning views of the city's skyline, historic landmarks, and beautiful waterfront. Here are some top Bosphorus cruises with detailed descriptions and tour providers:

1. Bosphorus Full-Day Cruise with Lunch

This full-day Bosphorus cruise provides an immersive experience of Istanbul's waterways. The tour includes stops at key sites such as Rumeli Fortress and the charming village of Anadolu Kavagi. Enjoy a delicious Turkish lunch on board while taking in the panoramic views of the Bosphorus Strait. This comprehensive tour offers both sightseeing and cultural insights, making it ideal for first-time visitors.

- **Tour Provider:** Istanbul Clues
- **Location:** Eminönü, Istanbul
- **Duration:** 8 hours
- **Phone:** +90 212 518 68 44

2. Bosphorus Sunset Cruise

The Bosphorus Sunset Cruise is perfect for those who want to experience the magic of Istanbul at dusk. As the sun sets over the city, passengers can enjoy breathtaking views of iconic landmarks such as the Maiden's Tower, Dolmabahçe Palace, and the Bosphorus Bridge illuminated against the evening sky. This cruise offers a romantic and serene atmosphere, complemented by light snacks and drinks served on board.

- **Tour Provider:** Istanbul Welcome Card
- **Location:** Kabataş, Istanbul
- **Duration:** 2 hours
- **Phone:** +90 212 243 43 92

3. Private Bosphorus Yacht Tour

For a more personalized and luxurious experience, the Private Bosphorus Yacht Tour offers an exclusive journey along the Bosphorus. This customizable tour allows guests to explore the strait at their own pace, with stops at various landmarks and attractions. The private yacht comes with a professional crew, ensuring a comfortable and memorable cruise. This option is ideal for special occasions or intimate gatherings.

- **Tour Provider:** Zoe Yacht Bosphorus Cruises
- **Location:** Bebek, Istanbul
- **Duration:** 2-3 hours
- **Phone:** +90 532 777 02 64

4. Bosphorus Dinner Cruise

The Bosphorus Dinner Cruise combines sightseeing with a delightful dining experience. Passengers can enjoy a gourmet Turkish meal while cruising past illuminated landmarks such as the Blue Mosque, Hagia Sophia, and the Bosphorus Bridge. The cruise also features live entertainment, including traditional Turkish music and dance performances, providing a lively and cultural evening on the water.

- **Tour Provider:** Bosphorus Tours Istanbul
- **Location:** Eminönü, Istanbul
- **Duration:** 3-4 hours

- **Phone:** +90 212 528 13 80

5. Short Bosphorus Cruise

Ideal for those with limited time, the Short Bosphorus Cruise offers a quick yet comprehensive tour of the strait. This 90-minute cruise provides views of major attractions such as the Topkapi Palace, Ortaköy Mosque, and the Rumeli Fortress. The tour is guided, offering insightful commentary on the history and significance of the sights along the Bosphorus.

- **Tour Provider:** Turyol
- **Location:** Eminönü, Istanbul
- **Duration:** 1.5 hours
- **Phone:** +90 212 512 25 61

6. Bosphorus Cruise and Golden Horn Tour

This combination tour includes a cruise along the Bosphorus as well as a tour of the Golden Horn. The tour covers historical sites such as the Eyüp Sultan Mosque and Pierre Loti Hill, providing a comprehensive look at Istanbul's rich history and stunning landscapes. The cruise offers a unique perspective of both the Bosphorus and the Golden Horn, making it a well-rounded experience.

- **Tour Provider:** Şehir Hatları
- **Location:** Eminönü, Istanbul
- **Duration:** 4 hours
- **Phone:** +90 212 444 18 36

7. Afternoon Bosphorus Cruise

The Afternoon Bosphorus Cruise offers a relaxing and scenic journey along the Bosphorus during the day. Passengers can enjoy views of Istanbul's palaces, mosques, and mansions while sipping on tea or coffee served on board. The cruise provides a peaceful and leisurely way to explore the strait, making it suitable for families and those looking to unwind.

- **Tour Provider:** Dentur Avrasya
- **Location:** Kabataş, Istanbul
- **Duration:** 2 hours
- **Phone:** +90 212 254 28 15

8. Bosphorus Strait and Black Sea Cruise

This extended cruise takes passengers from the Bosphorus Strait to the Black Sea, offering a unique and diverse experience. The tour includes stops at the picturesque village of Anadolu Kavagi and the ancient castle of Yoros. Passengers can enjoy lunch on board while taking in the beautiful scenery of the Bosphorus and the Black Sea coast.

- **Tour Provider:** Bosphorus Cruise Tours
- **Location:** Kabataş, Istanbul
- **Duration:** 6 hours
- **Phone:** +90 212 225 76 65

9. Bosphorus by Night Cruise

The Bosphorus by Night Cruise offers a unique and enchanting view of Istanbul's illuminated skyline. The cruise provides views of key landmarks such as the Bosphorus Bridge, the Ortaköy Mosque, and the Maiden's Tower. With the city lights reflecting on the water, this cruise offers a magical and memorable experience for all passengers.

- **Tour Provider:** Istanbul Bosphorus Tours
- **Location:** Eminönü, Istanbul
- **Duration:** 2 hours
- **Phone:** +90 212 512 25 96

10. Hop-On Hop-Off Bosphorus Tour

The Hop-On Hop-Off Bosphorus Tour allows passengers to explore the Bosphorus at their own pace. With multiple stops along the strait, passengers can disembark to visit attractions such as the Dolmabahçe Palace, Ortaköy, and the Rumeli Fortress. This flexible tour is ideal for those who want to explore the Bosphorus and its surroundings in more detail.

- **Tour Provider:** Şehir Hatları
- **Location:** Eminönü, Istanbul
- **Duration:** Varies
- **Phone:** +90 212 444 18 36

These Bosphorus cruises provide diverse experiences, from romantic sunset views to cultural dinner cruises, ensuring that visitors can find the perfect way to explore the stunning waterways of Istanbul.

Beaches and Swimming Spots

Istanbul, a city known for its rich history and vibrant culture, also offers several beaches and swimming spots perfect for a refreshing dip. Here are some of the best beaches and swimming spots in Istanbul:

1. Florya Güneş Beach

Florya Güneş Beach is a popular spot on the European side of Istanbul. It features a long stretch of sandy shore along the Sea of Marmara, offering a pleasant escape from the city's hustle and bustle. The beach is well-maintained and provides a range of amenities, including sun loungers, umbrellas, showers, and changing rooms. The shallow waters make it suitable for families with children. There are also several cafes and restaurants nearby where visitors can enjoy a meal or a drink while taking in the sea view.

- **Location:** Florya, Bakırköy
- **Season:** May to September
- **Facilities:** Sun loungers, umbrellas, showers, changing rooms, cafes, and restaurants

2. Kilyos Solar Beach

Kilyos Solar Beach is located on the Black Sea coast, north of Istanbul. Known for its vibrant atmosphere, it is one of the largest beaches in the area, offering a wide range of activities including water sports, beach volleyball, and live music events. The beach is well-equipped with sun loungers, umbrellas, showers, and changing rooms. There are also several bars and restaurants where visitors can relax and enjoy refreshments. The beach is popular among young people and is a great spot for both relaxation and entertainment.

- **Location:** Kilyos, Sarıyer
- **Season:** May to October
- **Facilities:** Sun loungers, umbrellas, showers, changing rooms, water sports, beach volleyball, bars, and restaurants

3. Suma Beach

Suma Beach, also located in Kilyos, is a trendy beach club that attracts a young and lively crowd. It features a spacious sandy beach with comfortable sun loungers and umbrellas. The beach club offers various activities such as yoga, beach volleyball, and water sports. There is also a lively nightlife scene with DJ performances and beach parties. The beach's relaxed and fun atmosphere makes it a popular choice for both daytime relaxation and nighttime entertainment.

- **Location:** Kilyos, Sarıyer
- **Season:** May to September
- **Facilities:** Sun loungers, umbrellas, showers, changing rooms, yoga, beach volleyball, water sports, DJ performances, bars, and restaurants

4. Büyükada Beach

Büyükada Beach is located on Büyükada, the largest of the Princes' Islands. The beach offers a peaceful and scenic environment, far from the noise of the city. Visitors can enjoy clear waters and beautiful views of the surrounding islands. The beach is equipped with sun loungers, umbrellas, and showers. There are also several cafes and restaurants nearby. To reach Büyükada, visitors need to take a ferry from the mainland, adding to the adventure of the trip.

- **Location:** Büyükada, Princes' Islands
- **Season:** June to September
- **Facilities:** Sun loungers, umbrellas, showers, cafes, and restaurants

5. Caddebostan Beach

Caddebostan Beach is a popular urban beach on the Asian side of Istanbul. It features a long stretch of sandy shore along the Sea of Marmara, providing a convenient and accessible escape for city dwellers. The beach is well-maintained and offers amenities such as sun loungers, umbrellas, showers, and changing rooms. There are also several parks and green areas nearby, making it a great spot for a family day out. The beach's proximity to the city center makes it a favorite among locals.

- **Location:** Caddebostan, Kadıköy
- **Season:** May to September
- **Facilities:** Sun loungers, umbrellas, showers, changing rooms, cafes, and restaurants

6. Ağva Beach

Ağva Beach is located in the picturesque town of Ağva, known for its beautiful rivers and serene environment. The beach features fine sand and clear waters, ideal for swimming and sunbathing. Visitors can also explore the surrounding nature, including the nearby rivers and forests. The beach is equipped with sun loungers, umbrellas, showers, and changing rooms. There are also several small cafes and restaurants offering local cuisine. Ağva Beach is perfect for a peaceful and relaxing getaway.

- **Location:** Ağva, Şile
- **Season:** June to September
- **Facilities:** Sun loungers, umbrellas, showers, changing rooms, cafes, and restaurants

7. Burc Beach

Burc Beach, operated by Boğaziçi University, is another popular beach in Kilyos. It features a long sandy shore with clear waters, making it perfect for swimming and sunbathing. The beach offers various facilities including sun loungers, umbrellas, showers, and changing rooms. There are also several activities available, such as beach volleyball, windsurfing, and kitesurfing. The lively atmosphere and range of amenities make Burc Beach a favorite among students and young people.

- **Location:** Kilyos, Sarıyer
- **Season:** May to September
- **Facilities:** Sun loungers, umbrellas, showers, changing rooms, beach volleyball, windsurfing, kitesurfing, cafes, and restaurants

8. Heybeliada Beach

Heybeliada Beach is located on Heybeliada, one of the Princes' Islands. The beach offers a tranquil setting with beautiful views of the Sea of Marmara. Visitors can enjoy swimming in clear waters and relaxing on the sandy shore. The beach is equipped with sun loungers, umbrellas, showers, and changing rooms. There are also several cafes and restaurants nearby, offering a range of food and drinks. The island's peaceful environment makes Heybeliada Beach a perfect spot for a relaxing day out.

- **Location:** Heybeliada, Princes' Islands
- **Season:** June to September
- **Facilities:** Sun loungers, umbrellas, showers, changing rooms, cafes, and restaurants

9. Şile Beach

Şile Beach is a long, sandy beach located on the Black Sea coast. Known for its clean waters and natural beauty, it is a popular destination for both locals and tourists. The beach is well-maintained and offers facilities such as sun loungers, umbrellas, showers, and changing rooms. There are also several cafes and restaurants where visitors can enjoy local seafood and other delicacies. The scenic environment and relaxed atmosphere make Şile Beach a great place for a peaceful day by the sea.

- **Location:** Şile, Istanbul
- **Season:** June to September
- **Facilities:** Sun loungers, umbrellas, showers, changing rooms, cafes, and restaurants

10. Uzunya Beach

Uzunya Beach is a secluded spot located in the Demirciköy area of Sarıyer. This hidden gem offers a quiet and serene environment, away from the crowded city beaches. The beach features fine sand and clear waters, perfect for swimming and relaxing. Facilities include sun loungers, umbrellas, showers, and changing rooms. There is also a beachside restaurant serving delicious seafood and other local dishes. The natural beauty and tranquility of Uzunya Beach make it an ideal location for a peaceful getaway.

- **Location:** Demirciköy, Sarıyer
- **Season:** June to September
- **Facilities:** Sun loungers, umbrellas, showers, changing rooms, restaurant

Chapter 13: Istanbul with Families

Parks, Playgrounds and Outdoor Spaces

Here are some of the best family-friendly parks and playgrounds in Istanbul:

1. Emirgan Park

Emirgan Park is one of Istanbul's oldest and largest public parks, offering stunning views of the Bosphorus. It spans over 117 acres and features beautiful landscaped gardens, walking paths, and three historic pavilions. The park is especially famous for its tulip festival in April, showcasing millions of tulips in various colors and designs. Children will enjoy the playgrounds scattered throughout the park, and families can have picnics in the designated areas.

- **Opening Hours:** 24 hours
- **Address:** Emirgan, 34467 Sarıyer/Istanbul
- **How to Get There:** Take the M2 metro line to Hacıosman and then a bus or taxi to Emirgan.
- **Insider Tip:** Visit in April to experience the spectacular tulip festival.

2. Yıldız Park

Yıldız Park, situated between Beşiktaş and Ortaköy, is a serene green space offering a peaceful escape from the city's hustle and bustle. The park covers a large area with beautiful landscapes, ponds, and historic Ottoman mansions. There are several playgrounds for children, as well as walking and jogging paths. The park also has designated picnic areas and cafes where you can relax and enjoy the surroundings.

- **Opening Hours:** 24 hours
- **Address:** Yıldız, 34349 Beşiktaş/Istanbul
- **How to Get There:** Take a bus to Beşiktaş from various parts of the city and walk to the park.
- **Insider Tip:** Visit the historic Yıldız Palace Museum within the park for an added cultural experience.

3. Maçka Park

Maçka Park, located in the heart of Istanbul, offers a lush green space for relaxation and recreation. The park is popular for its walking and jogging paths, dog park, and playgrounds.

It also features beautiful gardens, fountains, and an aerial cable car that provides stunning views of the Bosphorus. The park is a great place for a family day out, with plenty of open spaces for picnics and outdoor activities.

- **Opening Hours:** 24 hours
- **Address:** Maçka, 34367 Şişli/Istanbul
- **How to Get There:** Take the M2 metro line to Osmanbey and walk to the park.
- **Insider Tip:** Ride the cable car for a unique perspective of the city.

4. Fenerbahçe Park

Fenerbahçe Park is a charming seaside park located on the Asian side of Istanbul. It offers beautiful walking paths, lush greenery, and stunning views of the Sea of Marmara. The park has several playgrounds for children, as well as picnic areas and cafes. It's a popular spot for families to spend the day, especially during weekends. The peaceful ambiance and scenic beauty make it a favorite among locals.

- **Opening Hours:** 24 hours
- **Address:** Fenerbahçe, 34726 Kadıköy/Istanbul
- **How to Get There:** Take the M4 metro line to Kadıköy and then a bus or taxi to the park.
- **Insider Tip:** Visit the park in the early morning for a tranquil experience.

5. Bebek Park

Bebek Park, located in the upscale neighborhood of Bebek, is a beautiful seaside park along the Bosphorus. The park features well-maintained gardens, playgrounds, and walking paths. It's a popular spot for families, joggers, and those looking to enjoy the scenic views of the Bosphorus. The park also has cafes and restaurants nearby, making it a perfect place for a leisurely day out.

- **Opening Hours:** 24 hours
- **Address:** Bebek, 34342 Beşiktaş/Istanbul
- **How to Get There:** Take a bus to Bebek from various parts of the city.
- **Insider Tip:** Enjoy a coffee at one of the nearby cafes while overlooking the Bosphorus.

6. Gülhane Park

Gülhane Park, located near the Topkapi Palace, is one of Istanbul's oldest and most historic parks. The park offers beautiful gardens, walking paths, and playgrounds for children. It's a perfect spot for a stroll or a family picnic. The park also houses the Istanbul Museum of the History of Science and Technology in Islam. Gülhane Park provides a peaceful retreat in the heart of the city, with plenty of open spaces and scenic beauty.

- **Opening Hours:** 6:00 AM - 10:30 PM
- **Address:** Cankurtaran, 34122 Fatih/Istanbul
- **How to Get There:** Take the T1 tram line to Gülhane station.
- **Insider Tip:** Visit early in the morning to enjoy the park's tranquility before the crowds arrive.

7. Atatürk Arboretum

Atatürk Arboretum, located in the Sarıyer district, is a beautiful botanical garden and arboretum. The park features a wide variety of trees, plants, and flowers, making it a perfect place for nature lovers. There are several walking paths and small lakes, providing a serene environment for a relaxing day out. The arboretum is also a popular spot for photography enthusiasts.

- **Opening Hours:** 8:30 AM - 5:00 PM (Closed on Mondays)
- **Address:** Bahçeköy, 34473 Sarıyer/Istanbul
- **How to Get There:** Take the M2 metro line to Hacıosman and then a bus or taxi to the arboretum.
- **Admission Fee:** $2 for adults, $1 for students
- **Insider Tip:** Bring a camera to capture the stunning natural beauty and diverse plant life.

8. Nezahat Gökyiğit Botanical Garden

Nezahat Gökyiğit Botanical Garden, located in the Ataşehir district, is a peaceful oasis in the city. The garden features a wide variety of plants, flowers, and themed sections, including a Japanese garden and a medicinal plant garden. There are several walking paths and playgrounds for children, making it a great spot for a family day out. The garden also offers educational programs and workshops.

- **Opening Hours:** 9:30 AM - 6:00 PM (Closed on Mondays)

- **Address:** Barbaros, 34746 Ataşehir/Istanbul
- **How to Get There:** Take the M4 metro line to Kozyatağı and then a bus or taxi to the garden.
- **Insider Tip:** Check the garden's website for information on workshops and guided tours.

9. Belgrad Forest

Belgrad Forest, located in the Sarıyer district, is a large forested area offering a variety of outdoor activities. The forest features several walking and jogging trails, picnic areas, and playgrounds. It's a popular spot for nature lovers, hikers, and families looking to escape the city's hustle and bustle. The forest also has several ponds and a rich variety of flora and fauna.

- **Opening Hours:** 24 hours
- **Address:** Bahçeköy, 34473 Sarıyer/Istanbul
- **How to Get There:** Take the M2 metro line to Hacıosman and then a bus or taxi to the forest.
- **Insider Tip:** Visit during weekdays to avoid the weekend crowds and enjoy a peaceful hike.

10. Moda Park

Moda Park, located in the Moda neighborhood of Kadıköy, is a popular seaside park offering beautiful views of the Sea of Marmara. The park features walking paths, playgrounds, and picnic areas. It's a great spot for a family outing, with plenty of open spaces for children to play. The park is also a popular spot for locals to enjoy the sunset and the scenic views.

- **Opening Hours:** 24 hours
- **Address:** Moda, 34710 Kadıköy/Istanbul
- **How to Get There:** Take the M4 metro line to Kadıköy and then a bus or walk to the park.
- **Insider Tip:** Visit in the late afternoon to enjoy the stunning sunset views over the Sea of Marmara.

Kid-Friendly Museums

Istanbul offers a variety of kid-friendly museums that blend education and fun, making them perfect for family visits. Here are some of the best options:

1. Istanbul Toy Museum

Istanbul Toy Museum, founded by Turkish poet and novelist Sunay Akın, showcases a vast collection of toys from different eras and countries. The museum offers an enchanting journey through the history of toys, featuring items that will delight both children and adults. The collection includes antique dolls, tin toys, and toy trains, making it a captivating experience for kids. The museum also hosts creative workshops and educational programs.

- **Opening Hours:** 9:30 AM - 6:00 PM (Tue-Sun)
- **Address:** Ömerpaşa Caddesi Dr. Zeki Zeren Sokak No:17, Göztepe, Kadıköy
- **How to Get There:** Take the Marmaray to Göztepe station and walk for 10 minutes.
- **Admission Fee:** $5 (Adults), $3 (Children)
- **Insider Tip:** Visit the museum on weekdays to avoid the weekend crowds.

2. Rahmi M. Koç Museum

Rahmi M. Koç Museum is a fascinating industrial museum located along the Golden Horn. It offers a wide range of exhibits on transportation, industry, and communications, including vintage cars, submarines, and airplanes. Kids can enjoy interactive displays, a ride on a vintage train, and even explore a real submarine. The museum's diverse exhibits make it an educational and engaging experience for children of all ages.

- **Opening Hours:** 10:00 AM - 5:30 PM (Tue-Fri), 10:00 AM - 6:30 PM (Sat-Sun)
- **Address:** Hasköy Cad. No: 5, Hasköy, Beyoğlu
- **How to Get There:** Take the bus to Hasköy or the ferry to Hasköy Pier.
- **Admission Fee:** $7 (Adults), $4 (Children)
- **Insider Tip:** Don't miss the mini train ride and the submarine tour for an extra special experience.

3. Istanbul Aquarium

Istanbul Aquarium, one of the largest thematic aquariums in the world, offers a mesmerizing underwater journey. It features various thematic zones representing different seas and regions, from the Black Sea to the Pacific Ocean. Kids will love the interactive exhibits, the rainforest area, and the opportunity to see sharks, rays, and other marine creatures up close. The aquarium also has a 5D cinema and a souvenir shop.

- **Opening Hours:** 10:00 AM - 7:00 PM (Mon-Sun)
- **Address:** Şenlikköy Mahallesi, Yeşilköy Halkalı Cd. No:93, Florya, Bakırköy
- **How to Get There:** Take the Marmaray to Florya station and walk for 10 minutes.
- **Admission Fee**: $14 (Adults), $10 (Children)
- **Insider Tip:** Buy tickets online for discounts and shorter wait times.

4. Miniaturk

Miniaturk is a miniature park showcasing scaled-down models of Turkey's most famous landmarks and historical sites. The park is an excellent way for kids to learn about Turkey's rich history and culture in a fun and engaging way. The detailed miniatures include the Hagia Sophia, the Blue Mosque, and the ancient city of Ephesus. There is also a play area for children and a miniature railway.

- **Opening Hours:** 9:00 AM - 7:00 PM (Mon-Sun)
- **Address:** İmrahor Caddesi, Sütlüce, Beyoğlu
- **How to Get There**: Take the bus to Sütlüce or the ferry to Hasköy Pier.
- **Admission Fee:** $5 (Adults), $3 (Children)
- **Insider Tip:** Use the audio guide for interesting facts about each miniature.

5. Istanbul Modern

Istanbul Modern is Turkey's first museum of modern and contemporary art, offering a variety of exhibitions and educational programs. The museum has a dedicated children's section where kids can engage in art activities, workshops, and interactive exhibits. The diverse range of contemporary art pieces and installations provides an enriching cultural experience for young visitors.

- **Opening Hours**: 10:00 AM - 6:00 PM (Tue-Sun)
- **Address:** Asmalımescit Mahallesi, Meşrutiyet Caddesi No:99, Beyoğlu
- **How to Get There:** Take the metro to Şişhane station and walk for 5 minutes.
- **Admission Fee:** $7 (Adults), Free (Children under 12)
- **Insider Tip:** Check the museum's schedule for special kids' workshops and events.

6. Istanbul Sea Life Aquarium

Istanbul Sea Life Aquarium is home to over 15,000 sea creatures, including sharks, rays, and sea turtles. The aquarium features Europe's largest underwater tunnel, providing a unique and immersive experience. Kids can learn about marine life through interactive exhibits and touch pools where they can interact with starfish and other small creatures. The aquarium also offers educational programs and feeding shows.

- **Opening Hours:** 10:00 AM - 8:00 PM (Mon-Sun)
- **Address:** Forum Istanbul Shopping Mall, Kocatepe Mahallesi, Paşa Cd. No:5, Bayrampaşa
- **How to Get There:** Take the metro to Kocatepe station and walk for 5 minutes.
- **Admission Fee:** $14 (Adults), $10 (Children)
- **Insider Tip:** Arrive early to catch the feeding shows and avoid crowds.

7. Istanbul Aviation Museum

Istanbul Aviation Museum, also known as the Turkish Air Force Museum, offers an exciting glimpse into the history of aviation. The museum features a vast collection of aircraft, helicopters, and aviation equipment. Kids can explore the cockpits of old planes and learn about the development of aviation technology. The outdoor exhibition area allows children to see various aircraft up close, making it an educational and thrilling experience.

- **Opening Hours:** 9:00 AM - 4:30 PM (Tue-Sun)
- **Address:** Yeşilköy Mahallesi, Havaalanı Cd. No:17, Bakırköy
- **How to Get There:** Take the Marmaray to Yeşilköy station and walk for 15 minutes.
- **Admission Fee:** $5 (Adults), $3 (Children)
- **Insider Tip**: Bring a picnic to enjoy in the museum's outdoor area.

8. Madame Tussauds Istanbul

Madame Tussauds Istanbul offers an interactive experience where kids can meet lifelike wax figures of their favorite celebrities, historical figures, and characters. The museum features themed sections such as sports, music, history, and film, providing a fun and educational experience. Kids can pose with their favorite stars, learn about their achievements, and even participate in interactive exhibits.

- **Opening Hours:** 10:00 AM - 8:00 PM (Mon-Sun)
- **Address:** Grand Pera, İstiklal Caddesi No:56, Beyoğlu

- **How to Get There:** Take the metro to Taksim station and walk for 5 minutes.
- **Admission Fee:** $14 (Adults), $10 (Children)
- **Insider Tip:** Combine your visit with a trip to the nearby Istanbul Modern for a full day of fun and culture.

9. Istanbul Naval Museum

Istanbul Naval Museum, located in Beşiktaş, is one of the largest maritime museums in Turkey. It features a rich collection of artifacts related to the Ottoman Navy and Turkish maritime history, including ship models, naval uniforms, and historical documents. Kids will be fascinated by the impressive collection of imperial caiques (royal boats) and the grand hall displaying full-sized ships. The museum offers educational programs and interactive exhibits.

- **Opening Hours:** 9:00 AM - 5:00 PM (Tue-Sun)
- **Address:** Sinanpaşa Mahallesi, Beşiktaş Cd. No:6, Beşiktaş
- **How to Get There:** Take the bus to Beşiktaş or the ferry to Beşiktaş Pier.
- **Admission Fee:** $7 (Adults), $4 (Children)
- **Insider Tip:** Check the schedule for special exhibitions and educational workshops for kids.

10. Istanbul Planetarium

Istanbul Planetarium, located within the Istanbul Science and Technology Museum, offers an immersive astronomical experience. Kids can enjoy star shows, educational films, and interactive exhibits about space and the universe. The planetarium features a state-of-the-art dome theater that provides a 360-degree viewing experience. It's an excellent place for children to learn about astronomy and science in a fun and engaging way.

- **Opening Hours:** 10:00 AM - 5:00 PM (Tue-Sun)
- **Address:** Demirkapı Cd. No:2, Fatih
- **How to Get There:** Take the tram to Aksaray station and walk for 10 minutes.
- **Admission Fee:** $7 (Adults), $4 (Children)
- **Insider Tip:** Visit the museum's other science exhibits for a comprehensive educational experience.

Chapter 14: Health and Wellness

Spas and Wellness Centers

1. Çırağan Palace Kempinski Spa

Nestled within the luxurious Çırağan Palace Kempinski, this spa offers a regal experience in a historical setting by the Bosphorus. The spa features an extensive menu of treatments, including traditional Turkish hammam rituals, rejuvenating facials, and therapeutic massages. Guests can enjoy the serene ambiance of the indoor pool or relax in the steam rooms and saunas. The private suites offer a secluded space for couples or individuals seeking a more intimate experience. The spa's use of high-quality products and its attention to detail ensure a pampering experience that leaves guests feeling revitalized.

2. Ayasofya Hurrem Sultan Hamamı

Located in a historic building near the Hagia Sophia, Ayasofya Hurrem Sultan Hamamı is a meticulously restored 16th-century bathhouse commissioned by Sultan Suleiman the Magnificent for his wife, Roxelana. The hammam offers an authentic Turkish bath experience with traditional scrubbing, foam massages, and aromatherapy. The marble-clad interiors and historical ambiance provide a unique and immersive experience. The spa also features a tea lounge where guests can relax with a cup of Turkish tea after their treatments, further enhancing the sense of tranquility and rejuvenation.

3. Raffles Istanbul Spa

The Raffles Spa at the Raffles Istanbul offers a sanctuary of calm amidst the bustling city. The spa's design blends modern luxury with traditional Ottoman elements, creating a serene environment. Guests can indulge in a variety of treatments, including signature massages, anti-aging facials, and holistic wellness therapies. The spa also features a state-of-the-art fitness center, yoga studios, and an indoor pool with stunning city views. Personalized wellness programs and the use of premium skincare products ensure a tailored and luxurious spa experience that caters to individual needs.

4. The Ritz-Carlton Spa

Situated in the heart of Istanbul, The Ritz-Carlton Spa offers a luxurious retreat with a focus on holistic wellness. The spa features an array of treatments inspired by local traditions and global practices, including hot stone massages, revitalizing body scrubs, and detoxifying facials. The facilities include a serene indoor pool, relaxation lounges, and private treatment rooms with breathtaking views of the Bosphorus. The spa's skilled therapists use premium products and techniques to provide a rejuvenating experience that balances the body, mind, and spirit.

5. Four Seasons Hotel Istanbul at Sultanahmet Spa

This intimate spa located within the historic Four Seasons Hotel at Sultanahmet offers a luxurious escape with a focus on personalized service. The spa features a range of treatments, including deep tissue massages, revitalizing facials, and traditional Turkish hammam rituals. The beautifully designed treatment rooms provide a tranquil setting, and the use of high-quality products ensures a pampering experience. The spa also offers wellness consultations and bespoke treatment plans to address individual needs, enhancing the overall sense of well-being and relaxation.

6. Pürovel Spa & Sport at Swissôtel The Bosphorus

Pürovel Spa & Sport offers a holistic wellness experience with a focus on natural and organic treatments. The spa's facilities include an indoor pool, saunas, steam rooms, and a fitness center equipped with the latest technology. Guests can choose from a variety of treatments, such as invigorating massages, hydrating facials, and detoxifying body wraps. The spa's serene ambiance and expert therapists ensure a rejuvenating experience that promotes relaxation and well-being. The panoramic views of the Bosphorus from the spa add to the overall sense of tranquility.

7. Sanitas Spa at the Hyatt Regency Istanbul Ataköy

Sanitas Spa offers a serene and luxurious environment for relaxation and rejuvenation. The spa's extensive menu of treatments includes therapeutic massages, revitalizing facials, and traditional Turkish hammam rituals. The facilities feature an indoor pool, saunas, steam rooms, and a fully equipped fitness center. Guests can enjoy the tranquil ambiance and the expertise of the spa's therapists, who use high-quality products to ensure a pampering experience. The spa's focus on holistic wellness and personalized service makes it a perfect retreat for those seeking relaxation and rejuvenation.

8. The Spa at Mandarin Oriental Bosphorus

The Spa at Mandarin Oriental Bosphorus offers a luxurious retreat with a focus on holistic wellness and personalized service. The spa features a comprehensive menu of treatments, including signature massages, anti-aging facials, and traditional hammam rituals. The state-of-the-art facilities include a thermal suite, vitality pools, and relaxation lounges with stunning Bosphorus views. The spa's expert therapists use premium products and innovative techniques to provide a bespoke experience that promotes relaxation, rejuvenation, and overall well-being.

9. Nuspa at The St. Regis Istanbul

Nuspa at The St. Regis Istanbul offers a luxurious and contemporary spa experience with a focus on personalized wellness. The spa's facilities include an indoor pool, relaxation lounges, and private treatment rooms with modern design elements. Guests can choose from a variety of treatments, such as deep tissue massages, hydrating facials, and detoxifying body wraps. The spa's skilled therapists use premium products and techniques to provide a bespoke experience that caters to individual needs. The tranquil ambiance and attention to detail ensure a rejuvenating and relaxing experience.

10. The SPA at Marti Istanbul Hotel

The SPA at Marti Istanbul Hotel offers a luxurious and tranquil retreat with a focus on holistic wellness. The spa features a range of treatments, including therapeutic massages, revitalizing facials, and traditional Turkish hammam rituals. The facilities include an indoor pool, saunas, steam rooms, and a fully equipped fitness center. Guests can enjoy the serene ambiance and the expertise of the spa's therapists, who use high-quality products to ensure a pampering experience. The spa's focus on personalized service and attention to detail makes it a perfect retreat for relaxation and rejuvenation.

Turkish Baths and Hammams

1. Çemberlitaş Hamamı

Located in the historic heart of Istanbul, Çemberlitaş Hamamı is a quintessential Ottoman bath designed by the famed architect Mimar Sinan in 1584. This hammam is a perfect blend of tradition and modernity, with its stunning central dome, elegant marble interiors, and intricate tilework. Visitors can indulge in the traditional scrub and foam massage in separate sections for men and women. The ambiance is steeped in history, offering a serene escape from the bustling city outside. The services include a variety of massages, skin treatments, and relaxing lounges where guests can unwind post-treatment, savoring Turkish tea or refreshments.

2. Ayasofya Hurrem Sultan Hamamı

Nestled between Hagia Sophia and the Blue Mosque, Ayasofya Hurrem Sultan Hamamı is an opulent bathhouse commissioned by Sultan Suleiman the Magnificent for his beloved wife, Hurrem Sultan. This hammam exudes luxury with its exquisite marble, gold-accented fixtures, and plush interiors. The services are top-notch, featuring traditional scrubs, aromatic oil massages, and a range of skincare treatments. The atmosphere is one of refined elegance, offering an unparalleled relaxation experience amidst the historical grandeur. Each visitor is treated like royalty, reflecting the hammam's rich heritage and attention to detail.

3. Süleymaniye Hamamı

Built by Mimar Sinan in 1557, Süleymaniye Hamamı is part of the grand Süleymaniye Mosque complex. It stands as a testament to Ottoman architectural prowess with its large domed ceiling, intricate tilework, and spacious marble platforms. This hammam is unique as it offers a mixed bathing experience, ideal for couples and families. The traditional scrubbing and foam massages are complemented by a variety of additional services, such as clay masks and aromatherapy, making it a comprehensive wellness destination. The ambiance is both historic and welcoming, providing a genuine insight into Ottoman bathing culture.

4. Kılıç Ali Paşa Hamamı

Situated in the Tophane district, Kılıç Ali Paşa Hamamı was constructed by Mimar Sinan in the late 16th century for the Ottoman admiral Kılıç Ali Paşa. The hammam's stunning design includes a grand central dome, beautifully restored marble surfaces, and intricate details that reflect its naval patron's heritage. The bathing experience is luxurious, featuring traditional services like the kese (scrub) and köpük (foam) massages, as well as modern spa treatments.

The setting is serene and elegant, providing a tranquil haven where guests can experience centuries-old traditions in a meticulously preserved environment.

5. Cağaloğlu Hamamı

A favorite among locals and tourists alike, Cağaloğlu Hamamı is one of the last major hammams to be built in the Ottoman Empire, dating back to 1741. Located near the Grand Bazaar, this bathhouse features stunning Baroque architecture with lavish marble and intricate tile designs. The services include traditional scrubbing, foam massages, and various other treatments, such as aromatherapy and reflexology. The ambiance is one of grandeur and history, offering a unique blend of relaxation and cultural immersion. It's a perfect spot for those looking to experience a slice of Ottoman luxury and hospitality.

6. Galatasaray Hamamı

Located in the vibrant Beyoğlu district, Galatasaray Hamamı dates back to 1481, making it one of Istanbul's oldest hammams. It features a classic Ottoman design with a large central dome, marble basins, and a spacious hot room. The services offered include traditional kese and foam massages, along with a variety of other treatments like mud masks and aromatherapy. The atmosphere is lively and authentic, providing a true taste of Turkish bathing culture. Visitors can enjoy a relaxing and invigorating experience in a setting that has retained its historical charm and significance over the centuries.

7. Mihrimah Sultan Hamamı

Situated in the Edirnekapı neighborhood, Mihrimah Sultan Hamamı was built in the mid-16th century by Mimar Sinan for Mihrimah Sultan, the daughter of Sultan Suleiman the Magnificent. The hammam is renowned for its elegant design, featuring a central dome, marble interiors, and beautifully decorated ceilings. The services include traditional scrubbing and foam massages, as well as modern spa treatments. The ambiance is serene and regal, offering a peaceful retreat where guests can unwind and rejuvenate in a setting that reflects the grandeur of the Ottoman era. The hammam also features a range of skincare and beauty treatments, enhancing the overall experience.

8. Aziziye Hamamı

Located in the Kadıköy district on the Asian side of Istanbul, Aziziye Hamamı offers a blend of traditional Turkish bath services and contemporary spa treatments. This hammam features classic Ottoman architecture with a large dome, marble platforms, and a cozy, welcoming atmosphere. Services include the traditional kese and foam massages, along with modern treatments such as aromatherapy and reflexology. The setting is tranquil and elegant, providing a relaxing escape from the city's hustle and bustle. Guests can enjoy a range of treatments in a serene and beautifully designed environment, reflecting the rich bathing traditions of Istanbul.

9. Cinili Hamamı

Located in Üsküdar, Cinili Hamamı was constructed in 1640 by the order of Kösem Sultan, the influential mother of Sultan Murad IV. This hammam is named after its beautiful tiles (cinili) that adorn the interiors. The services include the traditional scrub and foam massage, along with various other treatments like aromatherapy and clay masks. The ambiance is historic and serene, providing a relaxing environment where guests can experience traditional Turkish bathing rituals. The beautifully tiled interiors and marble surfaces add to the overall charm, making it a popular choice for both locals and tourists.

10. Ağa Hamamı

Located in the Taksim area, Ağa Hamamı is one of the oldest Turkish baths in Istanbul, dating back to 1454. It was originally built as a private hammam for Fatih Sultan Mehmet and his sons. The hammam features a large central dome, marble basins, and traditional hot rooms. Services include the traditional scrub, foam massage, and various other treatments such as aromatherapy and mud masks. The atmosphere is authentic and welcoming, offering a unique glimpse into the rich history of Turkish bathing culture. Visitors can enjoy a relaxing and rejuvenating experience in a setting that has retained its historical charm and significance.

Yoga and Meditation Retreats

1. Kadikoy Yoga Shala

Located in the vibrant Kadikoy district, Kadikoy Yoga Shala offers serene retreats focused on yoga, meditation, and holistic wellness. Set amidst peaceful surroundings, their retreats combine daily yoga sessions with guided meditation practices. Accommodations are cozy and eco-friendly, promoting a sustainable lifestyle.

Participants can also enjoy organic meals and rejuvenating spa treatments, making it an ideal urban escape for those seeking inner balance and relaxation.

2. Anjali Yoga Istanbul

Anjali Yoga Istanbul, nestled in the heart of Beyoglu, offers transformative retreats blending yoga, meditation, and mindfulness practices. Their retreat programs cater to all levels, from beginners to advanced practitioners, focusing on alignment, breath work, and mental clarity. Participants stay in comfortable accommodations with access to communal spaces for reflection and relaxation. Healthy vegetarian meals are provided, enhancing the holistic experience aimed at fostering physical and spiritual well-being.

3. Istanbul Yoga Center

Istanbul Yoga Center, located near Taksim Square, hosts retreats that integrate yoga, meditation, and self-discovery workshops. Surrounded by the city's energy, this center offers a retreat oasis with daily yoga classes tailored to individual needs. Meditation sessions are complemented by lectures on mindfulness and stress reduction techniques. Accommodations are simple yet cozy, promoting a tranquil environment conducive to personal growth and inner peace.

4. Zen Yoga Istanbul

Zen Yoga Istanbul, situated in Nisantasi, offers immersive retreats designed to harmonize body, mind, and spirit. Their programs include dynamic yoga practices, guided meditation sessions, and healing therapies such as Reiki and aromatherapy. Accommodations are elegant and minimalist, providing a serene atmosphere for relaxation and introspection. Healthy meals are served, emphasizing organic and locally sourced ingredients, enhancing the holistic experience aimed at rejuvenation and self-discovery.

5. Yoga Şala Istanbul

Yoga Şala Istanbul, located in Levent, specializes in retreats that combine traditional yoga teachings with modern wellness practices. Their retreats emphasize mindful movement, deep relaxation techniques, and meditation sessions in a supportive community environment. Participants stay in comfortable accommodations with access to a tranquil garden and yoga studio. Nutritious vegetarian meals are served, promoting physical vitality and mental clarity, making it an ideal urban retreat for holistic rejuvenation.

6. Soulshine Istanbul

Soulshine Istanbul, nestled in Cihangir, offers transformative retreats blending yoga, meditation, and creative workshops. Their programs focus on inner exploration and personal growth through daily yoga sessions, guided meditations, and expressive arts therapies. Accommodations are stylish and cozy, featuring artistic decor and calming views of the city skyline. Participants enjoy nourishing meals prepared with organic ingredients, fostering a holistic experience aimed at renewal and self-expression.

7. Gaia Yoga Istanbul

Gaia Yoga Istanbul, located in Moda, offers retreats that integrate yoga, meditation, and nature excursions. Surrounded by greenery and breathtaking views of the Bosphorus, their retreats provide a serene escape from city life. Daily yoga classes cater to all levels, accompanied by meditation sessions and mindfulness practices. Accommodations are eco-friendly and comfortable, promoting a sustainable lifestyle. Nutritious vegetarian meals are served, enhancing the holistic experience aimed at rejuvenation and inner peace.

8. YogaHouse Istanbul

YogaHouse Istanbul, situated in Besiktas, hosts retreats focused on holistic wellness and spiritual renewal. Their programs include daily yoga sessions, guided meditations, and therapeutic workshops aimed at stress reduction and emotional balance. Accommodations are cozy and tranquil, featuring minimalist decor and serene garden views. Participants enjoy nourishing vegetarian meals, promoting physical vitality and mental clarity. The retreats offer a supportive environment for personal growth and introspection.

9. Lotus Yoga Istanbul

Lotus Yoga Istanbul, located in Ortakoy, offers retreats that combine yoga, meditation, and mindfulness practices in a peaceful setting. Their programs cater to both beginners and experienced practitioners, emphasizing alignment, breath awareness, and inner stillness. Accommodations are comfortable and serene, providing a relaxing environment for reflection and rejuvenation. Healthy meals are served, featuring organic ingredients sourced locally, enhancing the holistic experience aimed at holistic well-being.

Chapter 15: Istanbul Itinerary

5 Days in Istanbul: The Perfect Istanbul Itinerary

Istanbul, where East meets West, is a city rich in history, culture, and vibrant energy. Here's a 5-day itinerary that captures the essence of Istanbul:

Day 1: The Historical Heart of Istanbul

Your first day in Istanbul is all about diving deep into the rich history and architecture that has shaped this fascinating city. The Sultanahmet district, often referred to as the "Old City," is where most of Istanbul's top historical attractions are located. Prepare for a day of awe-inspiring sights, delicious food, and a touch of the city's vibrant nightlife.

Morning

7:30 AM - Breakfast at Café Rumist

Start your day early with breakfast at **Café Rumist**, a cozy spot just a short walk from Sultanahmet Square. The café offers a delightful Turkish breakfast spread that includes fresh bread, olives, tomatoes, cucumbers, cheeses, honey, and a variety of jams. Don't forget to try Menemen, a traditional Turkish scrambled egg dish cooked with tomatoes, green peppers, and spices. Enjoy your meal with a hot cup of Turkish tea or coffee, setting the tone for a day of exploration.

8:30 AM - Hagia Sophia

After breakfast, head to the iconic **Hagia Sophia** (Ayasofya), which opens at 9:00 AM. This UNESCO World Heritage site, originally built as a cathedral in 537 AD, was later converted into a mosque and now serves as a museum. Spend at least an hour marveling at its immense dome, intricate mosaics, and the fusion of Christian and Islamic art. The mixture of Byzantine and Ottoman influences creates a truly unique atmosphere. Take your time to explore the upper galleries, where you can get a closer look at the ancient mosaics, including the famous Deësis mosaic.

10:00 AM - Blue Mosque

Next, walk across the square to the **Blue Mosque** (Sultan Ahmed Mosque), one of Istanbul's most famous landmarks. This stunning mosque, completed in 1616, is known for its striking blue İznik tiles that adorn the interior. As you step inside, you'll be struck by the vast prayer hall, illuminated by sunlight streaming through the stained glass windows. The mosque is still active, so be mindful of prayer times, and ensure you're dressed modestly. Spend about 30-45 minutes here, soaking in the peaceful ambiance and architectural splendor.

Mid-Morning

11:00 AM - Basilica Cistern

From the Blue Mosque, it's a short walk to the **Basilica Cistern** (Yerebatan Sarnıcı), an ancient underground water reservoir built in 532 AD. The cistern is a cool and serene contrast to the bustling city above. As you descend into the dimly lit chamber, you'll find yourself among a forest of 336 marble columns. Look out for the two Medusa-head columns, which are particularly intriguing due to their mysterious origins. The soft lighting and the sound of dripping water create an almost otherworldly atmosphere. Spend about 30 minutes exploring this hidden gem.

Lunch

12:00 PM - Lunch at Deraliye Ottoman Cuisine

After the Basilica Cistern, make your way to **Deraliye Ottoman Cuisine**, located just a few minutes away. This restaurant offers a taste of traditional Ottoman dishes in an elegant setting. Start with appetizers like hummus and baba ganoush, followed by dishes such as hünkar beğendi (Sultan's delight), a creamy eggplant puree topped with succulent lamb. Pair your meal with a glass of refreshing ayran, a traditional Turkish yogurt drink. The restaurant's ambiance and attentive service make for a relaxing and satisfying lunch experience.

Afternoon

1:30 PM - Topkapi Palace

Post-lunch, head to **Topkapi Palace**, a short walk from Sultanahmet Square. This vast palace complex was the primary residence of the Ottoman sultans for nearly 400 years. The palace opens at 9:00 AM, and you'll want to allocate at least 2-3 hours to explore its many courtyards, gardens, and opulent rooms. Highlights include the Harem, where the sultan's family lived, the Imperial Treasury, which houses the famous Topkapi Dagger and Spoonmaker's Diamond, and the Sacred Relics room, where artifacts related to Prophet Muhammad are kept. The palace also offers stunning views over the Bosphorus and the Golden Horn.

4:00 PM - Gülhane Park

After the grandeur of Topkapi Palace, take a stroll through **Gülhane Park**, which is located adjacent to the palace grounds. This peaceful green space was once part of the palace gardens and offers a welcome respite from the busy city streets. Find a bench under the shade of the trees and enjoy the tranquility. The park is a great spot for a short rest before you continue your exploration.

Evening

5:00 PM - Grand Bazaar

No visit to Istanbul is complete without a visit to the **Grand Bazaar** (Kapalıçarşı), one of the largest and oldest covered markets in the world.

With over 4,000 shops, the Grand Bazaar is a labyrinth of narrow alleys filled with everything from Turkish carpets and lanterns to jewelry and spices. Spend a couple of hours wandering through the bazaar, practicing your haggling skills, and perhaps picking up a souvenir or two. Even if you don't plan on buying anything, the experience of navigating this bustling market is unforgettable.

Dinner and Nightlife

7:30 PM - Dinner at Seven Hills Restaurant

For dinner, make your way to **Seven Hills Restaurant**, located on a rooftop terrace offering spectacular views of both the Hagia Sophia and the Blue Mosque. The restaurant specializes in seafood, and their grilled fish is a must-try. As the sun sets, the monuments are beautifully illuminated, providing a magical backdrop for your meal. Pair your dinner with a glass of local wine or raki, a traditional Turkish anise-flavored spirit.

9:30 PM - Nightlife at Nardis Jazz Club

After dinner, head to **Nardis Jazz Club**, located near the Galata Tower, for a taste of Istanbul's nightlife. Nardis is one of the city's premier jazz venues, offering live performances in an intimate setting. Enjoy a cocktail or a glass of wine as you listen to talented local and international jazz musicians. The club has a cozy, laid-back atmosphere, perfect for unwinding after a full day of sightseeing.

12:00 AM - Nightcap at 5 Kat Bar

If you're up for one last drink, head to **5 Kat Bar** in the Cihangir neighborhood. This stylish rooftop bar offers panoramic views of the Bosphorus and the city skyline. Enjoy a cocktail while soaking in the city lights, reflecting on your first day in Istanbul.

Day 2: Discovering the Bosphorus

On your second day in Istanbul, the focus shifts to the Bosphorus, the waterway that divides Europe and Asia. This itinerary will take you along the Bosphorus, offering breathtaking views, cultural sites, and the vibrant atmosphere of Istanbul's waterfront neighborhoods. From a scenic cruise to exploring palaces, this day is designed to immerse you in the unique blend of history, nature, and modern life that defines Istanbul.

Morning

8:00 AM - Breakfast at Van Kahvaltı Evi

Start your day with a hearty Turkish breakfast at **Van Kahvaltı Evi** in the Cihangir neighborhood, a popular spot for locals and tourists alike. This café is known for its traditional Van-style breakfast, which includes a variety of cheeses, olives, eggs, fresh bread, honey, clotted cream (kaymak), and menemen (Turkish-style scrambled eggs). The lively atmosphere and delicious food will energize you for a day of exploration.

9:30 AM - Spice Bazaar

After breakfast, head to the **Spice Bazaar** (Mısır Çarşısı), one of Istanbul's most vibrant and fragrant markets. The Spice Bazaar, located in the Eminönü district near the Galata Bridge, is a feast for the senses, with stalls overflowing with spices, herbs, dried fruits, nuts, and sweets. Take your time to wander through the aisles, sample some Turkish delight, and perhaps pick up a few spices or teas to take home. The bazaar is a great place to immerse yourself in the local culture and do some shopping.

Mid-Morning

10:30 AM - Bosphorus Cruise

After exploring the Spice Bazaar, make your way to the nearby Eminönü ferry terminal to embark on a **Bosphorus Cruise**.

The cruise typically lasts about 1.5 to 2 hours and offers stunning views of Istanbul's skyline, dotted with palaces, mosques, and historical fortresses. As you glide along the Bosphorus, you'll see landmarks such as the Dolmabahçe Palace, Ortaköy Mosque, the Bosphorus Bridge, and the Rumeli Fortress. The ferry ride provides a unique perspective on the city, showcasing its blend of European and Asian influences. Be sure to bring your camera, as there will be plenty of photo opportunities along the way.

Lunch

12:30 PM - Lunch in Ortaköy

Disembark at the charming neighborhood of **Ortaköy**, known for its picturesque mosque and lively atmosphere. Ortaköy is famous for its street food, particularly kumpir, a stuffed baked potato filled with a variety of toppings like cheese, olives, corn, sausage, and pickles. Grab a kumpir from one of the many vendors and find a spot by the waterfront to enjoy your lunch with a view of the Bosphorus and the Ortaköy Mosque. If you prefer a sit-down meal, there are plenty of cafes and restaurants in the area offering Turkish and international cuisine.

Afternoon

2:00 PM - Dolmabahçe Palace

After lunch, take a short bus or taxi ride to **Dolmabahçe Palace**, one of Istanbul's most opulent landmarks.

Built-in the mid-19th century, Dolmabahçe Palace was the main administrative center of the Ottoman Empire and later the residence of Mustafa Kemal Atatürk, the founder of modern Turkey. The palace is renowned for its lavish interiors, including the Crystal Staircase, the grand Ceremonial Hall, and the world's largest Bohemian crystal chandelier. The palace grounds also feature beautifully landscaped gardens with stunning views of the Bosphorus. Allocate at least 1.5 to 2 hours to explore the palace and its grounds.

4:00 PM - Taksim Square and Istiklal Avenue

After visiting Dolmabahçe Palace, take a taxi or a short walk to **Taksim Square**, the heart of modern Istanbul. From Taksim Square, stroll down **Istiklal Avenue**, a bustling pedestrian street lined with shops, cafes, restaurants, and historic buildings. Istiklal Avenue is a great place to shop for souvenirs, explore art galleries, or simply people-watch. Along the way, you'll pass landmarks such as the 19th-century **Çiçek Pasajı** (Flower Passage), the **Galatasaray High School**, and the nostalgic **Tünel funicular**. Spend the late afternoon exploring this vibrant area, and perhaps stop for a Turkish coffee or a sweet treat at one of the many cafes.

Evening

6:30 PM - Dinner at Mikla

For dinner, head to **Mikla**, one of Istanbul's top fine dining restaurants, located on the rooftop of the Marmara Pera Hotel. Mikla offers a modern take on Turkish cuisine, with a menu that highlights local ingredients and flavors.

The restaurant's sleek design and panoramic views of the city and the Bosphorus make it a perfect spot for a special evening. Dishes such as lamb loin, sea bass, and Anatolian beef are beautifully presented and paired with an extensive selection of Turkish wines. Make sure to book a table in advance, especially if you want to dine at sunset when the views are particularly spectacular.

9:00 PM - Drinks at 360 Istanbul

After dinner, continue your evening at **360 Istanbul**, a trendy rooftop bar located on Istiklal Avenue. As the name suggests, 360 Istanbul offers a 360-degree view of the city, including the Bosphorus, the Golden Horn, and the historic peninsula. The bar has a vibrant atmosphere with live music or DJ sets on most nights. Enjoy a cocktail or a glass of wine while taking in the stunning nighttime views of Istanbul's skyline. The mix of modern beats, creative cocktails, and the panoramic setting makes 360 Istanbul a great spot to experience the city's nightlife.

Late Night

11:00 PM - Night Walk Across Galata Bridge

If you're not ready to call it a night, take a leisurely walk across the **Galata Bridge**. The bridge connects the old city with the Beyoğlu district and offers beautiful views of the **Golden Horn**, especially at night when the city's landmarks are illuminated. The bridge is also lined with fishermen and late-night snack vendors, adding to its lively atmosphere. This walk is a perfect way to wind down after a full day of exploring the Bosphorus.

Day 3: Exploring the Neighborhoods

On your third day in Istanbul, delve into the city's diverse and vibrant neighborhoods. From the bohemian vibes of Cihangir to the historic charm of Balat and the modern allure of Karaköy, each neighborhood offers its unique character and experiences.

Morning

8:00 AM - Breakfast at Cafe Privato

Start your day with a traditional Turkish breakfast at **Cafe Privato** in the Galata neighborhood. This cozy café, situated near the iconic Galata Tower, offers a rich breakfast spread featuring fresh bread, a variety of cheeses, olives, honey, jams, eggs, and menemen.

The café's warm ambiance and excellent views of the Bosphorus provide a perfect setting to begin your day of neighborhood exploration.

9:30 AM - Galata Tower

After breakfast, head to the **Galata Tower**, one of Istanbul's most famous landmarks. Originally built in the 14th century by the Genoese, this medieval stone tower offers panoramic views of the city, including the Golden Horn, the Bosphorus, and the historic peninsula. Take the elevator to the top and enjoy the breathtaking views, which are particularly stunning in the morning light. The tower also houses a small museum and a café.

Mid-Morning

10:30 AM - Explore Karaköy

From Galata Tower, make your way down to **Karaköy**, one of Istanbul's trendiest neighborhoods. Karaköy is known for its mix of modern cafes, art galleries, and boutique shops, set against a backdrop of historic buildings. Stroll through the narrow streets and discover hidden gems like **Mumhane Street**, known for its vibrant street art, and **French Street** (Fransız Sokağı), lined with quaint cafes and art galleries. Karaköy is also home to several historical sites, including the **Kılıç Ali Paşa Mosque**, a stunning 16th-century mosque designed by the famous Ottoman architect Mimar Sinan.

12:00 PM - Coffee Break at Karabatak

Take a break at **Karabatak**, a popular café in Karaköy. This charming café, set in a restored historic building, offers a relaxed atmosphere and excellent coffee. Karabatak is known for its Vienna-style coffee and delicious pastries, making it an ideal spot to recharge before continuing your exploration. The café's eclectic décor and outdoor seating add to its appeal, making it a favorite among locals and visitors alike.

Lunch

1:00 PM - Lunch at Naif Karaköy

For lunch, stay in Karaköy and dine at **Naif Karaköy**, a stylish restaurant that blends modern and traditional Turkish cuisine. Naif's menu features a range of dishes, from fresh salads and mezes to grilled meats and seafood. The restaurant's chic interior and cozy outdoor seating make it a great place to enjoy a leisurely lunch. Be sure to try some of their signature dishes, such as the grilled octopus or lamb kofta.

Afternoon

2:30 PM - Explore Balat

After lunch, take a short taxi ride to **Balat**, one of Istanbul's most colorful and historic neighborhoods.

Balat is known for its vibrant houses, cobblestone streets, and a rich cultural heritage that reflects the city's diverse past. Begin your exploration at the **Fener Greek Orthodox Patriarchate**, an important religious site for Orthodox Christians. Then, wander through the streets of Balat, where you'll find a mix of old churches, synagogues, and traditional Ottoman houses. The **Ahrida Synagogue** and the **Bulgarian St. Stephen Church** are notable landmarks that showcase the area's multicultural history.

As you explore, don't miss the chance to visit some of Balat's unique shops and cafes. **Cafe Vodina** is a popular spot for a coffee break, while **Merdivenli Yokuş** is a picturesque street lined with colorful houses that's perfect for photography. Balat's blend of history, culture, and local life makes it one of Istanbul's most fascinating neighborhoods to explore.

4:00 PM - Visit the Rahmi M. Koç Museum

End your afternoon with a visit to the **Rahmi M. Koç Museum**, located on the waterfront near Balat. This museum is dedicated to the history of transport, industry, and communications, and it offers a wide range of exhibits, from vintage cars and locomotives to maritime artifacts and model trains. The museum is housed in a beautifully restored Ottoman-era building, and its diverse collection makes it a fun and educational experience for visitors of all ages.

Evening

6:00 PM - Sunset at Pierre Loti Hill

As the day draws to a close, make your way to **Pierre Loti Hill** in the Eyüp district for a stunning view of the sunset over the Golden Horn. Named after the French writer Pierre Loti, who frequented this spot, the hill offers a panoramic view of the city and the water. You can reach the hill by taking a cable car from **Eyüp**, and once at the top, enjoy a cup of tea or Turkish coffee at the historic Pierre Loti Café while watching the sunset.

Dinner

7:30 PM - Dinner at Asitane Restaurant

For dinner, head to **Asitane Restaurant** in the historic Edirnekapı neighborhood near the Chora Church. Asitane specializes in Ottoman cuisine, offering a menu inspired by recipes from the imperial kitchens of the Topkapi Palace. The dishes are carefully prepared using traditional methods and ingredients, providing a unique dining experience that transports you back to the Ottoman era. Signature dishes include almond soup, mutancana (a lamb stew with dried fruits), and helva made with grape molasses. The restaurant's elegant setting and historic ambiance make it an ideal place to savor the rich flavors of Ottoman cuisine.

Nightlife

9:30 PM - Drinks in Cihangir

After dinner, return to the lively neighborhood of **Cihangir** for a nightcap. Cihangir is known for its bohemian vibe and is home to various bars and cafes that are popular with artists, writers, and creatives. **Geyik Coffee Roastery & Cocktail Bar** is a great cocktail spot, offering a cozy atmosphere and expertly crafted drinks. Alternatively, visit **Kahve 6**, a trendy café that transforms into a laid-back bar in the evenings, known for its friendly atmosphere and eclectic crowd.

Day 4: Asian Side Adventures

Morning

8:00 AM - Breakfast at Çiya Sofrası

Start your day with a traditional Turkish breakfast at **Çiya Sofrası** in the lively Kadıköy neighborhood. This beloved restaurant is known for its authentic Anatolian cuisine and offers a breakfast menu featuring a wide variety of regional specialties. Enjoy a spread of fresh bread, olives, cheeses, honey, jams, and eggs, along with a glass of traditional Turkish tea. The warm atmosphere and delicious food at Çiya Sofrası make it a perfect place to begin your day on the Asian side.

9:30 AM - Explore Kadıköy Market

After breakfast, take a stroll through the **Kadıköy Market**, one of the most vibrant and bustling markets in Istanbul. Here, you'll find an array of fresh produce, spices, olives, cheeses, and more. The market is also home to many specialty shops selling traditional Turkish delights, coffee, and tea. Take your time to explore the market's many stalls, sample local delicacies, and perhaps pick up some souvenirs. The lively atmosphere and friendly vendors make this a truly immersive experience.

Mid-Morning

10:30 AM - Visit the Moda Neighborhood

From Kadıköy Market, take a short walk to the **Moda neighborhood**, known for its laid-back vibe, tree-lined streets, and beautiful sea views. Moda is a popular spot for locals to relax, and it's easy to see why. Begin your exploration at **Moda Park**, a picturesque park located along the waterfront. The park offers stunning views of the Sea of Marmara and the Princes' Islands, making it an ideal spot for a stroll.

Continue your exploration by wandering through Moda's charming streets, where you'll find a mix of old Ottoman houses, modern cafes, and boutique shops. Be sure to stop by **Moda Sahnesi**, a cultural center that hosts theater performances, concerts, and art exhibitions. The neighborhood's relaxed atmosphere and creative energy make it a delightful place to explore.

12:00 PM - Coffee Break at Walter's Coffee Roastery

Before leaving Moda, take a break at **Walter's Coffee Roastery**, a unique café inspired by the TV series Breaking Bad. The café's laboratory-themed interior and baristas dressed in yellow lab coats create a fun and quirky atmosphere. Walter's is known for its specialty coffee and creative drinks, making it a great place to recharge before continuing your day.

Lunch

1:00 PM - Lunch at Kanaat Lokantası in Üsküdar

Next, head to the historic neighborhood of **Üsküdar** for lunch at **Kanaat Lokantası**, one of Istanbul's oldest and most famous traditional Turkish restaurants. Established in 1933, Kanaat Lokantası is renowned for its classic Ottoman and Turkish dishes. The restaurant's menu features a wide range of options, from hearty soups and stews to grilled meats and vegetable dishes. Be sure to try the hünkar beğendi (lamb stew served over creamy eggplant puree) or the classic Turkish meatballs (köfte). The restaurant's old-world charm and timeless dishes provide an authentic dining experience.

Afternoon

2:30 PM - Explore Üsküdar's Historic Sites

After lunch, explore the historic sites of **Üsküdar**, one of the oldest and most culturally rich neighborhoods on the Asian side. Begin at the **Mihrimah Sultan Mosque**, a stunning 16th-century mosque designed by the famous Ottoman architect Mimar Sinan. The mosque's elegant design and peaceful atmosphere make it a must-visit site.

From there, take a walk along the **Üsküdar waterfront**, where you'll find beautiful views of the Bosphorus and the European side of Istanbul. This area is also home to the **Kız Kulesi** (Maiden's Tower), an iconic landmark located on a small islet just off the coast. You can take a short boat ride to the tower, which now houses a café and restaurant. The tower's history dates back over a thousand years, and it has been used as a watchtower, lighthouse, and even a quarantine station over the centuries.

4:00 PM - Çamlıca Hill

After exploring Üsküdar, make your way to **Çamlıca Hill**, one of the highest points in Istanbul. The hill is divided into two sections: Büyük Çamlıca (Big Çamlıca) and Küçük Çamlıca (Small Çamlıca). From the top, you'll be rewarded with panoramic views of Istanbul, the Bosphorus, and the surrounding areas.

The lush gardens, walking paths, and serene atmosphere make Çamlıca Hill a popular spot for locals and tourists alike. There are also several traditional tea houses and cafes on the hill where you can relax and enjoy the view.

Evening

6:00 PM - Sunset Cruise on the Bosphorus

As evening approaches, return to the Kadıköy waterfront and embark on a **sunset cruise on the Bosphorus**. The cruise will take you along the strait, offering stunning views of the city as the sun sets over the horizon. You'll pass by historic palaces, mosques, and mansions, as well as the Bosphorus Bridge, beautifully illuminated in the evening. The gentle breeze and the sight of the city's skyline at dusk create a magical experience that you won't forget.

Dinner

8:00 PM - Dinner at Lacivert Restaurant

After the cruise, enjoy a fine dining experience at **Lacivert Restaurant**, one of the most prestigious restaurants on the Asian side. Located in a beautiful waterfront mansion in the Beykoz district, Lacivert offers stunning views of the Bosphorus and the European side. The restaurant specializes in Mediterranean and Turkish cuisine, with an emphasis on fresh seafood and high-quality ingredients. Dine on the terrace and savor dishes like grilled sea bass, octopus salad, and lamb chops, all while enjoying the romantic ambiance and panoramic views.

Nightlife

10:00 PM - Drinks at Kozmonot Pub

End your day with a nightcap at **Kozmonot Pub** in Kadıköy. This trendy pub, inspired by space exploration, offers a relaxed atmosphere and a wide selection of craft beers, cocktails, and snacks. The pub's quirky décor, featuring space-themed elements, adds to the fun vibe. Whether you're in the mood for a local brew or a creative cocktail, Kozmonot is a great place to unwind and reflect on your day of adventures on Istanbul's Asian side.

Day 5: Cultural Immersion in Istanbul

On your final day in Istanbul, immerse yourself in the city's rich cultural landscape. This day will be dedicated to exploring the traditional arts, music, and culinary delights that make Istanbul such a unique and vibrant city. From morning to night, you'll experience the authentic cultural essence of Istanbul, leaving you with lasting memories of this incredible city.

Morning

8:00 AM - Breakfast at Café Privato

Start your day with a traditional Turkish breakfast at **Café Privato**, located in the charming Galata neighborhood. This cozy café offers a delightful breakfast spread with homemade jams, fresh cheeses, olives, honey, eggs, and freshly baked bread. Pair your meal with a cup of Turkish tea or coffee while enjoying views of the iconic Galata Tower.

9:30 AM - Explore the Istanbul Archaeological Museums

After breakfast, make your way to the **Istanbul Archaeological Museums** in the Sultanahmet area. This complex of three museums is a treasure trove of ancient artifacts, with collections that span the Greek, Roman, Byzantine, and Ottoman periods. The Archaeological Museum houses magnificent statues, sarcophagi, and relics from ancient civilizations, while the Museum of the Ancient Orient showcases artifacts from Mesopotamia, Egypt, and Anatolia. Don't miss the Tiled Kiosk Museum, which displays stunning examples of Turkish ceramics. Spend the morning wandering through these museums and immersing yourself in the rich history of the region.

Mid-Morning

11:30 AM - Visit the Turkish and Islamic Arts Museum

Next, walk over to the **Turkish and Islamic Arts Museum**, located in the historic Ibrahim Pasha Palace, near the Blue Mosque. This museum offers a fascinating look into the cultural heritage of the Islamic world, with a focus on Turkey's rich artistic traditions. The museum's collection includes exquisite calligraphy, illuminated manuscripts, intricate carpets, and ceramics, providing a deep dive into the art and craftsmanship of the Islamic world. The museum's setting in a former Ottoman palace adds to the overall experience.

Lunch

1:00 PM - Lunch at Khorasani Restaurant

For lunch, head to **Khorasani Restaurant**, a well-regarded eatery in Sultanahmet that specializes in traditional Turkish kebabs and mezes. The menu features a variety of grilled meats, fresh salads, and flavorful dips, all prepared using authentic recipes and ingredients. The restaurant's warm and inviting atmosphere makes it a great spot to relax and enjoy a delicious meal after a morning of cultural exploration.

Afternoon

2:30 PM - Discover the Süleymaniye Mosque

After lunch, visit the **Süleymaniye Mosque**, one of Istanbul's most iconic landmarks. Designed by the famous Ottoman architect Mimar Sinan, this grand mosque is a masterpiece of Ottoman architecture and an important cultural site. The mosque complex includes a courtyard, gardens, and a series of tombs, including that of Sultan Suleiman the Magnificent and his wife, Hürrem Sultan. Take your time to explore the mosque and appreciate its stunning interior, adorned with intricate tilework and calligraphy.

3:30 PM - Stroll Through the Grand Bazaar

No cultural immersion in Istanbul would be complete without a visit to the **Grand Bazaar**, one of the largest and oldest covered markets in the world. The bazaar is a labyrinth of over 4,000 shops selling everything from jewelry, carpets, and textiles to spices, ceramics, and souvenirs. Take in the vibrant atmosphere as you wander through the bustling alleys, and don't hesitate to haggle with the shopkeepers for the best prices. The Grand Bazaar is a cultural experience in itself, offering a glimpse into the traditional commerce of Istanbul.

Evening

5:30 PM - Experience a Traditional Turkish Bath at Çemberlitaş Hamamı

As the day winds down, treat yourself to a traditional Turkish bath (hamam) experience at the **Çemberlitaş Hamamı**, one of the oldest and most famous hamams in Istanbul. Built in 1584 by Mimar Sinan, this historic bathhouse offers a luxurious and rejuvenating experience in an authentic Ottoman setting. Indulge in a full-body scrub, foam massage, and a relaxing soak in the warm marble baths. The Çemberlitaş Hamamı provides the perfect opportunity to unwind and reflect on your cultural journey through Istanbul.

Dinner

7:30 PM - Dinner at Asitane Restaurant

For your final dinner in Istanbul, dine at **Asitane Restaurant**, a renowned establishment known for its historical Ottoman cuisine. Located near the Chora Church, Asitane offers a unique dining experience that recreates the dishes served in the Ottoman palaces centuries ago. The menu features delicacies like almond soup, stuffed quince, and lamb with apricots, all prepared using recipes that date back to the Ottoman Empire. The elegant setting and attention to detail make Asitane a perfect choice for a memorable farewell dinner in Istanbul.

Nightlife

9:00 PM - Attend a Whirling Dervish Ceremony

End your day with a spiritual experience by attending a **Whirling Dervish ceremony** at the **Hodjapasha Cultural Center**. The Sema ceremony, performed by the Mevlevi order of dervishes, is a mesmerizing spiritual ritual that dates back over 700 years. The dervishes whirl in a meditative dance accompanied by traditional music, symbolizing the soul's journey towards God. The ceremony offers a deep insight into the mystical side of Turkish culture and is a powerful way to conclude your cultural immersion in Istanbul.

Top-Rated Guided Tours

Exploring Istanbul, a city that straddles two continents, offers visitors a rich tapestry of history, culture, and architectural wonders. Here are some top-rated guided tours in Istanbul, providing in-depth exploration of the city's iconic landmarks and hidden gems.

1. Full-Day Istanbul Classics Tour

This comprehensive full-day tour covers Istanbul's most famous landmarks, including the Hagia Sophia, Blue Mosque, Topkapi Palace, and the Hippodrome. The tour is perfect for first-time visitors who want to immerse themselves in the city's history and culture. You'll walk through Sultanahmet, the heart of the Old City, and learn about the Byzantine and Ottoman empires from an expert guide. The tour also includes a visit to the Grand Bazaar, where you can shop for local handicrafts and souvenirs.

- **Meeting Point:** Sultanahmet Square (Exact location shared after booking)
- **Highlights:** Hagia Sophia, Blue Mosque, Topkapi Palace, Hippodrome, Grand Bazaar
- **Tour Provider:** Istanbul Guided Tours
- **Duration:** 8 hours
- **Contact:** +90 212 522 3200 | Istanbul Guided Tours

2. Bosphorus Cruise and Spice Market Tour

This half-day tour offers a unique perspective of Istanbul from the water, combined with a sensory experience at the Spice Market. The tour begins with a stroll through the bustling Spice Market, where you can sample exotic spices, Turkish delights, and teas. Following this, you'll embark on a scenic cruise along the Bosphorus Strait, which divides Europe and Asia. From the boat, you'll have stunning views of Istanbul's skyline, including palaces, mosques, and the iconic Bosphorus Bridge.

- **Meeting Point:** Eminönü Square, near the Spice Market entrance
- **Highlights:** Spice Market, Bosphorus Strait, Bosphorus Bridge, Maiden's Tower
- **Tour Provider:** Bosphorus Cruise Tours
- **Duration:** 4 hours
- **Contact:** +90 212 444 9878 | Bosphorus Cruise Tours

3. Istanbul by Night: Food and Culture Tour

Experience Istanbul's vibrant nightlife on this evening food and culture tour. The tour takes you through the lively neighborhoods of Beyoğlu and Karaköy, where you'll visit local eateries, try traditional Turkish dishes, and sample street food. The tour also includes stops at historic sites and a rooftop terrace with panoramic views of the city's illuminated landmarks. Your guide will share stories about Istanbul's culinary traditions and nightlife, making this tour both delicious and enlightening.

- **Meeting Point:** Taksim Square, in front of the Republic Monument
- **Highlights:** Beyoğlu, Karaköy, Turkish street food, rooftop views
- **Tour Provider:** Istanbul Eats Food Tours
- **Duration:** 5 hours
- **Contact:** +90 212 251 7516 | Istanbul Eats Food Tours

4. Byzantine Relics Walking Tour

Dive deep into Istanbul's Byzantine heritage with this walking tour focused on the city's most significant Byzantine sites. The tour includes visits to the Hagia Sophia, the Basilica Cistern, and the Chora Church, famous for its stunning mosaics and frescoes. Your knowledgeable guide will provide insights into the architectural and historical significance of these sites, offering a glimpse into the city's rich past during the Byzantine Empire.

- **Meeting Point:** Sultanahmet Square, near the Hagia Sophia entrance
- **Highlights:** Hagia Sophia, Basilica Cistern, Chora Church
- **Tour Provider:** Walks of Istanbul
- **Duration:** 4 hours
- **Contact:** +90 212 638 9623 | Walks of Istanbul

5. Princes' Islands Day Trip

Escape the hustle and bustle of Istanbul with a day trip to the Princes' Islands, a group of nine islands in the Sea of Marmara. The tour typically includes a visit to Büyükada, the largest and most popular island, where you can explore by horse-drawn carriage or bicycle since motor vehicles are prohibited. Enjoy the serene environment, pine forests, and beautiful views of the sea. The tour also includes lunch at a local seafood restaurant and free time to explore the island at your leisure.

- **Meeting Point:** Kabataş Ferry Terminal, Istanbul
- **Highlights:** Büyükada Island, horse-drawn carriage ride, seafood lunch, Sea of Marmara views
- **Tour Provider:** Istanbul Day Trips
- **Duration:** 8 hours
- **Contact:** +90 212 517 5680 | Istanbul Day Trips

6. Istanbul's Hidden Gems Tour

This off-the-beaten-path tour is perfect for those who want to explore Istanbul beyond the typical tourist sites. The tour takes you to lesser-known neighborhoods, hidden courtyards, and ancient city walls that few visitors ever see. You'll visit the Fener and Balat districts, known for their colorful houses and historic churches, as well as the Süleymaniye Mosque, which offers breathtaking views over the Golden Horn. Your guide will share fascinating stories about the city's history and local life, making this a truly immersive experience.

- **Meeting Point:** Fener Ferry Terminal
- **Highlights:** Fener and Balat districts, Süleymaniye Mosque, ancient city walls
- **Tour Provider:** Hidden Istanbul Tours
- **Duration:** 5 hours
- **Contact:** +90 212 532 5656 | Hidden Istanbul Tours

7. Istanbul Photography Tour

Perfect for photography enthusiasts, this tour focuses on capturing the beauty of Istanbul through the lens. Whether you're a professional or an amateur, the tour will guide you through some of the city's most photogenic spots, including the colorful streets of Balat, the majestic domes of the Blue Mosque, and the bustling markets of Kadıköy. The tour also offers tips on how to improve your photography skills while exploring Istanbul's vibrant neighborhoods and historic sites.

- **Meeting Point:** Karaköy Square, near the Galata Bridge
- **Highlights:** Balat, Blue Mosque, Kadıköy Market, Galata Tower
- **Tour Provider:** Istanbul Photo Tours
- **Duration:** 4 hours
- **Contact:** +90 212 251 8833 | Istanbul Photo Tours

8. Culinary Backstreets: The Asian Side Food Tour

Discover the culinary delights of Istanbul's Asian side with this food-focused walking tour. Starting from the vibrant Kadıköy neighborhood, the tour takes you through local markets, bakeries, and eateries, where you can sample traditional Turkish dishes like simit, kebabs, and baklava. The tour also includes a visit to a traditional Turkish coffee house, where you'll learn about the art of Turkish coffee-making and enjoy a cup of freshly brewed coffee. This tour is a feast for the senses and a must for food lovers.

- **Meeting Point:** Kadıköy Ferry Terminal, Istanbul
- **Highlights:** Kadıköy Market, Turkish coffee house, local eateries
- **Tour Provider:** Culinary Backstreets
- **Duration:** 6 hours
- **Contact:** +90 212 456 6666 | Culinary Backstreets

9. Istanbul's Bosphorus by Private Yacht

For a luxurious experience, this private yacht tour along the Bosphorus offers stunning views of Istanbul's skyline from the water. The tour includes a knowledgeable guide who will share insights into the history and significance of the landmarks you pass, including Dolmabahçe Palace, Ortaköy Mosque, and the Rumeli Fortress. The private yacht provides an intimate and exclusive experience, perfect for special occasions or simply enjoying a peaceful cruise along the Bosphorus.

- **Meeting Point:** Bebek Marina, Istanbul
- **Highlights:** Dolmabahçe Palace, Ortaköy Mosque, Rumeli Fortress, Bosphorus Bridge
- **Tour Provider:** Bosphorus Luxury Yachts
- **Duration:** 3 hours
- **Contact:** +90 212 444 7777 | Bosphorus Luxury Yachts

10. Ottoman Istanbul: A Journey Through the Empire

Delve into the rich history of the Ottoman Empire with this guided tour, which focuses on Istanbul's most important Ottoman landmarks. The tour includes visits to the Topkapi Palace, the residence of Ottoman sultans for over 400 years, and the grand Süleymaniye Mosque, built by the famous architect Mimar Sinan.

You'll also explore the Spice Bazaar, where you can experience the vibrant atmosphere of a traditional Ottoman market. This tour is perfect for history buffs who want to learn more about the legacy of the Ottoman Empire in Istanbul.

- **Meeting Point:** Topkapi Palace Main Gate, Sultanahmet
- **Highlights:** Topkapi Palace, Süleymaniye Mosque, Spice Bazaar
- **Tour Provider:** Ottoman Heritage Tours
- **Duration:** 5 hours
- **Contact:** +90 212 513 4747 | Ottoman Heritage Tours

Chapter 16: Practical Information

Language and Communication

Official Language

The official language of Istanbul, as with the rest of Turkey, is Turkish. Turkish is a member of the Turkic language family and is spoken by nearly 85 million people worldwide. The language uses the Latin alphabet, which was adopted in 1928 as part of Atatürk's reforms.

Common Phrases

While many people in tourist areas speak English, learning a few basic Turkish phrases can enhance your travel experience and help you connect with locals. Here are some useful phrases:

- Hello - Merhaba
- Goodbye - Hoşça kal (if you're leaving) / Güle güle (if someone else is leaving)
- Please - Lütfen
- Thank you - Teşekkür ederim (formal) / Teşekkürler (informal)
- Yes - Evet
- No - Hayır
- Excuse me - Afedersiniz
- Do you speak English? - İngilizce biliyor musunuz?
- How much? - Ne kadar?
- Where is the bathroom? - Tuvalet nerede?

English Proficiency

In Istanbul, English is widely spoken in tourist areas, hotels, restaurants, and shops. Many younger Turks and those in the hospitality industry have a good command of English. However, in more residential neighborhoods and less touristy areas, English proficiency might be lower. Learning a few basic Turkish words and phrases can be very helpful and appreciated by locals.

Signage and Menus

Most signage in tourist areas, public transportation, and airports is bilingual, featuring both Turkish and English. Menus in restaurants, especially in touristy areas, are often available in English. In more local eateries, you might find only Turkish menus, but the staff are usually helpful in explaining dishes.

Mobile and Internet Connectivity

Staying connected in Istanbul is relatively easy. Free Wi-Fi is available in many hotels, cafes, and restaurants. For better coverage, especially if you plan to explore more remote areas, consider purchasing a local SIM card. Major Turkish mobile providers include Turkcell, Vodafone, and Türk Telekom. SIM cards can be bought at the airport, shopping malls, and mobile phone shops. Ensure your phone is unlocked before purchasing a local SIM card.

Communication Apps

Using communication apps like WhatsApp, Viber, and Telegram is common in Istanbul. Many locals use these apps for both personal and business communication. It's a convenient way to stay in touch with your tour guides, hotel staff, and fellow travelers.

Emergency Numbers

Knowing the local emergency numbers is crucial:

- Police - 155
- Fire Department - 110
- Ambulance - 112

These numbers are available 24/7, and operators typically speak Turkish. However, in tourist areas, they might be able to connect you to an English-speaking operator.

Language Learning Resources

Apps: Duolingo, Babbel, and Memrise offer Turkish language courses.

Online Courses: Websites like Coursera and Udemy provide comprehensive Turkish language courses.

Phrasebooks: Carrying a Turkish phrasebook or downloading one on your smartphone can be very helpful.

Cultural Etiquette

Understanding some basic cultural etiquette can improve your communication and interactions with locals:

Greetings: A common greeting in Turkey is a handshake. Close friends or family may greet each other with a kiss on both cheeks.

Politeness: Turkish people are generally very polite and hospitable. Using words like "please" (lütfen) and "thank you" (teşekkür ederim) is important.

Personal Space: Turks may stand closer to you than what you might be used to in your home country. This is normal and part of their culture.

Forms of Address: Use formal titles like "Bey" (Mr.) and "Hanım" (Mrs./Ms.) after a person's first name for a respectful address.

Body Language

Non-verbal communication is also important in Turkey:

Nodding and Shaking Head: Nodding the head up and down means "yes," while shaking it side to side means "no."

Gestures: Pointing with the index finger is considered rude. Use your whole hand to gesture.

Eye Contact: Direct eye contact is common and shows sincerity and interest. However, too much eye contact might be seen as challenging.

Safety Tips

Istanbul, a city that straddles two continents, is a vibrant and bustling metropolis with a rich history and culture. While it is generally a safe city for tourists, it's essential to stay vigilant and be aware of certain safety tips to ensure a pleasant and secure visit. Here are comprehensive safety tips for visitors to Istanbul:

1. General Safety Awareness

Stay Alert: Always be aware of your surroundings, especially in crowded areas such as markets, tourist attractions, and public transport.

Avoid Isolated Areas: Stick to well-lit and populated areas, especially at night. Avoid wandering into quiet, unfamiliar neighborhoods alone.

2. Personal Belongings and Pickpocketing

Secure Your Valuables: Use a money belt or a crossbody bag that can be worn in front to keep your valuables safe. Avoid carrying large amounts of cash.

Be Cautious in Crowds: Pickpocketing can be a problem in crowded places like the Grand Bazaar, public transport, and popular tourist sites. Keep your bag zipped and close to your body.

3. Public Transportation

Use Reputable Transport: Stick to official taxis (they are yellow) and reputable ride-sharing services. Agree on a fare before starting the journey or ensure the meter is running.

Be Aware of Public Transport: Trams, buses, and ferries can be crowded. Keep an eye on your belongings and be mindful of your surroundings.

4. Scams and Fraud

Avoid Street Scams: Be cautious of overly friendly strangers who offer unsolicited help or invite you to a nearby bar or café. This can sometimes lead to scams where tourists are overcharged or put in uncomfortable situations.

Check Prices: Always confirm prices before accepting any service or purchasing items, especially in markets and restaurants. Some establishments may inflate prices for tourists.

5. Health and Wellbeing

Drink Bottled Water: While tap water in Istanbul is chlorinated and safe for brushing teeth, it's advisable to drink bottled water to avoid any stomach discomfort.

Sun Protection: The summer sun can be intense. Wear sunscreen, sunglasses, and hats, and stay hydrated.

6. Cultural Sensitivity

Dress Modestly: While Istanbul is a cosmopolitan city, it's respectful to dress modestly, especially when visiting religious sites such as mosques. Women should cover their shoulders and knees, and a scarf might be required to cover the head.

Respect Local Customs: Remove your shoes when entering mosques and avoid loud conversations or disruptive behavior.

7. Emergency Contacts

Know Emergency Numbers: Familiarize yourself with local emergency numbers. In Istanbul, dial 112 for medical emergencies, 155 for police, and 110 for fire emergencies.

Embassy Information: Keep the contact information of your country's embassy or consulate handy in case of emergencies.

8. Natural Hazards

Be Earthquake Prepared: Istanbul is in an earthquake-prone region. Familiarize yourself with earthquake safety procedures, and know the evacuation routes of your accommodation.

9. Local Laws and Regulations

Understand Local Laws: Respect local laws and regulations. Avoid engaging in illegal activities, and be aware of the legal drinking age (18) and the ban on drug use.

No Drone Zone: Using drones in Istanbul requires permission. Unauthorized use can lead to legal consequences.

10. Accommodation Safety

Choose Safe Accommodations: Stay in reputable hotels or accommodations with good reviews and security measures.

Secure Your Room: Always lock your door and windows when you leave your room. Use the hotel safe to store your valuables.

11. Solo Travel Tips

Stay Connected: If you're traveling alone, keep in touch with family or friends and inform them of your daily plans.

Blend In: Try to blend in with locals by dressing conservatively and not drawing attention to yourself.

12. Technology and Connectivity

Protect Your Devices: Use a VPN when accessing the internet on public Wi-Fi networks to protect your personal information.

Local SIM Card: Consider purchasing a local SIM card for reliable mobile service and easy access to maps and emergency contacts.

13. Money and Transactions

Use ATMs Wisely: Use ATMs located inside banks or reputable establishments to avoid card skimming.

Carry Small Change: Having small denominations is useful for minor purchases and avoiding issues with receiving change.

14. Language Barrier

Learn Basic Turkish Phrases: Knowing a few basic Turkish phrases can be helpful and appreciated by locals. Phrases like "Merhaba" (Hello), "Teşekkür ederim" (Thank you), and "Lütfen" (Please) can go a long way.

Translation Apps: Use translation apps to help communicate with locals who may not speak English.

Health and Medical Services

Here is a comprehensive guide to health and medical services in Istanbul for visitors.

Healthcare System Overview

Istanbul's healthcare system includes a mix of public and private hospitals, clinics, and pharmacies. Public hospitals are generally more affordable, but they might have longer wait times and language barriers. Private hospitals and clinics offer higher standards of service, often with English-speaking staff, making them more suitable for international visitors.

Public Hospitals

Public hospitals in Istanbul provide a wide range of medical services at relatively low costs. They are well-equipped and staffed with qualified healthcare professionals. However, they can be crowded, and English-speaking staff may be limited. Some notable public hospitals include:

- Haseki Training and Research Hospital
- Şişli Etfal Training and Research Hospital
- Cerrahpaşa Medical Faculty Hospital

Tips:

- Be prepared for longer wait times.
- Carry your passport and travel insurance information.
- Use translation apps or seek assistance from bilingual staff if needed.

Private Hospitals

Private hospitals in Istanbul offer high-quality medical care, shorter wait times, and multilingual staff. These hospitals are more expensive but provide a comfortable and efficient healthcare experience. Some of the top private hospitals include:

- American Hospital
- Acıbadem Healthcare Group
- Memorial Hospital
- Florence Nightingale Hospital

Tips:

- Ensure your travel insurance covers treatment at private hospitals.
- Verify if the hospital has English-speaking staff when making an appointment.
- Carry a credit card for payment, as private hospitals may require upfront payment.

Pharmacies (Eczane)

Pharmacies are widely available throughout Istanbul and are well-stocked with both prescription and over-the-counter medications. Pharmacists are knowledgeable and can provide basic medical advice. Many pharmacies in tourist areas have English-speaking staff.

Tips:

- Look for the red "E" sign, indicating a pharmacy (eczane).
- Most pharmacies are open from 9 AM to 7 PM, with some open 24/7 (nöbetçi eczane).
- Carry a list of your medications and their generic names for easier communication.

Emergency Services

Emergency medical services in Istanbul are reliable and can be accessed by dialing 112 for an ambulance. Emergency rooms in both public and private hospitals provide urgent care.

Tips:

- Learn a few basic Turkish phrases related to medical emergencies.
- Always carry your identification and health insurance details.
- Inform the dispatcher if you need an English-speaking operator.

Travel Insurance

Travel insurance is highly recommended for visitors to Istanbul. It can cover medical expenses, emergency evacuation, and other unforeseen incidents. Make sure your insurance policy is valid in Turkey and covers both public and private healthcare facilities.

Tips:

- Check if your insurance includes emergency medical evacuation.
- Carry a copy of your insurance policy and emergency contact numbers.
- Understand the claim process and keep all receipts and medical reports.

Vaccinations and Health Precautions

There are no mandatory vaccinations for travelers to Turkey, but it's advisable to be up-to-date on routine vaccinations. Additionally, consider vaccinations for Hepatitis A and B, typhoid, and rabies if you plan to stay longer or travel to rural areas.

Tips:

- Consult your doctor before traveling for personalized advice on vaccinations.
- Practice good hygiene, drink bottled water, and be cautious with street food to avoid gastrointestinal issues.
- Use insect repellent to prevent mosquito-borne diseases.

Dental Care

Istanbul is known for high-quality dental care at affordable prices, attracting dental tourists. Many dental clinics offer a wide range of services, including routine check-ups, cosmetic dentistry, and surgical procedures.

Tips:

- Research and choose reputable dental clinics with good reviews.
- Ensure the clinic has English-speaking staff.
- Check if your travel insurance covers dental treatments.

Optical Services

Istanbul offers excellent optical services, including eye exams, prescription glasses, and contact lenses. Optical stores are widespread, and many have in-house optometrists.

Tips:

- Bring a copy of your prescription if you need new glasses or contact lenses.
- Verify if the optical store has English-speaking staff.
- Compare prices and services before making a purchase.

Mental Health Services

Mental health services are available in Istanbul, including counseling, therapy, and psychiatric care. Private hospitals and clinics often have mental health professionals who can provide services in English.

Tips:

- Seek recommendations for mental health professionals who speak English.
- Check if your insurance covers mental health services.
- Be aware of cultural differences in mental health treatment approaches.

Electricity and Adapters

Electricity Specifications in Istanbul

Voltage and Frequency:

- **Voltage:** The standard voltage in Istanbul, as in the rest of Turkey, is 220 volts.
- **Frequency:** The electrical frequency is 50 Hz.

Most modern electronic devices, such as smartphones, laptops, and cameras, are designed to handle a range of voltages (100-240V) and frequencies (50/60Hz).

Plug Types:

In Istanbul, the power sockets used are of type C and type F.

- **Type C:** Also known as the Europlug, this plug has two round pins.
- **Type F:** Also known as the Schuko plug, this plug has two round pins with two earth clips on the side.

Both types are common in most European countries, making it convenient for travelers from Europe. However, visitors from other regions will need appropriate adapters.

Adapters and Converters:

Plug Adapters:

- **Purpose:** A plug adapter allows you to plug your device into Istanbul's power sockets if your plug type is different from type C or F.
- **Types:** Universal adapters or specific adapters for type C and type F plugs.

Voltage Converters:

Purpose: A voltage converter (or transformer) is necessary if your device operates on a different voltage (e.g., 110V in the United States).

Usage: While many modern electronics are dual-voltage and only need a plug adapter, some devices, especially older or high-power appliances like hair dryers or straighteners, may require a voltage converter.

Universal Travel Adapter:

Versatility: For convenience, a universal travel adapter that supports multiple plug types and includes USB ports for charging multiple devices is recommended. These adapters often come with built-in surge protection.

Where to Buy Adapters and Converters:

Before Travel: It's best to purchase adapters and converters before your trip. They are widely available online and in electronics stores.

In Istanbul: If you forget to bring an adapter, you can find them in major electronics stores, travel accessory shops, and even some hotels. Popular stores include Media Markt and Teknosa.

Important Tips:

Check Device Specifications: Always check your device specifications for voltage and frequency compatibility. If your device is not dual-voltage, using it without a voltage converter can damage it.

Multiple Devices: If you plan to charge multiple devices simultaneously, consider bringing multiple adapters or a power strip with surge protection.

Hotel Availability: Some hotels provide adapters for their guests. Check with your hotel in advance to see if this service is available.

Power Surges: Istanbul, like many large cities, can experience power surges. Using an adapter with built-in surge protection can help protect your devices.

Charging Stations and Public Access:

Airports and Train Stations: Both Istanbul Airport and Sabiha Gökçen Airport have charging stations available. Major train stations also typically provide charging points.

Cafes and Restaurants: Many cafes, especially international chains like Starbucks, offer charging points for customers.

Public Transport: Modern trams, buses, and metro stations in Istanbul may have USB charging ports available.

Time Zone and Climate

Istanbul, the largest city in Turkey, operates on Turkey Time (TRT). This time zone is 3 hours ahead of Coordinated Universal Time (UTC+3). Istanbul does not observe Daylight Saving Time, meaning that the time remains consistent throughout the year without any shifts forward or backward.

Understanding Turkey Time (TRT)

Standard Time Zone: UTC+3

No Daylight-Saving Time: Unlike many other countries, Turkey has opted to keep a single time zone year-round.

This decision was implemented to better align business hours with daylight hours and to provide consistency for residents and visitors alike.

Comparison with Major Cities

To help you understand how Istanbul's time zone compares with other major cities around the world, here are some examples:

London: Istanbul is 3 hours ahead of London (UTC+0 during Standard Time, UTC+1 during British Summer Time).

New York: Istanbul is 8 hours ahead of New York (UTC-5 during Standard Time, UTC-4 during Daylight Saving Time).

Tokyo: Istanbul is 6 hours behind Tokyo (UTC+9).

Sydney: Istanbul is 7 hours behind Sydney (UTC+10 during Standard Time, UTC+11 during Daylight Saving Time).

Practical Implications for Visitors

Understanding Istanbul's time zone is crucial for planning your trip, especially if you are coordinating flights, tours, business meetings, or other activities.

Flight Arrivals and Departures

Arrival Times: Be aware that flight schedules will be listed in the local time of the departure and arrival cities. Make sure to adjust your watch or device to TRT upon arrival.

Connecting Flights: If you have connecting flights, ensure that you account for the time difference to avoid missing your connection.

Business Hours

General Hours: Most businesses, including shops, restaurants, and offices, typically operate from 9:00 AM to 6:00 PM TRT.

Banks: Banking hours are usually from 9:00 AM to 5:00 PM, Monday to Friday.

Tourist Attractions: Major tourist sites often open around 9:00 AM and close between 5:00 PM and 6:00 PM. Some may have extended hours during peak tourist seasons.

Communication with Home

Calling Home: When calling friends or family in different time zones, remember the time difference. For example, if it's noon in Istanbul, it's 9:00 AM in London, 4:00 AM in New York, and 8:00 PM in Tokyo.

Work Communications: If you need to conduct business or attend virtual meetings, plan accordingly. Schedule meetings at times that are convenient for both you and the other party, considering the time differences.

Events and Tours

Scheduling Tours: Many tours and excursions in Istanbul start early in the morning. Check the start times and ensure you're ready according to TRT.

Event Timings: If you're attending events such as concerts, shows, or cultural performances, make sure to note the local start time.

Technology and Devices

Updating Time: Most smartphones and smart devices will automatically update to the local time zone when you arrive in Istanbul. Ensure that your device settings are configured to adjust time zones automatically.

Manual Adjustments: If you're using a manual watch or a device that doesn't update automatically, set it to UTC+3 upon arrival.

Tipping Guidelines

Tipping, or "bahşiş" in Turkish, is a common practice in Istanbul and is generally expected in many service-oriented settings. Here's a comprehensive guide to understanding tipping etiquette in various scenarios during your visit to Istanbul:

Restaurants and Cafes

In Istanbul, it's customary to leave a tip in restaurants and cafes, although the percentage can vary based on the type of establishment and the quality of service received.

Fine Dining Restaurants: For upscale restaurants, a tip of 10-15% of the total bill is standard. Ensure that the service charge isn't already included in the bill, which is becoming more common.

Mid-range and Casual Dining: In more casual settings, a tip of around 5-10% is appropriate. If you're particularly pleased with the service, you can leave a bit more.

Cafes and Small Eateries: Tipping is more discretionary in smaller cafes or fast-food places. Leaving some small change or rounding up the bill is appreciated but not mandatory.

Bars and Nightclubs

When visiting bars or nightclubs, tipping is less structured but still appreciated:

Bartenders: It's common to leave a small tip of 5-10 Turkish Lira per drink, or round up the total bill.

Waitstaff: If you're served at a table, a tip of around 10% of the total bill is customary.

Hotels

Tipping in hotels varies based on the service and the level of the hotel:

Bellhops/Porters: It's customary to tip bellhops about 10-20 Turkish Lira per bag.

Housekeeping: Leaving 10-20 Turkish Lira per night for housekeeping is appreciated, especially if you stay for multiple nights.

Concierge: If the concierge provides special services such as booking reservations or arranging tours, a tip of 20-50 Turkish Lira is appropriate.

Taxis and Transportation

Tipping taxi drivers in Istanbul is not obligatory but is appreciated for good service:

Taxis: It's common to round up the fare to the nearest convenient amount, typically leaving a tip of about 5-10% of the fare.

Airport Transfers/Private Drivers: For private drivers or arranged airport transfers, a tip of 10-20 Turkish Lira is standard.

Tour Guides and Excursions

Tour guides and drivers often rely on tips as part of their income:

Tour Guides: For a half-day tour, tipping 50-100 Turkish Lira is customary, while for a full-day tour, 100-200 Turkish Lira is appropriate. If the guide provided exceptional service, consider tipping more.

Drivers: If you have a separate driver, a tip of 20-50 Turkish Lira for a half-day service and 50-100 Turkish Lira for a full day is standard.

Spas and Turkish Baths (Hamams)

Tipping in spas and Turkish baths is expected and appreciated:

Masseurs and Attendants: It's customary to tip around 10-20% of the total bill. If multiple attendants provide services, divide the tip accordingly.

Miscellaneous Services

In other service situations, tipping practices vary:

Public Restrooms: Attendants in public restrooms often expect a small tip, typically 1-2 Turkish Lira.

Street Performers: If you enjoy a performance, leaving some small change or a few Turkish Lira is a nice gesture.

Hairdressers and Barbers: Tipping around 10% of the bill is common practice.

General Tips for Tipping in Istanbul

Cash is Preferred: Tipping is usually done in cash, as it's the most convenient for service workers. It's a good idea to carry small denominations for this purpose.

Discretion is Appreciated: When tipping, do so discreetly by placing the tip in an envelope or handing it directly to the person.

Quality of Service: Adjust the tip according to the quality of service you receive. Exceptional service warrants a higher tip, while poor service may justify a smaller amount.

Local Customs: While tipping is appreciated, it's not as rigidly enforced as in some Western countries. Don't feel pressured to tip if the service is subpar.

Service Charges: Be aware of service charges included in the bill, especially in higher-end restaurants and hotels. If a service charge is already included, additional tipping is not necessary but still appreciated if the service is exceptional.

Internet and Wi-Fi Access

Istanbul, a bustling metropolis bridging Europe and Asia, offers a variety of internet and Wi-Fi access options to keep visitors connected. From free Wi-Fi spots to high-speed mobile internet, staying online in Istanbul is convenient and straightforward. Here's a detailed guide to help you navigate internet access during your visit.

Free Public Wi-Fi

1. Istanbul Airport (IST)

Istanbul Airport offers free Wi-Fi for travelers. Upon arrival, you can connect to the "IST-WIFI" network. The service is free for the first hour. After that, you may need to purchase additional time or use your mobile carrier's data plan.

2. Public Transportation

Many of Istanbul's public transportation hubs, including metro and tram stations, offer free Wi-Fi. Look for the "İBB WiFi" network. The service is provided by the Istanbul Metropolitan Municipality and is free, although it may require registration with a Turkish phone number.

3. Public Parks and Squares

Several parks and squares in Istanbul offer free Wi-Fi. Popular spots include Taksim Square, Sultanahmet Square, and Emirgan Park. Again, the "İBB WiFi" network is commonly available in these areas.

4. Cafés and Restaurants

Many cafés, restaurants, and coffee shops in Istanbul provide free Wi-Fi for customers. Chains like Starbucks, Gloria Jean's Coffees, and local favorites like Simit Sarayı often offer reliable internet access. Typically, you need to ask for the password when you make a purchase.

Hotel and Accommodation Wi-Fi

Most hotels in Istanbul, ranging from budget accommodations to luxury resorts, offer free Wi-Fi to guests.

Wi-Fi quality can vary, so it's a good idea to check reviews or ask the hotel staff about internet speeds if a reliable connection is crucial for your stay. Some upscale hotels may offer high-speed internet as part of their amenities package.

Mobile Internet

1. SIM Cards

Purchasing a local SIM card is a convenient option for tourists who need reliable mobile internet. Major Turkish mobile operators like Turkcell, Vodafone Turkey, and Türk Telekom offer prepaid SIM cards with data plans specifically designed for tourists. You can buy these at the airport, mobile stores, or authorized dealers across the city. Valid identification, such as a passport, is required for registration.

2. Mobile Wi-Fi Hotspots

Another option is renting a mobile Wi-Fi hotspot, also known as a pocket Wi-Fi device. These devices allow you to connect multiple devices to the internet simultaneously. You can rent them online before your trip or at the airport. Companies like Rent 'n Connect and Turkcell offer this service with various data plans.

Internet Cafés

While less common than in the past, internet cafés are still available in some parts of Istanbul. These cafés provide desktop computers with internet access and often have printing and scanning services. They are useful if you need to use a computer or don't have your device.

Tips for Staying Connected

1. VPN Services

For security and privacy, especially when using public Wi-Fi, consider using a VPN (Virtual Private Network) service. A VPN can help protect your data from potential hackers and allow you to access content that might be restricted in Turkey.

2. Offline Maps and Apps

To avoid data charges, download maps and travel guides for offline use before you leave. Apps like Google Maps and city-specific travel guides often have offline features that can be incredibly helpful when navigating Istanbul.

3. Data Plans

If you're using an international SIM card or roaming service, check with your provider for travel data plans to avoid excessive charges. Many carriers offer special packages for international travelers.

4. Wi-Fi Calling

To save on international call charges, use Wi-Fi calling services like WhatsApp, Skype, or Viber. Many of these apps allow free voice and video calls over the internet.

Local Customs and Etiquette

Greetings and Interaction

Greetings: Greetings are generally warm and friendly. Handshakes are common between people of the same gender. Men may kiss each other on the cheek (right cheek first) as a sign of friendship.

Addressing People: Use titles such as "Mr." (Bey) or "Mrs." (Hanım) followed by the person's surname when addressing formally. In informal settings, first names are used.

Dress Code

Modesty: Istanbul is a blend of modern and traditional values. When visiting mosques or religious sites, both men and women should dress modestly. Women should cover their heads with a scarf and wear clothing that covers their shoulders, arms, and legs. Men should avoid shorts and sleeveless shirts in religious places.

Casual Wear: Casual attire is generally acceptable in most parts of the city, but overly revealing clothing may attract unwanted attention, especially in conservative areas.

Dining Etiquette

Table Manners: Wait to be seated by the host or hostess. In more traditional settings, it's polite to wait for the eldest person at the table to start eating before you begin.

Sharing Meals: Turkish cuisine often involves shared plates. Wait for the host or elder to serve food or invite you to start eating.

Cultural Sensitivities

Religious Practices: During prayer times, especially on Fridays around midday, mosques may be crowded. Avoid visiting mosques during prayer times unless you intend to participate respectfully.

Alcohol Consumption: While alcohol is widely available in Istanbul, it's respectful to be discreet when consuming it in public places, especially during religious holidays or in conservative neighborhoods.

Social Norms

Personal Space: Turks may stand closer during conversations than what some visitors are used to. It's not considered intrusive but rather a sign of interest in the conversation.

Respect for Elders: Respect for elders is deeply ingrained in Turkish culture. Use formal language and gestures when addressing older individuals.

Gift Giving

Gifts: If invited to someone's home, consider bringing a small gift such as flowers or chocolates. It's a gesture of appreciation for the hospitality.

Language

Turkish Language: Learning a few basic Turkish phrases such as "Merhaba" (Hello), "Teşekkür ederim" (Thank you), and "Lütfen" (Please) can go a long way in showing respect for the local culture.

Practical Tips

Currency: The local currency is the Turkish Lira (TRY). While major credit cards are widely accepted, it's advisable to carry cash for smaller transactions.

Tipping: Tipping is customary in Istanbul. In restaurants, a tip of 5-10% of the bill is appreciated if a service charge isn't included. Tipping taxi drivers and hotel staff for good service is also common practice.

Photography: Always ask for permission before taking photos of people, especially in more conservative areas or religious sites.

Emergency Contacts and Numbers

Emergency Numbers

Emergency Services: For emergencies requiring police, ambulance, or fire services, dial 112.

Police: For non-emergency police assistance or to report a crime, dial 155.

Ambulance: For medical emergencies and ambulance services, dial 112.

Fire Department: For fire emergencies and rescue services, dial 110.

Tourism Information

Tourist Police: The Tourist Police in Istanbul can assist tourists with various issues, including lost belongings, tourist scams, and emergencies. They are generally located near major tourist areas.

Tourist Information Hotline: Istanbul Metropolitan Municipality provides tourist information and assistance through its hotline. You can reach them at +90 212 444 34 88.

Health and Medical Assistance

Medical Emergencies: For immediate medical assistance, dial 112 for an ambulance. Istanbul has several public and private hospitals and medical clinics.

Pharmacies: Pharmacies (Eczane) in Istanbul are widespread. Look for signs displaying a white cross on a green background. Some pharmacies operate 24/7, and there's usually a list displayed on pharmacy doors indicating the nearest 24-hour pharmacy.

Transportation

Public Transportation Information: For information on public transportation routes, schedules, and fares, contact Istanbul's public transportation authority, İETT. Their customer service number is +90 212 444 18 88.

Airport Information: Istanbul has two major airports: Istanbul Airport (IST) and Sabiha Gökçen International Airport (SAW). For flight information, contact the respective airport customer service.

Consulates and Embassies

Embassies and Consulates: For assistance related to passport issues, legal matters, or emergencies involving your country's citizens, contact your embassy or consulate in Istanbul. Here are some important embassy contacts:

- United States Embassy: +90 212 335 90 00
- British Consulate-General Istanbul: +90 212 334 64 00
- German Consulate General Istanbul: +90 212 334 61 00
- French Consulate General Istanbul: +90 212 393 92 00
- Canadian Consulate General Istanbul: +90 212 385 97 27

Other Useful Contacts

City Hall (Istanbul Metropolitan Municipality): For general inquiries about municipal services, transportation, and city events, contact +90 212 455 55 55.

Lost and Found: If you lose personal belongings in public places or on public transport, contact Istanbul Metropolitan Municipality's Lost and Found Office at +90 212 444 04 00.

Electricity and Gas Emergency: For issues related to electricity or gas supply disruptions, contact Istanbul's utility provider, İGDAŞ, at 187.

Useful Apps and Websites

Here are some essential resources to help you navigate Istanbul effectively:

Official Tourism Websites:

Istanbul Convention & Visitors Bureau: The official tourism website offers comprehensive information on attractions, events, accommodations, and practical tips for visitors.

Website: istanbul.com

Turkey Ministry of Culture and Tourism: Provides official information on cultural attractions, historical sites, and travel tips across Turkey, including Istanbul.

Website: goturkey.com

Transportation:

Istanbul Metropolitan Municipality (İETT): Information on public transportation options including buses, trams, and metro lines.

Website: Lett.Istanbul

Istanbul Airport: Details on flights, transportation to/from the airport, facilities, and services.

Website: istanbulhavalimani.com

Accommodations:

Booking.com: Offers a wide range of hotels, apartments, and hostels with user reviews and booking options.

Website: booking.com

Airbnb: Provides various accommodations including apartments and houses for short-term rentals.

Website: airbnb.com

Cultural and Historical Sites:

Topkapi Palace Museum: Official website for one of Istanbul's most iconic historical sites.

Website: topkapisarayi.gov.tr

Hagia Sophia Museum: Information on visiting the historic Hagia Sophia, now a museum.

Website: ayasofyamuzesi.gov.tr

Local Events and Festivals:

Istanbul.com Events: Listings of current events, festivals, concerts, and exhibitions happening in Istanbul.

Website: istanbul.com/events

Istanbul Foundation for Culture and Arts (İKSV): Organizer of Istanbul's major arts and cultural events.

Website: iksv.org/en

Emergency and Health Services:

Emergency Numbers: Includes police, ambulance, and fire department contacts.

Website: 112.gov.tr

Hospitals and Medical Services: Information on hospitals, clinics, and pharmacies in Istanbul.

Website: istanbulhospitals.com

Shopping and Markets:

Grand Bazaar: Information on one of the world's oldest and largest covered markets.

Website: grandbazaaristanbul.org

Istanbul Shopping Fest: Details on annual shopping festivals and discounts across Istanbul.

Website: istshopfest.com

Dining and Cuisine:

Zomato Istanbul: Restaurant reviews, ratings, and menus across various cuisines.

Website: zomato.com/istanbul

Istanbul Eats Food blog featuring authentic local eateries and culinary experiences.

Website: istanbuleats.com

Weather and Climate:

Meteorology General Directorate: Current weather forecasts and climate information for Istanbul.

Website: mgm.gov.tr

Basic Turkish Useful Phrases and Language Tips

Visiting Turkey and want to make the most of your experience by communicating effectively? Here's a practical guide to Turkish language essentials and useful phrases that will help you navigate your way around, interact with locals, and immerse yourself more deeply in Turkish culture.

Basic Turkish Language Essentials

- Hello - Merhaba (MEHR-hah-bah)
- Good morning - Günaydın (GOO-nah-yuh-dun)
- Good afternoon - İyi günler (EE-yee GOON-ler)
- Good evening - İyi akşamlar (EE-yee ahk-shahm-LAHR)
- Goodbye - Hoşça kalın (HOH-shah kah-LUHN) (formal); Güle güle (GOO-leh GOO-leh) (informal)
- Yes - Evet (EH-vet)
- No - Hayır (HIGH-uhr)
- Please - Lütfen (LUTE-fen)
- Thank you - Teşekkür ederim (tesh-EHK-kur eh-deh-REEM)
- You're welcome - Rica ederim (REE-jah eh-deh-REEM)
- Excuse me (getting attention) - Pardon (pahr-DON)
- Excuse me (apology) - Affedersiniz (ahf-feh-dehr-SEE-neez)
- I'm sorry - Üzgünüm (OOZ-goon-oom)
- Do you speak English? - İngilizce konuşuyor musunuz? (een-gee-LEEZ-jeh koh-noo-shoo-YOHR moos-oo-NOOZ?)
- I don't understand - Anlamıyorum (AHN-lah-muh-YOHR-oom)

Essential Travel Phrases

- Where is...? - ...Nerede? (...NEH-reh-deh?)
- Example: Where is the bathroom? - Tuvalet nerede?
- How much is this? - Bu ne kadar? (boo neh KAH-dahr?)
- I would like... - ...istiyorum (...iss-tee-YOHR-oom)
- Example: I would like a coffee. - Bir kahve istiyorum.
- What time is it? - Saat kaç? (saht KAHCH?)
- Can you help me? - Bana yardım edebilir misiniz? (BAH-nah yahr-duhm eh-deh-beel-EER mee-SEE-neez?)

Dining Out

- Menu - Menü (meh-NOO)
- Water - Su (soo)
- Bill, please - Hesap, lütfen (heh-SAH-p, LUTE-fen)
- Cheers! (when toasting) - Şerefe! (SHEH-reh-feh)

Transportation

- Taxi - Taksi (TAHK-see)
- Bus - Otobüs (oh-toh-BYOOS)
- Metro - Metro (MEH-tro)
- Train - Tren (trehn)
- Airport - Havalimanı (hah-vah-lee-MAH-nuh)

Emergencies

- Help! - İmdat! (EEM-daht)
- Police - Polis (poh-LEES)
- Hospital - Hastane (hahs-TAH-neh)
- I need a doctor - Doktora ihtiyacım var (DOHK-toh-rah eet-yah-jah-JUHM vahr)

Cultural Tips

Respectful Greetings - When greeting someone, use "Merhaba" or "Günaydın" in the morning, "İyi günler" during the day, and "İyi akşamlar" in the evening. Handshakes are common among men and between women, while men may wait for women to extend their hands first.

Shoes Off Indoors - It's customary to remove your shoes before entering someone's home, as well as in mosques and certain traditional establishments.

Practical Tips

- **Language Apps:** Consider downloading Turkish language apps like Duolingo or Memrise for basic vocabulary and phrases.
- **Phrasebook:** Carry a small phrasebook or use a language translation app to help with communication.
- **Practice:** Don't be afraid to practice speaking Turkish with locals; they appreciate the effort even if your Turkish is limited.

Packing List: What to Bring for Every Season in Istanbul

Spring (March to May)

Spring in Istanbul brings mild temperatures and blooming gardens, making it an ideal time to explore the city.

Clothing:

- Light layers: Bring lightweight, breathable clothing such as T-shirts, long-sleeve shirts, and light sweaters or jackets for cooler evenings.
- Comfortable shoes: Pack comfortable walking shoes or sneakers for exploring historical sites and cobblestone streets.
- Scarf or shawl: A scarf can be useful for covering shoulders when visiting mosques.

Accessories:

- Umbrella: Spring can be rainy, so pack a compact umbrella or a rain jacket.
- Sunglasses and sunscreen: Protect yourself from the increasing sunshine.

Miscellaneous:

- Electrical adapter: Istanbul uses European-style plugs (Type C and Type F).
- Reusable water bottle: Stay hydrated while reducing plastic waste.

Summer (June to August)

Summers in Istanbul are hot and sunny, with occasional thunderstorms.

Clothing:

- Lightweight clothing: Pack shorts, skirts, dresses, and lightweight pants or capris.
- Swimsuit: If your accommodation has a pool or if you plan to visit beaches along the Bosphorus.
- Hat and sunglasses: Protect yourself from the intense sun.

Accessories:

- Sunscreen: Use a high SPF sunscreen to protect against strong UV rays.
- Insect repellent: Especially if you plan to visit parks or outdoor areas in the evenings.

Miscellaneous:

- Portable fan or mister: Stay cool during hot days and humid evenings.

Autumn (September to November)

Autumn in Istanbul is mild and pleasant, with cooler temperatures towards November.

Clothing:

- Layers: Bring light sweaters, long-sleeve shirts, and a jacket for cooler evenings.
- Comfortable shoes: Sneakers or walking shoes for sightseeing.

Accessories:

- Scarf or light jacket: For cooler evenings.

Miscellaneous:

- Medications: Bring any necessary medications and a small first aid kit.

Winter (December to February)

Winters in Istanbul are cold and wet, with occasional snowfall.

Clothing:

- Warm layers: Pack heavy sweaters, coats, scarves, gloves, and thermal underwear.
- Waterproof boots: Especially if you visit during snowy periods.

Accessories:

- Umbrella: Rainfall is common during winter.
- Winter accessories: Hat, gloves, and scarf to stay warm.

Miscellaneous:

- Language guide or app: English is widely spoken, but learning a few basic Turkish phrases can enhance your experience.

General Tips:

Travel insurance: Consider purchasing travel insurance to cover unexpected events.

Local currency: Have some Turkish lira (TRY) for small purchases and tips.

Prescription glasses/contact lenses: If needed, bring an extra pair.

Travel documents: Passport, visa (if required), flight tickets, and accommodation details.

Visitor Information Centers

Istanbul Visitor Information Centers are essential hubs for travelers seeking guidance, maps, and local insights to enhance their experience in this vibrant city. These centers offer a range of practical services designed to facilitate a smooth and enjoyable stay for visitors from around the world.

Services Offered:

Maps and Brochures: Visitor Information Centers provide detailed maps of Istanbul, including city maps, transportation maps, and guides to key attractions. These resources help visitors navigate the city easily and plan their itinerary.

Tourist Information: Knowledgeable staff at the centers offer valuable information on Istanbul's top attractions, cultural sites, historical landmarks, and hidden gems. They can recommend tours, excursions, and activities based on visitors' interests.

Accommodation Assistance: Visitors can receive assistance with booking accommodations, whether it's finding hotels, hostels, or rental apartments that suit their preferences and budget.

Transportation Tips: Information on public transportation options (metro, tram, buses, ferries), including maps and schedules, is available to help visitors navigate Istanbul efficiently. They can also guide you on purchasing Istanbulkart (city transportation card) for seamless travel.

Event and Festival Updates: Staff members keep visitors informed about ongoing events, festivals, exhibitions, and cultural performances happening in Istanbul during their stay.

Multilingual Support: Many centers have staff fluent in multiple languages, including English, Arabic, German, and French, ensuring effective communication with international visitors.

Safety and Emergency Assistance: Visitors can receive guidance on safety tips, emergency contacts, and local regulations to ensure a secure experience while exploring Istanbul.

Locations and Opening Hours:

Sultanahmet Visitor Information Center: Located in the heart of Sultanahmet, near major attractions like the Hagia Sophia and the Blue Mosque. Open daily from 9:00 AM to 7:00 PM.

Taksim Visitor Information Center: Situated in Taksim Square, a bustling area with shops, restaurants, and nightlife. Open daily from 9:00 AM to 8:00 PM.

Atatürk Airport Visitor Information Center: Conveniently located at Istanbul Atatürk Airport (IST), serving arriving passengers with information on transportation, hotels, and city attractions. Open 24/7.

Istanbul Tourist Information Office (Sirkeci): Near the Sirkeci Train Station, catering to travelers arriving or departing by train. Open daily from 9:00 AM to 6:00 PM.

Additional Services:

Free Wi-Fi: Many centers offer free Wi-Fi access for visitors to quickly access online resources and maps.

Souvenirs and Gifts: Some centers have a small shop selling Istanbul-themed souvenirs, postcards, and gifts for visitors to take home.

Interactive Displays: Modern centers may feature interactive displays and multimedia presentations showcasing Istanbul's history, culture, and attractions.

Contact Information:

Sultanahmet Visitor Information Center

Address: Sultan Ahmet Mahallesi, Alemdar Caddesi No: 11, Fatih, Istanbul

Phone: +90 212 518 18 18

Taksim Visitor Information Center

Address: Taksim Gezi Parkı, Gümüşsuyu, Beyoğlu, Istanbul

Phone: +90 212 635 79 97

Atatürk Airport Visitor Information Center

Address: Atatürk Havalimanı, 34149 Yeşilköy, Bakırköy, Istanbul

Phone: +90 212 463 30 00

Istanbul Tourist Information Office (Sirkeci)

Address: Hobyar Mahallesi, Ankara Caddesi No: 32, Sirkeci, Fatih, Istanbul

Phone: +90 212 520 77 96

Chapter 17: Day Trips and Excursions

10 Amazing Day Trips from Istanbul

Istanbul offers a plethora of amazing day trips, allowing travelers to explore beyond the city's bustling streets. Here are ten fantastic day trips from Istanbul:

1. Bursa

Nestled at the foot of the Uludağ Mountain, Bursa is famed for its rich Ottoman heritage and lush greenery. The city is renowned for its thermal baths, particularly the historical Çekirge Baths, and the Green Mosque, which boasts exquisite tile work. Bursa is also known for its silk market in the Koza Han, where you can purchase high-quality textiles and traditional Turkish garments. For a panoramic view of the city, take the cable car up to Uludağ Mountain, where you can enjoy outdoor activities or simply bask in the natural beauty. The city is also a gateway to the serene Oylat Caves and thermal springs, offering a perfect blend of history, culture, and relaxation.

- **Distance:** 155 km (96 miles)
- **Travel Time:** Approximately 2 hours by car or bus

2. Edremit and Ayvalık

The charming coastal towns of Edremit and Ayvalık offer a blend of natural beauty and historical intrigue. Edremit is known for its lush olive groves and the nearby ancient city of Assos, where you can explore the well-preserved ruins of a temple and enjoy breathtaking sea views. Ayvalık, a picturesque town on the Aegean coast, features cobblestone streets, Ottoman-era architecture, and a vibrant market. The area is also renowned for its excellent seafood and olive oil. Nearby, you can visit Cunda Island, accessible via a bridge, which offers charming seaside cafes and beautiful beaches.

- **Distance:** 320 km (199 miles)
- **Travel Time:** Approximately 4 hours by car

3. Şile

Şile, a quaint coastal town on the Black Sea, is known for its stunning natural scenery and historical landmarks. The town's iconic Şile Lighthouse, which has been guiding ships since the 19th century, is a must-visit. The surrounding beaches, such as Ağlayan Kaya Beach, offer beautiful sandy stretches and clear waters, perfect for a relaxing day by the sea. Şile is also famous for its charming old town, where you can explore traditional Turkish houses and local markets. The nearby village of Ağva, located at the confluence of two rivers, provides opportunities for riverboat tours and nature walks.

- **Distance:** 70 km (43 miles)
- **Travel Time:** Approximately 1.5 hours by car

4. Princes' Islands

The Princes' Islands, an archipelago in the Sea of Marmara, offer a serene escape from the hustle and bustle of Istanbul. The largest and most popular island, Büyükada, features charming old wooden houses, horse-drawn carriages, and beautiful beaches. You can explore the island's historic mansions, such as the Greek Orthodox Monastery of Saint George, or relax in the tranquil gardens of the island's parks. Each island has its unique charm: Heybeliada is known for its lush pine forests, while Kınalıada offers a more rustic experience. The islands are a haven for those seeking a peaceful retreat with picturesque views.

- **Distance:** Varies by island (approx. 20 km / 12 miles from Istanbul)
- **Travel Time:** Approximately 1 hour by ferry

5. Sapanca and Maşukiye

Sapanca and Maşukiye, located in the Sakarya Province, are renowned for their stunning natural landscapes and outdoor activities. Sapanca Lake is a picturesque spot for picnicking, fishing, and boat rides. The surrounding area is ideal for nature lovers, with lush forests and hiking trails offering opportunities to explore the local flora and fauna. Maşukiye, a charming village nearby, is famous for its serene atmosphere and local restaurants serving delicious kebabs and traditional Turkish cuisine. The area also features a variety of thermal springs and resorts for a relaxing experience in nature.

- **Distance:** 130 km (81 miles)
- **Travel Time:** Approximately 1.5 hours by car

6. Çanakkale

Çanakkale, a city with a rich historical background, is a gateway to the ancient city of Troy and the Gallipoli Peninsula.

The site of ancient Troy, famously associated with Homer's epic poems, features extensive ruins, including the remains of its ancient walls and the iconic wooden horse. On the Gallipoli Peninsula, you can explore the poignant memorials and cemeteries dedicated to soldiers from World War I. Çanakkale itself offers a charming waterfront, historic sites, and vibrant local markets. The city's location along the Dardanelles Strait provides stunning views and a rich maritime heritage.

- **Distance:** 320 km (199 miles)
- **Travel Time:** Approximately 4 hours by car

7. Yalova

Yalova, located on the coast of the Sea of Marmara, is known for its thermal baths and natural beauty. The city's thermal spa facilities, such as the Terminal region, offer relaxing hot springs and wellness treatments in a picturesque setting. Yalova is also home to the historic Atatürk Mansion, a former residence of Turkey's founder, Mustafa Kemal Atatürk, which provides insights into his life and legacy. The nearby Karaca Arboretum showcases a diverse range of plant species and offers pleasant walking trails through beautifully landscaped gardens.

- **Distance:** 90 km (56 miles)
- **Travel Time:** Approximately 1.5 hours by car or ferry

8. Kocaeli

Kocaeli, situated along the northeastern coast of the Marmara Sea, offers a mix of historical and natural attractions. The city's historic sites include the İzmit Clock Tower and the ancient Roman aqueducts. Kocaeli is also home to Seka Park, a large urban park with beautiful green spaces, walking paths, and views of the sea. For nature enthusiasts, the nearby Kartepe Mountain provides opportunities for hiking and skiing during the winter months. The region's proximity to both urban and natural attractions makes it an ideal destination for a diverse day trip experience.

- **Distance:** 100 km (62 miles)
- **Travel Time:** Approximately 1.5 hours by car

9. Kilyos

Kilyos, a coastal village on the Black Sea, is known for its stunning beaches and relaxed atmosphere. The sandy shores of Kilyos Beach are perfect for a day of sunbathing and swimming, while the surrounding area offers a range of seaside restaurants and cafes. The village is also home to the Kilyos Castle, which provides panoramic views of the Black Sea and the surrounding landscape. For a more adventurous experience, you can explore the nearby coastal trails and enjoy a range of water sports in the clear waters of the Black Sea.

- **Distance:** 40 km (25 miles)
- **Travel Time:** Approximately 1 hour by car

10. Edirne

Edirne, a city near the Turkish-Bulgarian border, is steeped in Ottoman history and architectural marvels. The Selimiye Mosque, a UNESCO World Heritage site, is renowned for its magnificent dome and intricate tile work, a masterpiece of the architect Mimar Sinan. The city is also home to the Old Mosque, built in the 15th century, and the Üç Şerefeli Mosque, known for its unique minaret design. Edirne's lively bazaars and traditional markets offer a variety of local crafts and delicacies. The city's historical significance and vibrant cultural scene make it a fascinating destination for a day trip.

- **Distance:** 230 km (143 miles)
- **Travel Time:** Approximately 2.5 hours by car

Chapter 18: Conclusion

Tips for a Fantastic Stay in Istanbul

Istanbul, with its rich history, vibrant culture, and stunning architecture, offers a plethora of experiences for travelers. To ensure an exceptional stay, here are some valuable tips:

1. Explore Both Continents: Istanbul is the only city in the world that straddles two continents—Europe and Asia. Take a ferry across the Bosphorus to experience both sides. The Asian side offers a more local, less touristy vibe with charming neighborhoods like Kadıköy and Üsküdar.

2. Stay in Sultanahmet for Historical Sites: If you're interested in Istanbul's rich history, consider staying in Sultanahmet. This area is home to major attractions like the Hagia Sophia, Blue Mosque, and Topkapi Palace, all within walking distance.

3. Use Public Transportation: Istanbul's public transportation system is efficient and affordable. The Istanbulkart, a reloadable card, can be used on trams, buses, ferries, and the metro. It's a convenient way to get around the city.

4. Indulge in Turkish Cuisine: Istanbul is a paradise for food lovers. Don't miss trying traditional dishes like kebabs, mezes, and baklava. Visit local eateries and street food vendors for an authentic taste. For a special experience, try a fish sandwich at Eminönü or a classic Turkish breakfast.

5. Visit Mosques Respectfully: When visiting mosques, dress modestly—women should cover their heads, shoulders, and legs, while men should wear long pants. Be mindful of prayer times when the mosques may be closed to visitors.

6. Shop at the Grand Bazaar: The Grand Bazaar is a must-visit, but it can be overwhelming. Take your time to explore its many shops and be prepared to haggle—bargaining is expected and part of the fun!

7. Take a Bosphorus Cruise: A cruise on the Bosphorus offers a unique perspective of the city's skyline and landmarks. Consider an evening cruise to enjoy the city lights and the serene ambiance of the Bosphorus at sunset.

8. Discover the Hidden Gems: Beyond the main attractions, explore lesser-known sites like the Chora Church for its stunning mosaics, or the Rüstem Paşa

Mosque for its beautiful tile work. Wander through neighborhoods like Balat and Fener for colorful streets and a glimpse of local life.

9. Learn Some Basic Turkish Phrases: While many people in tourist areas speak English, learning a few basic Turkish phrases can enhance your experience and endear you to locals. Simple greetings like "Merhaba" (hello) and "Teşekkür ederim" (thank you) go a long way.

10. Be Aware of Scams: As with any major tourist destination, be cautious of scams. Avoid unsolicited offers from strangers, particularly for tours or goods. Always agree on prices upfront, and if something feels off, trust your instincts.

11. Experience Turkish Tea and Coffee Culture: Take time to enjoy Turkish tea (çay) or coffee at a local café. Istanbul has a rich café culture, and sipping a hot beverage while people-watching is a quintessential experience. Try the traditional Turkish delight as an accompaniment.

12. Plan Your Visit to Major Attractions: Major attractions like the Hagia Sophia and Topkapi Palace can get very crowded, especially during peak tourist season. Arrive early in the morning or later in the afternoon to avoid long lines and enjoy a more relaxed visit.

13. Visit a Hammam: For a unique cultural experience, visit a traditional Turkish bath, or hammam. Enjoy the ritual of steaming, scrubbing, and relaxing in an atmospheric setting. There are both historic and modern hammams to choose from.

14. Enjoy Istanbul's Nightlife: Istanbul has a vibrant nightlife with something for everyone, from rooftop bars with stunning views to lively nightclubs and traditional meyhanes (taverns) with live music. Explore areas like Beyoğlu, Karaköy, and Kadıköy for a night out.

15. Watch a Whirling Dervish Show: Experience a mesmerizing Sufi whirling dervish ceremony, a spiritual dance that is deeply rooted in Turkish culture. Performances can be found at venues like the Galata Mevlevi Museum.

16. Pack for the Weather: Istanbul's weather can be unpredictable. Pack layers, including a light jacket, as evenings can be cool, especially near the Bosphorus. An umbrella is also handy, as rain showers can occur unexpectedly.

17. Use Local Apps: Download local apps like BiTaksi (for taxis) and Yemeksepeti (for food delivery) to make navigating the city easier. Google Maps is also invaluable for finding your way around.

18. Respect Local Customs: Turkish people are generally warm and hospitable, but it's important to respect local customs. This includes dressing modestly in certain areas, asking for permission before taking photos of people, and being polite in interactions.

19. Take a Day Trip: Consider a day trip outside the city to explore nearby attractions like the Princes' Islands, the ancient city of Troy, or the serene Sapanca Lake. These offer a refreshing break from the hustle and bustle of the city.

20. Keep Your Valuables Secure: Istanbul is generally safe, but as in any big city, it's wise to keep an eye on your belongings, especially in crowded areas like markets and public transport. Use a money belt or a secure bag to keep your valuables safe.

Farewell and Safe Travels

As your journey through Istanbul comes to an end, it's time to bid farewell to this city of contrasts, where the East meets the West, and ancient traditions blend seamlessly with modern life. From the bustling bazaars and the majestic Hagia Sophia to the tranquil shores of the Bosphorus, Istanbul has surely left an indelible mark on your heart. I hope that you've not only discovered its iconic landmarks but also its hidden gems, tasted its vibrant cuisine and connected with its warm and welcoming people.

Remember, Istanbul is a city that continues to reveal its mysteries with every visit. Whether it's your first time or a return trip, there's always something new to explore, learn, and love. As you depart, take with you the memories of its mesmerizing skyline, the sounds of the call to prayer echoing across the city, and the flavors of a tea shared with friends.

Wishing you safe travels and a heart full of wonderful memories until you find yourself wandering these streets once again.

Warm regards,

Sebastian Felix

Made in the USA
Las Vegas, NV
24 January 2025

16939270R00203